Strategic Planning
Threats and Opportunities
for Planners

Strategic Planning

Threats and Opportunities for Planners

Edited by
JOHN M. BRYSON
and
ROBERT C. EINSWEILER

PLANNERS PRESS
AMERICAN PLANNING ASSOCIATION
Chicago, Illinois   Washington, D.C.

This book is being published in cooperation with the
Journal of the American Planning Association, whose winter
1987 symposium on strategic planning formed the core of
this book.

Copyright 1988 by the American Planning Association
1313 E. 60th St., Chicago, IL 60637
ISBN 0-918286-54-9
Library of Congress Catalog Card Number 87-73537

Contents

Figures

Tables

Preface

Strategic planning is a hot topic—the subject of an increasing number of professional conference sessions, journal articles, and practitioner-oriented texts. This book offers policymakers and professional planners some of the best thinking available on what strategic planning is, how it might apply to public sector situations, and how it relates to the public planning profession. How strategic planning might apply to nonprofit situations also is discussed, but to a lesser extent.

Strategic planning provides some of the concepts, procedures, and tools that can help organizational and political leaders cope with an increasingly turbulent and interconnected world in which they are held accountable for the performance of their organizations or communities.

Most of the recent work on strategic planning has focused on its applicability to all or part of a for-profit corporation. Strategic planning, however, can be applied to a number of public and nonprofit purposes as well.

The book is intended for two main groups. The first consists of policymakers, managers, and planners in public and nonprofit organizations and communities who are responsible for strategic planning and want to learn more about it. The text will help them understand most of the important concepts, procedures, and tools of strategic planning, will present several case applications to facilitate understanding, and will offer several conclusions

about the field of public sector strategic planning and its future.

The second group consists of planning academics and students of strategic planning. A small, but growing, number of courses on strategic planning are offered in schools of public affairs, public administration, planning, and public policy. This book offers participants in such courses a survey of the public and nonprofit strategic planning field and reflections on the field's future. Business people and citizens interested in learning how to improve the operations of public and nonprofit organizations and communities also would find the book useful.

The contributions of many people and organizations made this book possible. The idea for the book can be traced to a conversation John Bryson had with Ray Burby and Ed Kaiser in Minneapolis during the 1984 annual conference of the American Planning Association. Ray and Ed are coeditors of the *Journal of the American Planning Association* and thought that a symposium in the *Journal* on strategic planning would be useful and timely. They then suggested that Frank So of the American Planning Association's national office might be interested in sponsoring a strategic planning session at the APA's annual conference in Los Angeles in May 1986. The papers presented at the session would be sent out for review for possible inclusion in a *Journal* symposium. (A maximum of five out of twelve papers could be included in the *Journal*.) The entire set of papers, plus perhaps some others, would be considered for possible publication as a book by the APA's Planners Press.

Frank did think the topic was timely and important and helped put together a highly successful day-long session in Los Angeles. As editor of the APA's Planners Press, he also heartily encouraged the idea of a book based on the papers presented at the conference. The 1987 *Journal* symposium and this book could not have been produced without the strong encouragement, support, and involvement of Ray, Ed, and Frank. We would like to express our deepest thanks to each.

The chapters by John M. Bryson and William D. Roering, Jerome L. Kaufman and Harvey M. Jacobs, Barton Wechsler and Robert W. Backoff, Backoff and Paul C. Nutt, and Ann M. Pflaum and Timothy J. Delmont appeared in the *Journal of the American Planning Association*, Volume 53, Number 1, Winter 1987. (The Bryson-Roering and Kaufman-Jacobs chapters both were named the *Journal*'s two "Best Articles of 1987.") We are grateful to the *Journal* for allowing republication of these articles (some in revised form) in this book. The introductory and concluding chapters were prepared for this book, as was the chapter by Bryan W. Barry. The other chapters were presented at the APA conference session and appear here in revised form.

Both of us also must thank the Hubert H. Humphrey Institute of Public Affairs at the University of Minnesota, which gave us substantial encouragement and support to pursue our interest in strategic planning. We are particularly grateful to Royce Hanson, former associate dean of the Institute and now dean of the School of Social Science at the University of Texas at Dallas, for his enthusiasm. We also thank the current associate dean, Richard Bolan, for his encouragement and support.

The London Business School (LBS) also helped with the project. John Bryson was a visiting professor in the Institute for Public Sector Management at LBS during the 1986–1987 academic year and much of the coediting task, therefore, involved transatlantic correspondence. Andrew Likerman, the director of the Institute, and Norman Flynn, a lecturer at LBS, were especially valued colleagues during various stages of the editing of the book.

Finally, John Bryson wants to thank Jossey-Bass Inc., publishers, of San Francisco, California, for their permission to include in the introductory and concluding chapters material from his book, *Strategic Planning for Public and Nonprofit Organizations: A Guide for Strengthening and Sustaining Organizational Achievement*, published in May, 1988.

John M. Bryson and Robert C. Einsweiler
Minneapolis, Minnesota
June 1, 1988

Contributors

Robert W. Backoff is an associate professor in the School of Public Administration at Ohio State University.

Bryan W. Barry is a senior vice-president at the Amherst H. Wilder Foundation and the author of *Strategic Planning Workbook for Nonprofit Organizations.*

Barry Bozeman is a professor in the Department of Public Administration, The Maxwell School, Syracuse University.

John M. Bryson is an associate professor of planning and public affairs in the Hubert H. Humphrey Institute of Public Affairs and is associate director of the Strategic Management Research Center at the University of Minnesota.

Michael Crow is assistant professor of political science and director of science policy and research in the Department of Political Science at Iowa State University.

Gregory A. Daneke is professor of public affairs and business administration at Arizona State University.

Timothy Delmont is director of the master of arts in management program at St. Mary's College of Minnesota.

Philip C. Eckhert is director of the Hennepin County Office of Planning and Development, Minneapolis, Minnesota.

Robert C. Einsweiler is professor of planning and public affairs in the Hubert H. Humphrey Institute of Public Affairs at the University of Minnesota.

Kathleen Haines is a data administrator in the Information Services Department of Hennepin County, Minnesota.

Harvey M. Jacobs is an assistant professor in the Department of Urban and Regional Planning at the University of Wisconsin–Madison.

David A. Johnson is a professor of planning at the University of Tennessee.

Jerome L. Kaufman is a professor in the Department of Urban and Regional Planning at the University of Wisconsin–Madison.

Joseph C. King is city manager of Lexington, Virginia, and former assistant city manager of Oak Ridge, Tennessee. He was project manager of Oak Ridge's comprehensive plan.

Paul C. Nutt is a professor of management at Ohio State University.

xiii

Ann M. Pflaum is associate dean of external affairs in continuing education and extension at the University of Minnesota and a visiting fellow at the university's Hubert H. Humphrey Institute of Public Affairs.

Peter Smith Ring is an associate professor in the Department of Strategic Management and Organization, the Carlson School of Management, at the University of Minnesota.

William D. Roering is an assistant professor of strategic management in the College of Business Administration at the University of Florida.

Michael S. Rubin is director of research and consulting at the Fels Center of Government at the University of Pennsylvania.

Barton Wechsler is an assistant professor in the Department of Public Administration at Florida State University.

Introduction

JOHN M. BRYSON
ROBERT C. EINSWEILER

Interest in strategic planning has surged because of several developments. First, leaders of governments, public agencies, nonprofit organizations, and communities face serious difficulties and challenges as their various environments become increasingly turbulent (Emery and Trist 1965) and interconnected (Luke 1988). Not only do changes occur more frequently and unpredictably in today's world, but changes in one area dramatically affect other areas. Second, despite the increasing difficulty of controlling their environments, organizational and community leaders are held accountable for the performance of their organizations and communities. These leaders, therefore, need help to manage complexity and change. Strategic planning provides some of the concepts, procedures, and tools they need.

STRATEGIC PLANNING

Strategic planning is a disciplined effort to produce fundamental decisions and actions that shape and guide what an organization (or other entity) is, what it does, and why it does it (Bryson 1988; cf. Olsen and Eadie 1982). Strategic planning is designed to help leaders and decision makers think and act strategically. The best examples of strategic planning—as is true of any good planning—demonstrate effective, focused information gathering; extensive communication among and participation by key decision makers and opinion leaders; the accommodation of divergent interests and values; the development and analysis of alternatives; an emphasis on the future implications of present decisions and actions; focused, reasonably analytic, and orderly decision making; and successful implementation.

The public sector roots of strategic planning are deep, but few in number. Strategic planning in the public sector has been applied primarily to military purposes and the practice of statecraft on a grand scale (Quinn 1980; Bracker 1980). In contrast, most of the work on strategic planning in this century has focused on its applicability to the for-profit organization.

Strategic planning, however, can be applied to a number of public and nonprofit purposes in addition to military, foreign policy, and diplomatic aims. (Chapter 2 will review the applicability of private sector strategic planning to public and nonprofit purposes.) Specifically, strategic planning can be applied to at least the following: (1) a public agency, department, or major organizational division; (2) a general purpose government, such as a city, county, or state government; (3) a nonprofit organization providing what are basically public services; (4) a specific function, such as transportation, health, or education that bridges organizational and governmental boundaries; and (5) an entire community, an urban or metropolitan area, or a region or state. The cases presented in this book illustrate each type of application.

The strategic planning process detailed in this book is applicable to all of the public and nonprofit entities listed above, but the specifics of application can differ. When strategic planning is focused on all or part of an organization, it is likely that "insiders" will make up a major fraction of the key decision makers who must be involved in the process. Certainly this would be true if the focus of attention were a public agency, department, or major organizational division, a general purpose government, or a nonprofit organization basically delivering public services. When most of the key decision makers are insiders—as opposed to outsiders—the hope is that at least it will be easier to get people together to discuss and decide important matters, to bargain and negotiate differences, and to coordinate the activities and actions of involved or affected parties. (Of course, whether an organization's board of directors or governing body consists of insiders or outsiders may be an open question, particularly if the members are publicly elected. For instance, are the members of a city council insiders, outsiders, or both? Regardless of the answer to this specific question, the general point remains true: A major proportion of the key decision makers probably will be insiders.)

In contrast, when strategic planning is focused on a function that crosses organizational or governmental boundaries, or on a community, an urban or metropolitan area, or a region or state, most of the key decision makers will be outsiders. In these situations, the focus will be on how to organize collective thought and action within an interorganizational or interinstitutional network where no one person, group, organization, or institution is in charge, but in which many are involved, affected, or have a partial responsibility to act. One should expect that it may be more difficult to organize an effective strategic planning process in such a shared power context (Bryson and Einsweiler 1988). Much more time probably will have to be spent on organizing forums for discussion, involving various diverse constituencies, bargaining and negotiating agreements, and coordinating the activities and actions of numerous relatively independent people, groups, organizations, and institutions (see Chapter 10, the Oak Ridge, Tennessee, case).

BENEFITS OF STRATEGIC PLANNING

Organizations and other entities engage in strategic planning for many reasons. Proponents of strategic planning often try to persuade their colleagues with statements such as the following (Barry 1986):

> We face so many conflicting demands we need a process for figuring out our priorities.

> We can expect a severe budget deficit next year unless we drastically rethink the way we do business.

> Issue X is staring us in the face and we need some way to help us think about its resolution, or else we will be badly hurt.

> Our funders (or elected officials, or board of directors) have asked us to prepare a strategic plan.

> Our organization (or community) has an embarrassment of riches, but we still need to figure out how we can do better; we owe it to our stakeholders.

Everyone is doing strategic planning these days; we'd better do it, too.

Regardless of why organizations or other entities engage in strategic planning, they are likely to gain similar benefits. A number of authors (Steiner 1979; Barry 1986; Bryson et al. 1986; Bryson et al. 1987; Bryson 1988) argue that strategic planning can help an organization:
• Think strategically and develop effective strategies.
  • Clarify future direction.
  • Establish priorities.
  • Make today's decisions in light of their future consequences.
  • Develop a coherent and defensible basis for decision making.
  • Exercise maximum discretion in the areas under organizational control.
  • Make decisions across levels and functions.
  • Solve major organizational problems.
  • Improve organizational performance.
  • Deal effectively with rapidly changing circumstances.
  • Build teamwork and expertise.
Although strategic planning can provide all these benefits, there is no guarantee it will. For one thing, strategic planning is simply a set of concepts, procedures, and tools. Planners need to be very careful about how they engage in strategic planning because all approaches are not equally useful and a number of conditions govern the successful use of each approach. This book will offer various ways to think about strategic planning, several different techniques, and a number of strategic planning cases. But the process will work in any given organization only if decision makers and planners use it with common sense and a sensitivity to the particulars of their situation.

Furthermore, strategic planning is not always advisable (Barry 1986). First, strategic planning will be of little use if the costs of the process are likely to outweigh any benefits, or the process takes time and money that might be used better elsewhere. Second, many organizations prefer to rely on the intuition of extremely gifted leaders instead of formal planning processes. If these leaders are strategically minded and experienced, the organizations may not need more formalized strategic planning. Third, other organizations—particularly those that have enormous difficulty reaching decisions that cut across levels, functions, or programs—may find that "muddling" is the only process that will work. Muddling legitimizes the existing distribution of power and resources in the organization and allows the separate parts of the organization to pursue opportunities, or suffer threats, as they arise.

Fourth, strategic planning may not be the best first step for an organization whose roof has fallen. For example, the organization may need to remedy a cash flow crunch or fill a key leadership position before undertaking strategic planning. Fifth, if the organization lacks the skills, resources, or commitment of key decision makers to produce a good plan, strategic planning will be a waste of time. Finally, strategic planning should not be undertaken if implementation is extremely unlikely.

PLANNING TYPES AND DIFFERENCES

Strategic planning should be distinguished from two other kinds of planning: organizationally based long-range planning and comprehensive planning for cities and regions.

Strategic vs. Long-Range Planning

Strategic planning for organizations and long-range planning for organizations often are treated as synonyms, but they are not (Bryson 1988; Taylor 1984). While there may be little difference in the outcomes of strategic planning and the best long-range planning, in practice they usually differ in four fundamental ways:

1. Both strategic and long-range planning focus on an *organization* and what it should do to improve its performance; however, strategic planning typically relies more on the identification and resolution of *issues* while long-range planning focuses more on the specification of goals and objectives and their translation into current budgets and work programs. Strategic planning is more suitable for politicized circumstances since identifying and resolving issues does not presume an all-encompassing consensus on organizational purposes and actions. The specification of goals and objectives and related budgets and work programs does presume such consensus if the goals, objectives, budgets, and work programs are to be anything other than an organizational New Year's resolution.

2. Strategic planning emphasizes *assessment of the organization's internal and external environments* far more than long-range planning does. Long-range planners tend to assume that current trends will continue, while strategic planners expect new trends, discontinuities, and a variety of surprises (Ansoff 1980). Strategic plans, therefore, are more likely than long-range plans to embody qualitative shifts in direction and to include a broader range of contingency plans.

3. Strategic planners are more likely than long-range planners to summon forth an idealized version of the organization—the organization's "vision of success" (Taylor 1984)—and ask how it might be achieved. The vision of success typically includes the future organization, its environment, and the way the organization will operate in that environment. Further, the vision often encompasses the strategies by which the organization will *change* its environment. Because they often are guided by a vision of success, strategic plans for organizations often represent qualitative shifts in direction, while long-range plans typically are linear extrapolations of the present. These linear extrapolations often are embodied in goal statements that represent projections of existing trends, rather than qualitative shifts in direction.

4. Strategic planning is much more action oriented than long-range planning. Strategic planners usually consider a *range* of possible futures, and focus on the implications—in relation to that range—of present decisions and actions. Long-range planners, on the other hand, tend to assume a *most likely* future, and then work backward to map out a sequence of decisions and actions necessary to reach the assumed future. Long-range planners and plans therefore are less oriented to present decisions and actions and are less prepared to handle contingencies.

Strategic vs. Comprehensive Planning

There may be little difference in outcomes between strategic planning and the best comprehensive planning for communities—if the agency doing the comprehensive planning is tied directly to key governmental decision makers. In our experience, however, the two tend to be quite different (Bryson and Einsweiler 1987). Urban comprehensive planning (often called long-range community or master planning) typically is focused on a preferred future situation. The situation usually is based on a fairly narrow set of environmental trends (e.g., population, employment, land use, and traffic forecasts) and the preferences of those involved in the process who have been advised by professional experts on how the system currently functions and how it can be expected to function in the future. A comprehensive plan along with supporting materials outline how to get from the present to the desired end state, but the actors and actions necessary to achieve the end state rarely are named.

In contrast, the most common focus of strategic planning in the public sector is on decisions that must be made about issues confronting organizations. The issues emerge from forces and trends in both the external and internal environments (and interactions of the two) and are shaped by the value preferences of various organizational decision makers, including the strategic planners. Strategic plans are then prepared that outline specific strategies to be pursued by specific actors (typically organizations) within specific time frames.

Thus, traditional urban comprehensive planning often has as much of a vision component as strategic planning, while strategic planning has more emphasis on actors and their actions, organizational changes required to achieve preferred actions, the internal environment, and a broader range of external environmental changes. In strategic planning, the view of the outside is not limited to a relatively standard list of forecasts.

Other Differences

There are other differences between traditional comprehensive planning and strategic planning for communities. For example, compre-

hensive planning usually confines its agenda to a few of government's existing roles. For that reason it is of less use to key decision makers than strategic planning, which embraces all of government's actual and potential roles before deciding where, how, and why to act. Strategic planning is being used by key governmental decision makers precisely because drastic changes in the public sector are forcing them to think strategically about what government *ought* to be doing. In other words, decision makers now are asking themselves what effective private sector executives always ask: What businesses should we be in?

The reasons for the divergence between strategic planning and comprehensive planning result partly from the fact that strategic planning is a *set* of concepts, procedures, and tools, and partly from the typical nature of public sector planning practice on the local level. On the theoretical side, public planning theorists have been urging public planners to behave more "strategically" for some time. But strategic planning is not a unitary set of concepts, procedures, and tools. There are a variety of approaches to strategic planning, and they are not all equally applicable to public situations. Although strategic planning is important and likely to become part of the standard repertoire of public planners, public planners must be very careful to tailor strategic planning approaches to serve their purposes and situations.

On the practice side, comprehensive planners often have difficulty behaving strategically because the practice of comprehensive planning is often channeled by the legislation governing its use, by program guidelines, and by the structural location of planning agencies within government. As a result of legislative requirements and program guidelines, comprehensive planning typically is not comprehensive at all, but is tied to land use, public facilities, transportation, utilities, housing, and perhaps a few other functions. The functional plans often are not tied together, and they typically ignore what government *ought* to be doing as contrasted with what it already does. The comprehensiveness now seems to come from adding up the separate functional parts (what in the 1960s and early 1970s was called hardening of the categories) and not from thinking comprehensively and strategically about a community and what its government might do to improve it.

Comprehensive planning also can be limited by the structural location of the planning agency within government. If the planners are not linked directly to the government's key decision makers, they typically are given responsibility for less than the full agenda of government. Further, because planners may be limited—through no fault of their own—in the kind of comprehensive planning they can practice, key decision makers may reach the unwarranted conclusion that public planners *cannot* be strategic planners.

Simply put, strategic planning requires a more comprehensive view of what may be important than that which normally guides comprehensive planning. At the same time, strategic planning produces a more selective action focus.

ORGANIZATION OF THE BOOK

The book is organized into three sections that are introduced by this chapter and end with a conclusions chapter. The chapters in the first section present an overview of what strategic planning and strategy are and place them within the context of (1) private sector strategic planning theory and practice, (2) urban and regional planning theory and practice, and (3) public sector strategic management theory and practice. The second section presents two papers devoted to important techniques of organizational strategic planning. The third section offers a number of strategic planning case studies that focus on different levels of government, and one recounts the strategic planning efforts of a nonprofit organization. The cases create an interesting collage of strategic planning efforts in a variety of circumstances.

An Overview of Concepts

The six chapters in this section cover a variety of conceptual issues. In Chapter 2, John M. Bryson and William D. Roering present a model process for public sector strategic planning and then compare and contrast six approaches to private sector strategic planning within the context of the public sector process. (The process also is applicable to nonprofit organizations; see Bryson 1988). They go on to discuss the public sector applicability of each of the private sector approaches along with the contingencies governing its successful use in the public sector.

Jerome L. Kaufman and Harvey M. Jacobs, in Chapter 3, place the discussion of strategic planning within the context of public planning theory and, to a lesser extent, of public planning practice. They are concerned principally with strategic planning for a *community* not for an *organization*. Organizations are the focus of most private sector literature. They find that the various elements of strategic planning have deep roots in the public sector. Strategic planning is unique, however, in that it joins all the elements as part of a strategic thinking and acting process. Kaufman and Jacobs also argue that public planners may do better by taking up the banner of strategic planning because of its links to the private sector so favored in today's political climate.

Two caveats are important here. First, using symbols that improve the acceptance of planning is well and good, but we believe that strategic planning actually should be done when people *say* that is what they are doing. Strategic planning is an identifiable set of practices, and if people say they are engaged in strategic planning, they should not be doing something else in the guise of strategic planning.

Second, the rise of strategic planning by governments and public agencies in the United States is occurring at the same time that private U.S. corporate planning staffs have been cut (*Business Week* 1984; Porter 1987) and public strategic planning has gone into decline in the United Kingdom. Do private corporations and the British know something we do not? Two explanations suggest that both U.S. corporations and British planners still value strategic thinking. The private sector realized that strategic thinking and acting by key decision makers—policymakers and line managers—was what really mattered; they found that corporate staffs that emphasized excessively quantitative and cumbersome strategic plans hampered effective decision making by policymakers and line managers. Accordingly, corporations kept strategic thinking and cut corporate planners. And in Britain, thoughtful critics are making a case for a reinstitution of public sector strategic planning and a reemphasis on strategic thinking by public planners (Brehny and Hall 1984, p. 99).

In Chapter 4, Michael Crow and Barry Bozeman return us to an organizational (rather than a community) focus for strategic planning. In contrast to Bryson and Roering, Crow and Bozeman pay less attention to the process and tools and more attention to the allocation of responsibilities for strategy formulation and implementation across levels, particularly in the federal government. They also address the likely differences in these allocations between private corporations on the one hand and governments and public agencies on the other.

Crow and Bozeman argue for a three-level conception of strategic public management: strategic, tactical, and operational. The strategic level concerns the organization's purpose and mission. Policymakers, legislators, elected officials, and political executives typically play a major role in establishing organizational purpose and mission. Senior public managers are especially important in the development of tactics to implement the strategies established by the policymakers. Lower level managers implement the tactics by creating operational procedures. Crow and Bozeman discuss a number of differences between public and private sectors, review several strategic management efforts within the federal government, and then present a number of useful propositions for the application of strategic public management by governments and public agencies.

Several comments on Crow and Bozeman's chapter are in order. First, Crow and Bozeman (like Barton Wechsler and Robert W. Backoff discussed below) are representative of the majority of private and public strategic management authors in that they do not emphasize strategic *planning* at all, except as part of a more encompassing process of strategic *management*. These authors also rarely refer to strategic *planners*. It is clear they assume official policymakers and line managers are the strategic planners, and that if some people have the title "planner" they are there primarily to facilitate decision making by policymakers and line managers. Public strategic management, in this view, is much broader than traditional urban and regional (or even national) planning, and includes all of government's actual or potential agenda; the policymakers, managers, and planners; and the implementation of adopted policies and strategies. Further, people with the job title of planner typically are seen as minor players on the strategic public management stage. Implicit in this expansive view of strategic public management—and in downplaying the importance of plann*ers* while upgrading the importance of plann*ing*—are a number of opportunities, as well as threats, for those who care about planners and the practice of planning for governments, public agencies, and nonprofit organizations. These opportunities and threats will be discussed in greater detail in the final chapter.

Second, readers must be careful about the meaning of terms used in Crow and Bozeman's chapter—as they should be with other chapters. Different authors use different words to mean the same thing, or the same word to mean different things, and readers must pay attention to these similarities and differences in meaning. The main area for caution in Crow and Bozeman's chapter is their use of labels for the three levels of strategic public management, i.e., strategic, tactical, and operational. These three levels correspond to the levels Kraemer (1973) labels normative, strategic, and operational, and to what we, the editors, usually refer to as the policymaking, strategic, and tactical levels. While the underlying distinctions are the same, the potential for semantic confusion is great.

Finally, the variety in the practice of strate-

gic public management at the federal level is worth noting. (That variety will be discussed more in Gregory A. Daneke's Chapter 13 on federal efforts to construct national energy policy.) Because of the need to tailor strategic planning and management to specific organizations and situations, we should expect considerable variety in how concepts, procedures, and tools are applied, and we also should expect considerable variation in the effectiveness of those applications. We would expect this variety no matter what the level of application (i.e., federal, state, regional, or local).

Peter Smith Ring, in Chapter 5, presents a useful framework and process that can help planners identify strategic issues and their sources. Ring argues that models of the public policy process, along with analytic frameworks developed initially for private sector application, can be combined to help public planners identify strategic issues. The identification of strategic issues is important because it is the heart of much strategic planning, at least in the public sector. (The centrality of strategic issues may be seen in Bryson's strategic planning process outlined in Chapter 2.) The strategies produced through planning typically are designed to resolve important issues faced by an organization.

The process proposed by Ring may strike many planners as too complicated to be of much use. They may argue that few line managers—and even fewer policymakers—could be expected to go through all of the steps Ring suggests. They may be right. But the importance of Ring's chapter is not so much the particular process he proposes (though it is interesting and agencies no doubt would benefit from its application) but his making readers aware of the variety of sources of strategic issues and pointing out that different analytical tools will highlight different issues. As to the application of the proposed process, while policymakers and line managers might not go through it in detail, support staff might—in preparation for or to follow up discussions of strategic issues by key decision makers. In addition, the proposed process is a useful start for developing simpler yet effective approaches to the identification of strategic issues.

Also in Ring's chapter, the reader must distinguish between the different meanings different authors hold for the same word. In particular, Ring accepts Paul C. Nutt and Robert W. Backoff's definition of an issue as "a difficulty or problem that has a significant influence on the way the organization functions or on its ability to achieve a desired future, for which there is no agreed-on response." He goes on to argue, following Chandler (1962, p. 13) that an issue becomes strategic if it involves decisions and actions related to changes in "the basic long-term goals and objectives of an [organization], and the adoption of courses of action and the allocation of resources necessary for carrying out these [changed] goals." Other authors define strategic issues differently. For example, Bryson and Roering define them as "fundamental policy choices affecting the organization's mandates, mission, or product and service level and mix, cost, financing, organization, or management."

Finally, in the future it will be particularly important to explore the interrelationship of strategic issues, goals, and visions of what an organization might be like in the future. Strategic planning is important because it focuses attention on the tough choices of great importance to agencies, governments, or communities, but the right way to focus attention on those choices probably varies depending on the situation. These interrelationships are not explored explicitly in the book, but individual chapters contain examples of different approaches geared to achieve a better fit to a specific situation. We explore the idea further here, because it is contrary to the dominant view in the planning literature—that planning should begin with stating goals.

Bryson (1988), for example (based partly on the work of Barry 1986 and the advice of Einsweiler 1987), argues that there are at least three approaches to the identification of strategic issues: the direct approach, the goals approach, and the vision of success approach. He then outlines a series of conditions, or hypotheses, about the kinds of situations in which each is likely to work best.

The direct approach involves going straight from a review of mandates, mission, and SWOTs (i.e., strengths, weaknesses, opportunities, and threats) to the identification of strategic issues. It appears that the direct approach works best when there is no agreement on goals, or if the goals on which there is agreement are too abstract to be useful. In other words, the approach appears best when there is no value congruence. (Once issues are resolved and agreements reached, of course, the results may be written in the form of goals and objectives.) The direct approach probably is best if there is no preexisting vision of success and developing a consensually based vision would be too difficult. The approach also works when no hierarchical authority can impose goals on other actors. And finally, the approach probably is best when the environment is so turbulent that limited actions in response to issues seem preferable to development of goals or visions that quickly may be rendered obsolete. The direct approach, in other words, can work in the pluralistic, partisan, politicized, and relatively fragmented worlds of most public organizations and communities—as long as there is a dominant coalition (Thompson 1967) strong enough and interested enough to make it work.

The goals approach is more in line with conventional planning theory, which stipulates that an organization or community should establish goals and objectives for itself and then develop strategies to achieve those goals and objectives. The approach can work if there is fairly broad and deep agreement on the organization's goals and objectives—and if those goals and objectives are detailed and specific enough to guide the development of strategies. The approach also can be expected to work when there is a hierarchical authority structure with leaders at the top who can impose goals on the rest of the system. When there is agreement on goals and objectives, strategies may be implemented fairly easily, since the field of choice will be greatly narrowed. (In fact, it may be possible for strategies to be implemented almost automatically without further policy intervention.) Strategic issues, if they are developed in such situations, may focus on how to translate goals and objectives into viable strategies.

Finally, there is the vision of success approach, whereby an organization or community develops a best or ideal picture of itself. The strategic issues then concern how the organization or community should move from the way it is now to how it would look and behave according to its vision. The vision of success approach appears most useful if dissension is mild, if it will be difficult to identify strategic issues directly, if no detailed and

specific agreed-upon goals and objectives exist and would be difficult to develop, and if drastic change is likely to be necessary. As conception precedes perception (May 1969), development of a vision can provide the concepts to enable people to see necessary changes. Here, too, strategic issues might be identified, but they would concern issues in translating the scenario into effective action.

The statement that there are three different approaches to the identification of strategic issues may raise the hackles of some planning theorists and practitioners who believe the start should *always* be with issues or goals or an idealized scenario for the organization or community. We argue, however, that what will work best probably depends on the situation, and that the wise planner will assess the situation carefully and choose an approach accordingly (Bryson and Delbecq 1979; Galloway 1979; Alexander 1984; Christensen 1985). Obviously, however, it would be useful to know a great deal more about exactly when and how to focus on issues, goals, or scenarios. For example, does the timing of the external environmental assessment affect the choice of approach? That is, if an environmental scan precedes issue identification or goal formulation, does one approach or the other become more likely or useful?

In Chapter 6, Michael Rubin presents an extremely interesting typology of strategies in the public sector. The typology is based on the juxtaposition of two dimensions: temporal horizon (short versus long) and environmental character (anticipated versus disruptive). The resulting strategic types (ventures, quests, parlays, and sagas) and subtypes provide clues about how to respond to what Rubin calls presenting situations, or circumstances requiring a strategic response. Rubin's typology is a useful addition to the other two typologies offered in this book. In Chapter 7, Barton Wechsler and Robert W. Backoff present a typology based on a set of organizational responses to environmental circumstances (i.e., developmental, political, or protective) in which time is not explicitly included as a strategic dimension. Backoff and Nutt, in Chapter 8, present another typology based on the requirements or expectations of strategy (i.e., quality, acceptance, innovation, or preservation of the status quo), in which again time is not an explicit strategic dimension.

The most important comment to make about these typologies is that they must be thought of primarily as heuristics designed to aid the strategist as he or she confronts particular situations. While there is a certain amount of empirical support for each of the typologies, none should be used without great caution and thoughtfulness. We are quite a long way from being able to prescribe with any certainty precisely which strategies to pursue in specific situations. Nonetheless, the three typologies do offer the strategist some very useful concepts and perspectives on strategy.

In addition to presenting their typology, Wechsler and Backoff in Chapter 7 present an interesting empirical study of the dynamics of strategy in public agencies. Their cases (all involving Ohio state agencies) graphically illustrate the interaction between an agency's understanding of its environment and its efforts at making strategy. It is clear that planners rarely can do everything they want strategically, but it is also clear that with careful thought and effective action agencies can achieve as much as their situations will allow—and in some cases can change their situations.

Techniques

The section on techniques consists of two chapters. The special contribution of Backoff and Nutt's Chapter 8 is the framework they present for using various tools in a strategic planning process. First, they present a model process, broken into stages, that is similar to the one presented by Bryson and Roering. Then Backoff and Nutt observe that each stage should have three steps—search, synthesis, and selection—so that the chances of finding effective answers to the questions in each stage are increased. They then list techniques that might be used in each step. Finally, they present their typology of strategies and indicate the implications each type of strategy holds for the use of techniques. The result is a valuable and practical approach to strategic planning that Backoff and Nutt have used successfully on many occasions.

In Chapter 9, Ann M. Pflaum and Timothy J. Delmont present an excellent practical approach to environmental scanning. One of the special features of strategic planning is that it requires attention be paid to the external environment. Pflaum and Delmont show how environmental scanning can be done pragmatically, inexpensively, and effectively.

Cases

Four cases illustrate how strategic planning concepts, procedures, and tools have been applied in different situations. Each of the cases is in some ways unique—but then so is every planning practice situation. The importance of the cases as a set is that they: (1) give a clear picture of what strategic planning might look like in practice, (2) show how strategic planning might be applied to different levels of government and to a nonprofit organization, (3) illustrate how strategic planning might be used to handle different substantive topics, and (4) allow for comparisons and contrasts of experience in different situations. Some of these comparisons and contrasts will be discussed shortly, while others will be covered in the final chapter.

In Chapter 10, Joseph C. King and David A. Johnson present the successful-to-date efforts of Oak Ridge, Tennessee, to combine strategic planning and comprehensive planning. The process Oak Ridge pursued combined most of the elements that characterize strategic planning (see Chapter 3) with those of more conventional comprehensive planning. The result demonstrates that strategic planning and comprehensive planning need not be mutually exclusive; they can be complementary. The case also demonstrates, at least implicitly, how the two types of planning normally differ.

The outcome of the Oak Ridge effort is unclear since implementation has just begun. Further, one must question whether the elements of the effort could be applied generally since the city has a unique history as a new town created during World War II as part of the Manhattan Project. The federal government and defense contractors have played important roles there. Nonetheless, the case offers some interesting clues as to how strategic planning for a *place* might be pursued, or rather, how a concern for place and affected stakeholders—including the local government—might be pursued simultaneously.

Chapter 11 (by Philip C. Eckhert, Kathleen Haines, Timothy J. Delmont and Ann M. Pflaum) presents a more typical strategic planning exercise focused on a government and what it should do. The case covers the efforts of Hennepin County, Minnesota (the county that contains Minneapolis), to employ a strategic issues management approach (see Chapter 2) across all levels and functions of the county government. While there have been difficulties with the approach, there also have been numerous successes, and the county administrator and his cabinet remain committed to strategic planning.

The case is important for several reasons. First, the scope and scale of the effort are impressive. The county government is large by almost any standards, yet it has been able to tackle effectively a broad range of issues. Second, the case demonstrates the political, managerial, and technical usefulness of an issues-management approach, in which individual issues follow their own time frame and decision path. The case is also important, however, in pointing out that the number of issues addressed must be limited or else the government's capacity for attention and management can be overwhelmed. Finally, the case points out that some of the most important benefits of a strategic planning effort include team building, morale and esteem boosts for participants, and overall organizational development. These benefits were unexpected by Hennepin County's managers, but have in fact turned out to be among the most important results of the process.

Chapter 12, by Bryan Barry, presents a successful example of strategic planning by a nonprofit organization (or rather, a governmental unit that became a nonprofit organization). The case is interesting for several reasons. First, it shows the applicability of strategic planning to nonprofit organizations. Second, the planning group followed a very simple process to produce an effective strategic plan and successful action. Third, the group pursued a scenario approach instead of the more common strategic issues approach. In other words, because a radical change from the present was considered likely, and because the group had strong leadership and could work together, the group began by imagining an idealized vision for the organization and then developed a strategic plan to realize the vision. They did not formulate strategic issues or goals prior to creation of the vision. Fourth, the organization's actual strategic plan is presented. The plan is interesting because it is simple, highly focused, and includes a number of components, such as plans for services, staffing, budgets, facilities, linkages with other organizations, and specific implementation steps. The case therefore presents a very clear picture of what strategic planning and plans can be.

In Chapter 13, Gregory A. Daneke recounts the largely ineffective federal efforts to undertake national strategic energy planning. This set of efforts contrasts with the other cases in that the energy planning efforts were focused on strategic planning for a function, rather than for an organization or a place. Daneke is able to glean from these efforts a number of important lessons that should help guide future federal-level attempts to plan strategically for specific functions. The lessons revolve around the interrelationships among rhetoric, crises, goals, issues, processes, and methods, and may apply to state and local levels as well.

All of the cases represent relatively early efforts by a variety of institutions and organizations to engage in strategic planning for public or nonprofit purposes. Local, county, metropolitan, state (if you include Wechsler and Backoff's Ohio state agency cases), and national cases, and a nonprofit example are

included. The focus is usually an organization, but in some cases the focus is a place or function. In addition to variations in focus, the cases also differ considerably in their scale of effort. As such, it is difficult to draw firm conclusions from the cases as to the effectiveness of strategic planning (although the same might be said of any other form of planning; see Bryson 1983). Nonetheless, one does get the clear impression that strategic planning can be effective if strong leaders want it to succeed, and if a sensible process is pursued.

Conclusions

The book's final chapter presents a number of conclusions. The principal conclusions are: (1) that strategic planning for public and nonprofit purposes is important and probably will become part of the standard repertoire of public and nonprofit planners, and (2) that, nevertheless, public and nonprofit planners must be very careful how they engage in strategic planning, since not all approaches are equally useful and since a number of conditions govern the successful use of each approach. In addition, we offer some observations on what it takes to succeed with strategic planning and what strategic planning practices organizations and communities are most likely to be able to institutionalize. We close with a number of conclusions related to strategic planning and planners' roles, planning education, and the future of planning.

We think these fourteen chapters present a useful overview of the variety of approaches to strategic planning for public and nonprofit purposes and the relationship of strategic planning to more traditional public planning (that is, traditional comprehensive or master planning) and to public management generally.

They also help detail the nature and source of strategic issues; the varieties and dynamics of strategy in public and nonprofit organizations; the linkage between a strategic planning process and specific techniques; the process and tools of environmental scanning; and the variety of experiences organizations at various levels have had with strategic planning. It should be clear from the chapters that public and nonprofit planners can and often do practice good strategic planning. We hope they will do more, so that public and nonprofit purposes and the skills and standing of the planning profession may be advanced.

REFERENCES

Alexander, E. R. 1984. After rationality, what? A review of responses to paradigm breakdown. *Journal of the American Planning Association* 50: 62–69.

Ansoff, I. 1980. Strategic issue management. *Strategic Management Journal* 1, 2: 131–148.

Barry, Bryan W. 1986. *Strategic planning workbook for nonprofit organizations.* St. Paul, Minn.: Amherst H. Wilder Foundation.

Bracker, J. 1980. The historical development of the strategic management concept. *Academy of Management Review* 5, 2: 219–224.

Brehny, Michael and Peter Hall. 1984. The strange death of strategic planning and the victory of the know-nothing school. *Built Environment* 10, 2: 95–99.

Bryson, John M. 1983. Representing and testing procedural planning methods. In *Evaluating Urban Planning Efforts.* Aldershot, England: Gower Publishing Company.

Bryson, John M. 1988. *Strategic planning for public and nonprofit organizations: A guide to strengthening and sustaining organizational achievement,* San Francisco, Calif.: Jossey-Bass.

Bryson, J. M. and A. L. Delbecq. 1979. A contingent approach to strategy and tactics in project planning. *Journal of the American Planning Association* 45: 167–179.

Bryson, John M. and Robert C. Einsweiler. 1987. Editors' introduction to the strategic planning symposium. *Journal of the American Planning Association* 53, 6–8.

Bryson, John M. and Robert C. Einsweiler, eds. 1988,

forthcoming. *Shared Power: What Is It? How Does It Work? How Can We Make It Work Better?* Lanham, Md.: University Press of America.

Bryson, J. M., R. E. Freeman, and W. D. Roering. 1986. Strategic planning in the public sector: Approaches and directions. In *Strategic Perspectives on Planning Practice,* edited by B. Checkoway. Lexington, Mass.: Lexington Books, pp. 65–85.

Bryson, J. M., A. H. Van de Ven, and W. D. Roering. 1987. Strategic planning and the revitalization of the public service. In *Toward a New Public Service,* edited by R. Denhardt and E. Jennings. Columbia, Mo.: Extension Publications, University of Missouri, pp. 55–75.

Business Week. 1984. The new breed of strategic planners. 2680: 62–68.

Chandler, A. 1962. *Strategy and structure.* Cambridge, Mass.: MIT Press.

Christensen, K. S. 1985. Coping with uncertainty in planning. *Journal of the American Planning Association* 51, 1: 63–73.

Einsweiler, Robert C. 1987. Personal communication.

Emery, Fred and Eric Trist. 1965. The causal texture of organizational environments, *Human Relations* February 18, pp. 21–31.

Galloway, T. D. 1979. Comment on comparison of current planning theories: Counterparts and contradictions by B. M. Hudson. *Journal of the American Planning Association* 45, 4: 399–402.

Kraemer, Kenneth. 1973. *Policy analysis in local government.* Washington, D.C.: International City Management Association.

Luke, J. 1988, forthcoming. Managing interconnectedness: The challenge of shared power. In *Shared Power: What Is It? How Does It Work? How Can We Make It Work Better?* edited by J. M. Bryson and R. C. Einsweiler. Lanham, Md.: University Press of America.

May, Rollo. 1969. *Love and will.* New York, N.Y.: Norton.

Olsen, J. B. and D. C. Eadie. 1982. *The game plan: Governance with foresight.* Washington, D.C.: Council on State Planning Agencies.

Porter, M. 1987. The state of strategic thinking. *The Economist,* May 23, pp. 21–28 passim.

Quinn, J. B. 1980. *Strategies for change: Logical incrementalism.* Homewood, Ill.: R. D. Irwin.

Steiner, George A. 1979. *Strategic planning—What every manager must know.* New York, N.Y.: Free Press.

Taylor, B. 1984. Strategic planning—Which style do you need? *Long Range Planning* 17: 51–62.

Thompson, J. D. 1967. *Organizations in action.* New York, N.Y.: McGraw-Hill.

2

Applying Private Sector Strategic Planning in the Public Sector

JOHN M. BRYSON
WILLIAM D. ROERING

Strategic planning approaches developed in the private sector can help governments become more effective—at least that is the claim of many authors, including us. Proponents claim that strategic planning provides a set of concepts, procedures, and tools that can help public sector organizations deal with the recent dramatic changes in their environments. As two early proponents of strategic planning by governments note, "Strategic planning is a disciplined effort to produce fundamental decisions shaping the nature and direction of governmental activities within constitutional bounds" (Olsen and Eadie 1982, p. 4).

What distinguishes strategic planning from more traditional planning (particularly traditional long-range comprehensive or master planning for a community) is its emphasis on (1) action, (2) consideration of a broad and diverse set of stakeholders, (3) attention to external opportunities and threats and internal strengths and weaknesses, and (4) attention to actual or potential comptetitors (Bloom 1986; Kaufman and Jacobs 1987).

That does not mean, however, that all approaches to what might be called corporate-style strategic planning (that is, strategic planning approaches developed in the private sector) are equally applicable to the public sector. The purposes of this article, therefore, are (1) to compare and contrast six approaches to corporate-style strategic planning, (2) discuss their applicability to the public sector, and (3) to identify the most important contingencies that govern the successful use of these approaches in the public sector. (Actually, we present nine approaches, grouped into six categories.)

Before beginning, we should note that corporate strategic planning typically focuses on an *organization* and what it should do to improve its performance, and not on a *community,* the traditional object of attention for comprehensive planners, or on a *function,* such as transportation or health care within a community (Tomazinis 1985). We, too, focus primarily on a government corporation or agency and on how it might plan to improve its performance. But we also note where applications to

15

communities or functions seem appropriate.

We must observe as well that careful tests of corporate-style strategic planning in the public sector are few in number. (The same, of course, can be said about approaches to comprehensive, functional, and project planning; see Bryson 1983.) Nevertheless, there is enough experience with corporate strategic planning in the private sector—and increasingly in the public sector—to reach some tentative conclusions about what seems to work under what conditions.

This chapter is divided into three main sections. The first presents an outline of a public sector strategic planning process that can incorporate the six private sector approaches to strategic planning. The second is a discussion of the six approaches: the Harvard policy model, strategic planning systems, stakeholder management, content models (portfolio models and competitive analysis), strategic issues management, and process strategies (strategic negotiations, "logical incrementalism," and innovation). We compare and contrast those approaches along several dimensions, including their key features, assumptions, strengths, weaknesses, applicability to the public sector, and contingencies governing their use in the public sector.

The third section presents conclusions about the applicability of private sector strategic planning to public sector organizations and purposes. The principal conclusions are: (1) that public sector strategic planning is important and probably will become part of the standard repertoire of public planners, and (2) that, nevertheless, public planners must be very careful how they engage in strategic planning.

A PUBLIC SECTOR STRATEGIC PLANNING PROCESS

An outline of a public sector strategic planning process provides a framework for discussing the six corporate-style strategic planning approaches and their applicability to the public sector as shown in Figure 2–1. The process begins with an initial agreement (or "plan for planning") among decision makers whose support is necessary for successful plan formulation and implementation. Typically they would agree on the purpose of the effort, who should be involved, what should be taken as "given," what topics should be addressed, and the form and timing of reports. The support and commitment of management and the chief executive are vital if strategic planning in an organization is to succeed (Olsen and Eadie 1982). Further, the involvement of key decision makers outside the organization usually is crucial to the success of public programs if implementation will involve multiple parties and organizations (McGowen and Stevens 1983).

The second step is identification of the mandates, or "musts," confronting the government corporation or agency. Third comes clarification of the organization's mission and values, or "wants," because they have such a strong influence on the identification and resolution of strategic issues, as discussed below (Peters and Waterman 1982; Gilbert and Freeman 1985). The process draws attention in particular to similarities and differences among those who have stakes in the outcome of the process and in what the government's or agency's mission ought to be in relation to those stakeholders. *Stakeholder* is defined as any individual, group, or other organization that can place a claim on the organization's attention, resources, or output or is affected by that output. Examples of a government's stakeholders are citizens, taxpayers, service recipients, the governing body, employees, unions, interest groups, political

Figure 2–1. Strategic Planning Process

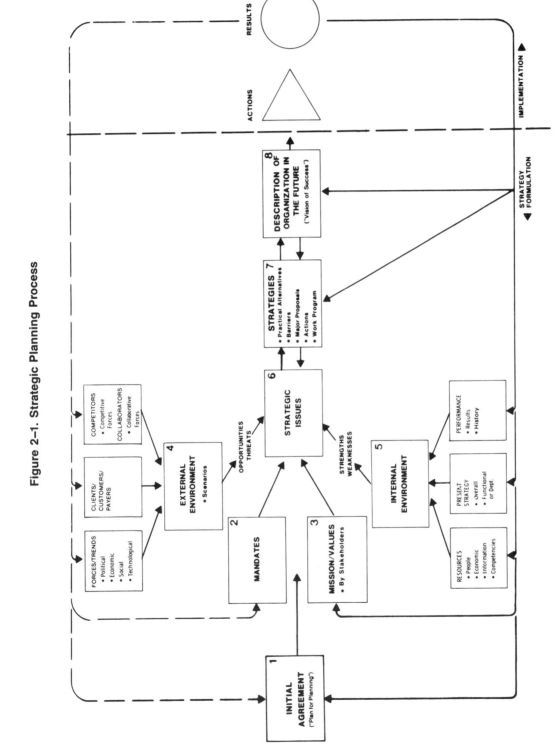

Sources: Bryson, Freeman, and Roering 1986; Bryson, Van de Ven, and Roering 1987.

parties, the financial community, and other governments.

Next come two parallel steps: identification of the *external* opportunities and threats the organization faces, and identification of its *internal* strengths and weaknesses. The distinction between what is inside and what is outside hinges on whether the organization controls the factor, which places it inside, or does not, which places it outside (Pfeffer and Salancik 1978). To identify opportunities and threats one might monitor a variety of political, economic, social, and technological forces and trends as well as various stakeholder groups, including clients, customers, payers, competitors, or collaborators. The organization might construct various scenarios to explore alternative futures in the external environment, a practice typical of private sector strategic planning (Linneman and Klein 1983). To identify strengths and weaknesses, the organization might monitor resources (inputs), present strategy (process), and performance (outputs).

Strategic planning focuses on achievement of the best fit between an organization and its environment. Attention to mandates and the external environment, therefore, can be thought of as planning from the outside in. Attention to mission and values and the internal environment can be considered planning from the inside out.

Together, the first five elements of the process lead to the sixth, identification of strategic issues (i.e., fundamental policy questions affecting the organization's mandates, mission, values, product or service level and mix, clients or users, cost, financing, or management). Usually, it is vital that strategic issues be dealt with expeditiously and effectively if the organization is to survive and prosper. Failure to address a strategic issue typically will lead to undesirable results from a threat, failure to capitalize on an important opportunity, or both.

Strategy development, the seventh step in our outline process, begins with the identification of practical alternatives for resolving the strategic issues. Then it moves to the enumeration of barriers to the achievement of those alternatives, rather than directly to development of proposals to realize the alternatives. A focus on barriers at this point is not typical but is one way of assuring that any strategies developed deal directly rather than haphazardly with implementation difficulties.

After strategy development comes an atypical eighth step: describing the organization's potential future. This description is the organization's vision of success (Taylor 1984), an outline of how the organization would look if it successfully implemented its strategies and achieved its full potential. The importance of such descriptions as a guide for performance has long been recognized by well-managed companies (Ouchi 1981; Peters and Waterman 1982) and organizational psychologists (Locke et al. 1981). Typically included in such descriptions are the organization's mission, its basic strategies, its performance criteria, some important decision rules, and the ethical standards expected of the organization's employees.

Those eight steps complete the strategy formulation process. Next come actions and decisions to implement the strategies and, finally, the evaluation of results.

Although our outline shows the process in a linear, sequential manner, we emphasize that the process in practice is iterative. Participants typically rethink what they have done several times before they reach final decisions. Moreover, the process does not always begin at the beginning. Instead, organizations typically find themselves confronted with a strategic issue that leads them to engage in strategic planning. Once engaged, the organization then is likely to go back and begin at the beginning.

The process is applicable to public organizations, functions, and communities. The only general requirement is a dominant coalition (Thompson 1967) willing to follow the process. For each of the approaches to corporate strategic planning we note specific contingencies that affect its application in the public sector.

Table 2–1. Comparison and Applicability of Private Sector Approaches to Strategic Planning in the Public Sector

Approach	Key features	Assumptions	Strengths	Weaknesses	Applicability to the public sector
Harvard policy model (Andrews 1980; Christensen et al. 1983)	Primarily applicable at the strategic business unit level SWOT analysis Analysis of management's values and social obligations of the firm Attempts to develop the best "fit" between a firm and its environment; i.e., best strategy for the firm	Analysis of SWOTs, management values, and social obligations of firm will facilitate identification of the best strategy Agreement is possible within the top management team responsible for strategy formulation and implementation Team has the ability to implement its decisions Implementation of the best strategy will result in improved firm performance (an assumption held in common with all strategic planning approaches)	Systematic assessment of strengths and weaknesses of firm and opportunities and threats facing firm Attention to management values and social obligations of the firm Systematic attention to the "fit" between the firm and its environment Can be used in conjunction with other approaches	Does not offer specific advice on how to develop strategies Fails to consider many existing or potential stakeholder groups	Organizations: Yes, if a strategic public planning unit can be identified and additional stakeholder interests are considered, and if a management team can agree on what should be done and has the ability to implement its decisions Functions: SWOT analysis is applicable Communities: SWOT analysis is applicable if what is "inside" and "outside" can be specified
Strategic planning systems (Lorange 1980; Lorange et al. 1986)	Systems for formulating and implementing important decisions across levels and functions in an organization Allocation and control of resources within a strategic framework and through rational decision making Attempts to comprehensively cover all key decision areas	Strategy formulation and implementation should be rational and anticipatory An organization's strategies should form an integrated whole The organization can control centrally all or most of its internal operations Goals, objectives, and performance indicators can be specified clearly Information on performance is available at reasonable cost	Coordination of strategy formulation and implementation across levels and functions Can be used in conjunction with other approaches	Excessive comprehensiveness, prescription, and control can drive out attention to mission, strategy, and organizational structure The information requirements of planning systems can exceed the participants' ability to comprehend the information	Organizations: Less comprehensive and rigorous forms of private-sector strategic planning systems are applicable to many public-sector organizations Functions: Necessary conditions for strategic planning systems to succeed are seldom met Communities: Unlikely
Stakeholder management (Freeman 1984)	Identification of key stakeholders and the criteria they use to judge an organization's performance Development of	An organization's survival and prosperity depend on the extent to which it satisfies its key stakeholders An organization's strategy will be successful only if it meets the needs of key stakeholders	Recognition that many claims, both complementary and competing, are placed on an organization Stakeholder analysis (i.e., a listing of key stakeholders and of the	Absence of criteria with which to judge different claims Need for more advice on how to develop strategies to deal with divergent stakeholder claims	Organizations: Yes, as long as agreement is possible among key decision makers over who the stakeholders are and what the organization's responses to them

Table 2–1. (Continued)

Approach	Key features	Assumptions	Strengths	Weaknesses	Applicability to the public sector
	strategies to deal with each stakeholder		criteria they use to judge an organization's performance) Can be used in conjunction with other approaches		should be. Functions: Yes, with the same caveats Communities: Yes, with the same caveats
Content approaches					
Portfolio methods (Henderson 1979; Wind and Mahajian 1981; MacMillan 1983)	A corporation's businesses are categorized into groups based on selected dimensions for comparison and development of corporate strategy in relation to each business Attempts to balance a corporation's business portfolio to meet corporate strategic objectives	Aggregate assessment of a corporation's various businesses is important to the corporation's success Resources should be channeled into the different businesses to meet the corporation's cash flow and investment needs A few key dimensions of strategic importance can be identified against which to judge the performance of individual businesses A group exists that can make and implement decisions based on the portfolio analysis	Provides a method for evaluating a set of businesses against dimensions that are deemed to be of strategic importance to the corporation Provides a useful way of understanding some of the key economic and financial aspects of corporate strategy Can be used as part of a larger strategic planning process	Difficult to know what the relevant strategic dimensions are, what the relevant entities to be compared are, and how to classify entities against dimensions Unclear how to use the tool as part of a larger strategic planning process	Organizations: Yes, if economic, social, and political dimensions of comparison can be specified, entities to be compared can be identified, and a group exists that can make and implement decisions based on the portfolio analysis Functions: Yes, with the same caveats Communities: Yes, with the same caveats
Competitive analysis (Porter 1980; 1985; Harrigan 1981)	Analysis of key forces that shape an industry, e.g., relative power of customers, relative power of suppliers, threat of substitute products, threat of new entrants, amount of rivalrous activity, exit barriers to firms in the industry	Predominance of competitive behavior on the part of firms within an industry The stronger the forces that shape an industry, the lower the general level of returns in the industry The stronger the forces affecting a firm, the lower the profits for the firm Analysis of the forces will allow one to identify the best strategy whereby an industry can raise its general level of returns and whereby a firm within an industry can maximize its profits	Provides a systematic method of assessing the economic aspects of an industry and the strategic options facing the industry and specific firms within it Gives relatively clear prescriptions for strategic action Can be used as part of a larger strategic planning process	Sometimes difficult to identify what the relevant industry is Excludes consideration of potentially relevant noneconomic factors Tends to ignore the possibility that organizational success may turn on collaboration, not competition	Organizations: Yes, for organizations in identifiable industries (e.g., public hospitals, transit companies, recreation facilities) if a competitive analysis is coupled with a consideration of noneconomic factors and if the possibility of collaboration is also considered Functions: Yes, if the function equates to an industry Communities: No
Strategic issues management (Ansoff 1980; King 1982; Pflaum and Delmont 1987)	Attention to the recognition and resolution of strategic issues	Strategic issues are issues that can have a major influence on the organization and must be managed if the organization is to meet its objectives Strategic issues can be identified by the use of a variety of tools (e.g., SWOT analyses and environmental scanning methods) Early identification of issues will result in more favorable resolution and greater likelihood of enhanced organizational performance A group exists that is able to engage in the process and manage the issue	Ability to identify and respond quickly to issues Has a "real time" orientation and is compatible with most organizations Can be used in conjunction with other approaches	No specific advice is offered on how to frame issues other than to precede their identification with a situational analysis	Organizations: Yes, as long as there is a group able to engage in the process and manage the issue Functions: Yes, with the same caveat Communities: Yes, with the same caveat
Process strategies					
Strategic negotiations	Bargaining and negotiation among	Organizations are "shared power" settings in which	Recognizes that there are many actors in the	Little advice on how to ensure technical	Organizations: Yes Functions: Yes

Table 2–1. (Continued)

Approach	Key features	Assumptions	Strengths	Weaknesses	Applicability to the public sector
(Pettigrew 1982; Fisher and Ury 1981; Allison 1971)	two or more players over the identification and resolution of strategic issues	groups must cooperate, bargain, and negotiate with each other in order to achieve their ends and assure organizational survival Strategy is created as part of a relatively constant struggle among competing groups in an organization Strategy is the emergent product of the partial resolution of organizational issues	strategy formulation and implementation process and that they often do not share common goals Recognizes the desirability of bargaining and negotiation in order for groups to achieve their ends and to assure organizational survival Can be used in conjunction with other approaches	workability and democratic responsibility—as opposed to political acceptability—of results No assurance that overall organizational goals can or will be achieved; there may not be a whole equal to, let alone greater than, the sum of the parts	Communities: Yes
Logical incrementalism (Quinn 1980; Lindblom 1959)	Emphasizes the importance of small changes as part of developing and implementing organizational strategies Fuses strategy formulation and implementation	Strategy is a loosely linked group of decisions that are handled incrementally Decentralized decision making is both politically expedient and necessary Small, decentralized decisions can help identify and fulfill organizational purposes	Ability to handle complexity and change Attention to both formal and informal processes Political realism Emphasis on both minor and major decisions Can be used in conjunction with other approaches	No guarantee that the loosely linked, incremental decisions will add up to fulfillment of overall organizational purposes	Organizations: Yes, as long as overall organizational purposes can be identified to provide a framework for incremental decisions Functions: Yes, with the same caveat Communities: Yes, with the same caveat
Framework for innovation (Taylor 1984; Pinchot 1985)	Emphasis on innovation as a strategy Reliance on many elements of the other approaches and specific management practices	Change is unavoidable, and continuous innovation to deal with change is necessary if the organization is to survive and prosper A "vision of success" is necessary to provide the organization with a common set of superordinate goals toward which to work Innovation as a strategy will not work without an entrepreneurial company culture to support it	Allows innovation and entrepreneurship while maintaining central control on key outcomes Fosters a commitment to innovation Can be used in conjunction with other approaches	Costly mistakes usually are necessary as part of the process of innovation Decentralization and local control result in some loss of accountability	Organizations: Yes, but the public is unwilling to allow public organizations to make the mistakes necessary as part of the process and development of an overall framework within which to innovate and maintain central control over key outcomes is difficult Functions: Yes, but with the same caveats Communities: Yes, with same caveats

APPROACHES TO CORPORATE STRATEGIC PLANNING

Although the roots of public sector strategic planning are deep, most of the history and development of the concepts, procedures, and tools of strategic planning in this century have occurred in the private sector.[1] This history has been amply documented by others (Bracker 1980). We briefly set forth six schools of thought or models of strategic planning developed in the private sector and discuss their key features, assumptions, strengths, weaknesses, applicability to the public sector, and contingencies governing their use.

As noted above, strategic planning as a concept involves general policy and direction set-ting, situation assessments, strategic issue identification, strategy development, decision making, action, and evaluation. We begin with the approaches that cover more of the process and highlight policy and direction setting; then we move to approaches that focus more nar-rowly on elements in the later stages of the pro-cess we have outlined.

The Harvard Policy Model

The Harvard policy model was developed as part of, and has been included in, the business policy course taught at the Harvard Business School since the 1920s (Christensen et al. 1983 and earlier versions). The approach provides the principal inspiration behind the most widely cited recent models of public sector stra-tegic planning (e.g., Olsen and Eadie 1982; Sor-kin, Ferris, and Hudak 1984). (See Table 2–1.)

The main purpose of the Harvard model is to help a firm develop the best fit between it-self and its environment; that is, to develop the best strategy for the firm. As articulated by Andrews (1980), strategy is "a pattern of pur-poses and policies defining the company and its business." One discerns the best strategy by analyzing the internal strengths and weak-nesses of the company and the values of sen-ior management, then identifying the external threats and opportunities in the environment and the social obligations of the firm.

Effective use of the model presumes that agreement is possible among the members of a top management team about the firm's situ-ation and the appropriate strategic response. Further, the model presumes the team has enough authority to enforce its decisions. A final important assumption of the model—common to all approaches to strategic plan-ning—is that if the appropriate strategy is iden-tified and implemented, the organization will be more effective.

The process presented in Figure 2–1 is strongly influenced by the Harvard model. Central to the process is attention to the inter-nal strengths and weaknesses of the govern-ment or agency, to the values of key stake-holders (not just senior managers), and to the external threats, opportunities, and mandates (not just social obligations) affecting the gov-ernment or agency.

In the business world, the Harvard model appears to be best applied at the level of the strategic business unit. A strategic business unit is a distinct business that has its own com-petitors and can be managed somewhat inde-pendently of other units within the organiza-tion (Rue and Holland 1986). The strategic business unit, in other words, provides an im-portant yet bounded and manageable focus for the model. The public sector equivalent of the strategic business unit is the strategic public planning unit, which typically would be an agency or department that addresses issues fundamentally similar in nature to one another (Montanari and Bracker 1986).

The Harvard model is also applicable at the higher and broader corporate level—in both private and public sectors—particularly if it is used with other approaches, such as the port-folio approaches to be discussed below. A port-folio approach is needed because a principal strategic concern at the corporate level is over-sight of a portfolio of businesses in the private sector or a portfolio of agencies or departments in the public sector.

The systematic assessment of strengths, weaknesses, opportunities, and threats—or SWOT analysis—is the primary strength of the

Harvard model. This element of the model appears to be applicable in the public sector to organizations, functions, and communities (Sorkin, Ferris, and Hudak 1984), although in the case of communities the distinction between inside and outside may be problematic. The main weakness of the Harvard model is that it does not offer specific advice on how to develop strategies, except to note that effective strategies will build on strengths, take advantage of opportunites, and overcome or minimize weaknesses and threats.

Strategic Planning Systems

Strategic planning often is conceived as a system whereby managers go about making, implementing, and controlling important decisions across functions and levels in the firm. Lorange (1980), for example, has argued that any strategic planning system must address four fundamental questions: (1) Where are we going? (mission), (2) How do we get there? (strategies), (3) What is our blueprint for action? (budgets), and (4) How do we know if we are on track? (control).

Strategic planning systems vary along several dimensions: the comprehensiveness of decision areas included, the formal rationality of the decision process, and the tightness of control exercised over implementation of the decisions (Armstrong 1982). The strength of these systems is their attempt to coordinate the various elements of an organization's strategy across levels and functions. Their weakness is that excessive comprehensiveness, prescription, and control can drive out attention to mission, strategy, and organizational structure (Frederickson and Mitchell 1984; Frederickson 1984) and can exceed participants' ability to comprehend them (Bryson, Van de Ven, and Roering 1987).

Strategic planning systems are applicable to public sector organizations for, regardless of the nature of the particular organization, it makes sense to coordinate decision making across levels and functions and to concentrate on whether the organization is implementing its strategies and accomplishing its mission. It is important to remember, however, that a strategic planning system characterized by substantial comprehensiveness, formal rationality in decision making, and tight control will work only in an organization that has a clear mission, clear goals and objectives, centralized authority, clear performance indicators, and information about actual performance available at reasonable cost (Stuart 1969; Galloway 1979). Few public sector organizations—or functions or communities—operate under such conditions. As a result, public sector strategic planning systems typically focus on a few areas of concern, rely on a decision process in which politics plays a major role, and control something other than program outcomes (e.g., budget expenditures) (Wildavsky 1979).

Bryson, Van de Ven, and Roering (1987) offer an example, based on the approach used by the 3M Corporation, of how such a control system might be implemented across levels in a government corporation or agency (see Figure 2–2). In the system's first cycle, there is bottom-up development of strategic plans within a framework established at the top, followed by reviews and reconciliations at each succeeding level. In the second cycle, operating plans are developed to implement the strategic plans.

A similar cyclic system is used by Hennepin County, Minnesota (the county that contains Minneapolis), to address 14 areas of strategic concern (e.g., finance, employment and economic development, transportation, and pro-

Figure 2–2. Annual Strategic Planning Process

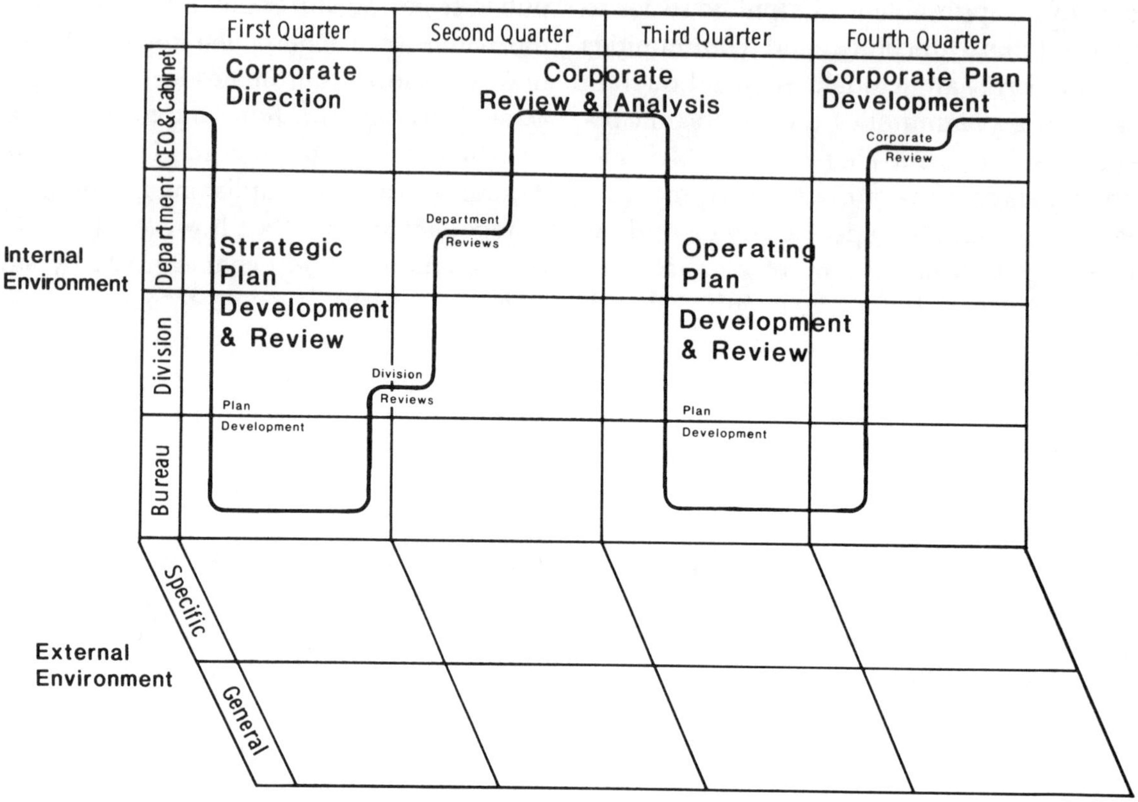

		First Quarter	Second Quarter	Third Quarter	Fourth Quarter
Internal Environment	CEO & Cabinet	Corporate Direction	Corporate Review & Analysis		Corporate Plan Development
					Corporate Review
	Department	Strategic Plan Development & Review	Department Reviews	Operating Plan Development & Review	
	Division	Plan Development	Division Reviews	Plan Development	
	Bureau				
External Environment	Specific				
	General				

Source: Bryson, Van de Ven, and Roering 1987

gram fragmentation and coordination). The system includes three cycles: strategic issue identification, strategy development, and strategy implementation (Eckhert et al. 1986).

Stakeholder Management Approaches

Freeman (1984) has argued that corporate strategy can be understood as a corporation's mode of relating or building bridges to its stakeholders. A stakeholder is "any group or individual who is affected by or who can affect the future of the corporation." Customers, employees, suppliers, owners, governments, financial institutions, and critics are examples. Freeman argues that a corporate strategy will be effective only if it satisfies the needs of multiple groups. Traditional private sector models of strategy have focused only on economic actors, but Freeman argues that changes in the current business environment require that other political and social actors must be considered as well.

Because it integrates economic, political, and social concerns, the stakeholder model is one of the approaches most applicable to the public sector. Many interest groups have stakes in public organizations, functions, and communities. For example, local economic development planning typically involves government, developers, bankers, the chamber of commerce, actual or potential employers, neighborhood groups, environmentalists, and so on. Local economic development planners would be wise to identify key stakeholders, their interests, what they will support, and strategies and tactics that might work in dealing with them (Kaufman 1979).

Bryson, Freeman, and Roering (1986) argue that an organization's mission and values ought to be formulated in stakeholder terms. That is, an organization should figure out what its mission should be in relation to each stakeholder group; otherwise, it will not be able to differentiate its responses well enough to satisfy its key stakeholders. This advice to public organizations is matched by private sector practice in several well-managed companies (O'Toole 1985). For example, the Dayton Hudson Corporation, a large retailer, identifies four key stakeholders—customers, employees, stockholders, and the communities in which it does business—and specifies what its mission is in relation to each. Dayton Hudson assumes that if it performs well in the eyes of each of those stakeholders, its success is assured.

The strengths of the stakeholder model are its recognition of the many claims—both complementary and competing—placed on organizations by insiders and outsiders and its awareness of the need to satisfy at least the key stakeholders if the organization is to survive. The weaknesses of the model are the absence of criteria with which to judge competing claims and the need for more advice on how to develop strategies to deal with divergent stakeholder interests.

Freeman has applied the stakeholder concept primarily at the corporate and industrywide levels in the private sector, but it seems applicable to all levels in the private and public sectors. Researchers have not yet made rigorous tests of the model's usefulness in the private or public sector, but there are several public sector case studies that indicate stakeholder analyses are quite useful as part of a strategic planning effort. Examples are the city government of St. Louis Park, Minnesota (Klumpp 1986), and the Ramsey County (Minnesota) Nursing Service (Allan 1985). If the model is to be used successfully, it must be possible to achieve reasonable agreement among key decision makers about who the key stakeholders are and what the response to their claims should be.

Content Approaches

The three approaches presented so far have to do more with process than with content. The process approaches do not prescribe answers, though good answers are presumed to emerge from appropriate application of them. In contrast, the tools to be discussed next—portfolio models and competitive analysis—have to do primarily with content and do yield answers. In fact, the models are antithetical to process when process concerns get in the way of developing the "right" answer.

Portfolio Models. The idea of strategic planning as managing a portfolio of businesses is based on an analogy with investment practice. Just as an investor assembles a portfolio of stocks to manage risk and realize optimum returns, a corporate manager can think of the corporation as a portfolio of businesses with diverse potentials that can be balanced to manage return and cash flow. The intellectual history of portfolio theory in corporate strategy is complex (Wind and Mahajan 1981). For our purposes it is adequate to use as an example the portfolio model developed by the Boston Consulting Group: the famous BCG Matrix (Henderson 1979).

Bruce Henderson, founder of the Boston Consulting Group, argued that all business costs followed a well-known pattern: unit costs dropped by one-third every time volume (or turnover) doubled. Hence, he postulated a relationship, known as the *experience curve*, between unit costs and volume. This relationship leads to some generic strategic advice: gain market share, for if a firm gains market share, its unit costs will fall and profit potential will increase. Henderson argued that any business could be categorized into one of four types depending on how its industry was growing and how large a share of the market it had: (1) high growth/high share businesses ("stars"), which generate substantial cash but also require large investments if their market share is to be maintained or increased; (2) low growth/high share businesses ("cash cows"), which generate large cash flows but require low investment and therefore generate profits that can be used elsewhere; (3) low growth/low share businesses ("dogs"), which produce little cash and offer little prospect of increased share; and (4) high growth/low share businesses ("question marks"), which would require substantial investment in order to become stars or cash cows (the question is whether the investment is worth it). Generic business strategies can be adopted to meet the whole corporation's cash flow and investment needs.

Although the applications of portfolio theory to the public sector may be less obvious than those of the three approaches described above, they are nonetheless just as powerful (MacMillan 1983). Many public sector organizations consist of multiple businesses that are only marginally related. Often resources from a single source are committed to these unrelated businesses. That means public sector managers must make portfolio decisions, though usually without the help of analytical portfolio models that frame those decisions strategically. The BCG approach, like most private sector portfolio models, uses only economic criteria, not the political or social criteria that might be necessary for public sector applications. Private sector portfolio approaches, therefore, must be modified substantially for public sector use.

The Philadelphia Investment Portfolio is a public sector example of a portfolio approach applied at the community level (Center for Philadelphia Studies 1982a; 1982b). The portfolio consists of 56 investment options (i.e., investments of public and private time and resources) arranged according to the degree to which they take advantage of ongoing trends (their "position") and the degree to which they facilitate the strategic objectives of the greater Philadelphia area (their "attractiveness"). (The judgments of position and attractiveness were formulated through the collaborative efforts of about 750 people in public, private, and nonprofit organizations who participated in the "Philadelphia: Past, Present, and Future" project.) Each of the two dimensions consists of a set of economic, political, and social criteria. The creators of the portfolio view Greater Philadelphia as a community of interests and stakeholders; they strive to loosely coordinate the activities of disparate parties to achieve community goals by offering specific investment options that are attractive to specific organizations or coalitions. An organization or coalition would pursue an option because that option fit its needs or desires; but the city as a whole also would benefit from the organization's decision to invest.

The strength of portfolio approaches is that they provide a method for measuring entities of some sort (e.g., businesses, investment options, proposals, or problems) against dimensions that are deemed to be of strategic importance (e.g., share and growth or position and attractiveness) for purposes of analysis and recommendation. The weaknesses of such approaches include the difficulty of knowing what the appropriate strategic dimensions are; difficulties of classifying entities against dimensions; and the lack of clarity about how to use the tool as part of a larger strategic planning process.

If modified to include political and social factors, portfolio approaches can be used in the public sector to inform strategic decisions about organizations, functions, and communities. The approaches can be used in conjunction with process approaches, such as the one outlined in Figure 2–1, to provide useful information as part of an assessment of an organization, function, or community in relation to its environment. Unlike the process models, however, portfolio approaches provide an answer as to what that relationship should be once the dimensions of comparison and the entities to be compared are specified. The answer would be accepted only if a dominant coalition could be convinced that the answer was correct.

Competitive Analysis. Another important content approach to assist with strategy selection has been developed by Michael Porter (1980, 1985) and his associates. Called competitive analysis, it assumes that by analyzing the forces that shape an industry, one can predict the general level of profits throughout the industry and the likely success of any particu-

lar strategy for a strategic business unit. Porter (1980) hypothesizes that five key forces shape an industry: relative power of customers, relative power of suppliers, threat of substitute products, threat of new entrants, and the amount of rivalrous activity among the players in the industry. Harrigan (1981) has argued that "exit barriers"—that is, the barriers that would prevent a company from leaving an industry—are a sixth force influencing success in some industries. There are two main propositions in the competitive analysis school: (1) the stronger the forces that shape an industry, the lower the general level of returns in the industry; and (2) the stronger the forces affecting a strategic business unit, the lower the profits for that unit.

For many public sector organizations, there are equivalents to the forces that affect private industry. Client or customer power often is exercised in the public arena, and suppliers of services (e.g., organizations providing contract services and the government's or agency's own labor supply) also can exercise power. There are fewer new entrants, but recently the private sector has begun to compete more forcefully with public organizations. And governments and agencies also often compete with one another (e.g., public hospitals for patients, or states and localities for the General Motors Saturn plant). An effective organization in the public sector, therefore, must understand the forces at work in its "industry" in order to compete effectively. On another level, planning for a specific public sector function (e.g., health care, transportation, and recreation) can benefit from competitive analysis if the function can be considered an industry. In addition, economic development agencies must understand the forces at work in given industries and on specific firms if they are to understand whether and how to nurture those industries and firms. Finally, although communities often compete with one another, competitive analysis does not apply at that level because communities are not industries in any meaningful sense.

The strength of competitive analysis is that it provides a systematic way of assessing industries and the strategic options facing strategic business units within those industries. For public sector applications, the weaknesses of competitive analysis are that (1) it is often difficult to know what the industry is and what forces affect it, and (2) the key to organizational success in the public sector is often collaboration instead of competition. Competitive analyses in the public sector, therefore, must be coupled with a consideration of social and political forces and the possibilities for collaboration.

Strategic Issue Management

We now leave content approaches to focus again on process approaches. Strategic issue management approaches are process components or pieces of the larger strategic planning process presented in Figure 2–1. Strategic issue management is primarily associated with Ansoff (1980) and focuses attention on the recognition and resolution of *strategic issues* — "forthcoming developments, either inside or outside the organization, which are likely to have an important impact on the ability of the enterprise to meet its objectives." The concept of strategic issues first emerged when practitioners of corporate strategic planning realized a step was missing between the SWOT analysis of the Harvard model and the development of strategies. That step was the identification of strategic issues. Many firms now include a

strategic issue identification step as part of full-blown strategy revision exercises and also as part of less comprehensive annual strategic reviews (King 1982). Full-blown annual revision has proved impractical because strategy revision takes substantial management energy and attention, and most strategies take several years to implement anyway. Instead, most firms are undertaking comprehensive strategy revisions several years apart (typically five) and in the interim are focusing their annual strategic planning processes on the identification and resolution of a few key strategic issues that emerge from SWOT analyses, environmental scans (Hambrick 1982; Pflaum and Delmont 1987), and other analyses.

In recent years many firms have developed strategic issue management processes actually separated from their annual strategic planning processes. Many important issues emerge too quickly to be handled as part of an annual process. A separate, quick response is necessary. Typically task forces reporting directly to top management are used to develop responses to pressing issues that unexpectedly turn up.

Strategic issue management clearly is applicable to governments and agencies as well, since the agendas of these organizations consist of issues that should be managed strategically (Ring and Perry 1985). In other words, they should be managed based on a sense of mission and mandates and in the context of an environmental assessment. The strength of the approach is its ability to recognize and analyze key issues quickly. The weakness of the approach is that no specific advice is offered on exactly how to frame the issues other than to precede their identification with a situational analysis of some sort. The approach also applies to functions and places or communities, as long as some group, organization, or coalition is able to engage in the process and to manage the issue.

Process Strategies

The final three process approaches to be discussed are, in effect, strategies. They are strategic negotiations, logical incrementalism, and strategic planning as a framework for innovation.

Strategic Negotiations. Several writers view corporate strategy as the partial resolution of organizational issues through a highly political process (Pettigrew 1977; Mintzberg and Waters 1985). As envisioned by Pettigrew (1977), strategic negotiations are very much contextually based, as strategy is viewed as the flow of actions and values embedded in a context.

The applicability of this view of strategy to the public sector is clear when one realizes that Allison's (1971) study of the Cuban Missile Crisis provided much of the stimulus for this line of private sector work. Negotiation has become an increasingly important focus of planning research and practice (Susskind and Ozawa 1984). An example of planning-related strategic negotiations is the Negotiated Investment Strategy project of the Charles F. Kettering Foundation (1982), in which federal, state, and local agencies in several cities worked out a coordinated investment strategy designed to meet the strategic objectives of each.

The strength of a negotiation approach is that it recognizes that power is shared in most public situations; no one person, group, or organization is "in charge," and cooperation and negotiation with others is often necessary in order for people, groups, and organizations to achieve their ends (Bryson and Einsweiler 1986). The main weakness of negotiation approaches—as expounded, for example, by Fisher and Ury (1981) in *Getting to Yes*—is that although they can show planners how to reach politically acceptable results, they are not very helpful in assuring technical workability or democratic responsibility of results.

Logical Incrementalism. Incremental approaches view strategy as a loosely linked group of decisions that are handled incrementally. Decisions are handled individually below the corporate level because such decentralization is politically expedient—corporate leaders should reserve their political clout for crucial decisions. Decentralization also is necessary—those closest to decisions are the only ones with enough information to make good decisions.

The incremental approach is identified principally with Quinn (1980), though the influence of Lindblom (1959) is apparent. Quinn developed the concept of *logical incrementalism*—or incrementalism in the service of overall corporate purposes—and as a result transformed incrementalism into a strategic approach. Logical incrementalism is a process approach that, in effect, fuses strategy formulation and implementation. The strengths of the approach are its ability to handle complexity and change, its emphasis on minor as well as major decisions, its attention to informal as well as formal processes, and its political realism. The major weakness of the approach is that it does not guarantee that the various loosely linked decisions will add up to fulfillment of corporate purposes. Logical incrementalism would appear to be very applicable to public sector organizations, functions, and places or communities—the situations in which, and for which, Lindblom first developed the incremental model—as long as it is possible to establish some overarching set of strategic objectives to be served by the approach.

Strategic Planning as a Framework for Innovation. Above we discussed strategic planning systems and noted that excessive comprehensiveness, prescription, and control could drive out attention to mission, strategy, and organizational structure. The systems, in other words, can become ends in themselves and drive out creativity, innovation, and new product and market development, without which most businesses would die (Schon 1971). Many businesses, therefore, have found it necessary to emphasize innovative strategies as a counterbalance to the excessive control orientation of many strategic planning systems. In other words, while one important reason for installing a strategic planning system is the need to exercise control across functions and levels, an equally important need for organizations is to design systems that promote creativity and entrepreneurship at the local level and prevent centralization and bureaucracy from stifling the wellsprings of business growth and change (Taylor 1984).

The framework-for-innovation approach to corporate strategic planning relies on many of the elements of the approaches discussed above, such as SWOT analyses and portfolio methods. This approach differs from earlier ones in that it emphasizes (1) innovation as a strategy, (2) specific management practices to support the strategy (e.g., project teams; venture groups; diversification, acquisition, and divestment task forces; research and development operations; new product and market groups; and a variety of organizational development techniques), (3) development of a vision of success that provides the decentralized and entrepreneurial parts of the organization with a common set of superordinate goals toward which to work, and (4) nurture of an entrepreneurial company culture (Pinchot 1985).

The strength of the approach is that it allows for innovation and entrepreneurship while maintaining central control. The weaknesses of the approach are that typically—and perhaps necessarily—a great many, often costly, mistakes are made as part of the innovation process and that there is a certain loss of accountability in very decentralized systems (Peters and Waterman 1982). Those weaknesses reduce the applicability of the approach to the public sector, in which mistakes are less acceptable and the pressures to be accountable for details (as opposed to results) are often greater (Ring and Perry 1985).

Nonetheless, the innovation approach would appear to be applicable to public sector organizations when the management of innovation is needed (e.g., Zaltman, Florio, and Sikorski 1977), as in the redesign of a public service (e.g., Savas 1982). Innovation as a strategy also can and should be pursued for functions and communities. Too often a distressing equation has operated in the public sector: more money equals more service, less money equals less service. As public budgets have become increasingly strapped, there has not been enough innovation and public service redesign. The equation does not need to be destiny; it is possible that creative effort and innovation might actually result in more service for less money.

CONCLUSIONS

Our purpose in this chapter has been to compare and contrast six approaches to corporate-style strategic planning, to discuss their applicability to the public sector, and to identify major contingencies governing their use. Several conclusions emerge from our review and analysis.

First, it should be clear that corporate strategic planning is not a single concept, procedure, or tool. In fact, it embraces a range of approaches that vary in their applicability to the public sector and in the conditions that govern their successful use. The public sector strategic planning process outlined above provides a useful framework for review and critique of the private sector approaches to strategic planning and their applicability to the public sector. The process comprises broad policy or direction setting, internal and external assessments, attention to key stakeholders, the identification of key issues, development of strategies to deal with each issue, decision making, action, and continuous monitoring of results. The process is applicable to organizations, functions, and places or communities. The private sector approaches to corporate strategic planning, in contrast, emphasize different parts of this whole strategic planning process, and each is focused on a given organization.

Second, although the public sector strategic planning process is a useful framework to guide thought and action, it must be applied with care to any given situation, as is true of any planning process (Bryson and Delbecq 1979; Galloway 1979; Christensen 1985). Because every planning process should be tailored to fit specific situations, every process in practice will be a hybrid. We have outlined a number of general assumptions and conditions governing successful use of the private sector strategic planning approaches in the public sector in order to facilitate construction of such hybrids.

Third, we think familiarity with strategic planning should be a standard part of the intellectual and skill repertoire of all public planners. Given the dramatic changes in the environments of public organizations in recent years, we expect elected public officials, public managers, and planners to pay increased attention to the formulation and implementation of effective strategies to deal with the changes. When applied appropriately to public sector conditions, strategic planning provides a set of concepts, procedures, and tools for doing just that. We suspect the most effective public planners are now—and will be increasingly in the future—the ones who are best at *strategic* planning.

Fourth, our assertion about the increased importance of strategic planning raises the question of the appropriate role of the strategic planner. In many ways this is an old debate in the planning literature. Should the planner be a technician, politician, or hybrid, i.e., both a technician and a politician (Howe and Kaufman 1979; Howe 1980)? Or should the planner not be a planner at all, at least formally, but instead be a line manager (Bryson, Van de Ven, and Roering 1987)? We believe the strategic planner can be solely a technician only when content approaches are used. When all other approaches are used, the strategic planner should be a hybrid, so that there is some assurance that both political and technical concerns are addressed. Furthermore, since strategic planning tends to fuse planning and decision making, it is helpful to think of decision makers as strategic planners and to think of strategic planners as facilitators of strategic decision making across levels and functions in organizations and communities.

Finally, research must explore a number of

theoretical and empirical issues in order to advance the knowledge and practice of public strategic planning. In particular, contingent models for public strategic planning must be developed and tested. These models should specify key situational factors governing use; provide specific advice on how to formulate and implement strategies in different situations; be explicitly political; indicate how to deal with plural, ambiguous, or conflicting goals or objectives; link content and process; indicate how collaboration as well as competition is to be handled; and specify roles for the strategic planner. Progress has been made on all of those fronts (Checkoway 1986), but more is necessary if public sector strategic planning is to help public organizations, functions, and communities fulfill their missions and serve their stakeholders effectively, efficiently, and responsibly.

AUTHORS' NOTE

The authors would like to gratefully acknowledge the helpful advice of Bob Einsweiler, Ray Burby, Ed Kaiser, and three anonymous reviewers of earlier drafts of this chapter. Whatever readability the paper has we owe principally to the efforts of Barbara Crosby.

NOTE

1. The word "strategy" comes from the Greek word *stratego*, a combination of *stratos*, or army, and *ego*, or leader (O'Toole 1985). Strategic planning thus began as the art of the general and now has become the art of the general manager.

REFERENCES

Allan, J. H. 1985. A case study of the Ramsey County Nursing Service strategic planning process. Plan B paper. Minneapolis, Minn.: School of Public Health, University of Minnesota.

Allison, G. T. 1971. *Essence of decision.* Boston, Mass.: Little, Brown.

Andrews, K. 1980. *The concept of corporate strategy.* Rev. ed. Homewood, Ill.: R. D. Irwin.

Ansoff, I. 1980. Strategic issue management. *Strategic Management Journal* 1, 2: 131–148.

Armstrong, J. S. 1982. The value of formal planning for strategic decisions: Review of empirical research. *Strategic Management Journal* 3, 2: 197–211.

Bloom, C. 1986. Strategic planning in the public sector. *Journal of Planning Literature* 1, 2: 253–59.

Bracker, J. 1980. The historical development of the strategic management concept. *Academy of Management Review* 5, 2: 219–224.

Bryson, J. M. 1983. Representing and testing procedural planning methods. In *Evaluating Urban Planning Efforts*, edited by Ian Masser. Hampshire, England: Gower Publishing Company.

———— and A. L. Delbecq. 1979. A contingent approach to strategy and tactics in project planning. *Journal of the American Planning Association* 45, 2: 167–179.

———— and R. C. Einsweiler, eds. 1986. *Shared power: What is it? How does it work? How can we make it work better?* Lanham, Md.: University Press of America.

————, R. E. Freeman, and W. D. Roering. 1986. Strategic planning in the public sector: Approaches and directions. In *Strategic Perspectives on Planning Practice*, edited by B. Checkoway, Lexington, Mass.: Lexington Books.

————, A. H. Van de Ven, and W. D. Roering. 1987. Strategic planning and the revitalization of the public service. In *Toward a New Public Service*, edited by R. Denhardt and E. Jennings. Columbia, Mo.: University of Missouri Press (forthcoming).

Center for Philadelphia Studies. 1982a. *A Philadelphia prospectus.* Philadelphia, Penn.: University of Pennsylvania.

————. 1982b. *Philadelphia investment portfolio.* Philadelphia, Penn.: University of Pennsylvania.

Charles F. Kettering Foundation. 1982. *Negotiated investment strategy.* Dayton, Ohio: Charles F. Kettering Foundation.

Checkoway, B., ed. 1986. *Strategic perspectives on planning practice.* Lexington, Mass.: Lexington Books.

Christensen, K. S. 1985. Coping with uncertainty in planning. *Journal of the American Planning Association* 51, 1: 63–73.

Christensen, R., K. Andrews, J. Bower, R. Hammermesh, and M. Porter. 1983. *Business policy: Text and cases.* Homewood, Ill.: R. D. Irwin.

Eckhert, P., K. Korbelik, T. Delmont, and A. Pflaum. 1986. *Strategic planning in Hennepin County, Minnesota:*

An issues management approach. Paper presented to the American Planning Association, National Planning Conference, Los Angeles. April.

Fisher, R. and W. Ury. 1981. *Getting to yes: Negotiating agreement without giving in.* New York, N.Y.: Penguin Books.

Fredrickson, J. W. 1984. The comprehensiveness of strategic decision processes. *Academy of Management Journal* 27, 2: 445–466.

———— and T. R. Mitchell. 1984. Strategic decision processes: Comprehensiveness and performance in an industry with an unstable environment. *Academy of Management Journal* 27, 2: 399–423.

Freeman, R. E. 1984. *Strategic management: A stakeholder approach.* Boston, Mass.: Pitman.

Galloway, T. D. 1979. Comment on "Comparison of Current Planning Theories: Counterparts and Contradictions," by B. M. Hudson. *Journal of the American Planning Association* 45, 4: 399–402.

Gilbert, D. R. and R. E. Freeman. 1985. Strategic management and responsibility: A game theoretic approach. Discussion paper 22. Minneapolis, Minn.: Strategic Management Research Center, University of Minnesota.

Hambrick, D. C. 1982. Environmental scanning and organizational strategy. *Strategic Management Journal* 3, 2: 159–174.

Harrigan, K. 1981. Barriers to entry and competitive strategies. *Strategic Management Journal* 2, 4: 395–412.

Henderson, B. 1979. *Henderson on corporate strategy.* Cambridge, Mass.: Abt Books.

Howe, E. 1980. Role choices of urban planners. *Journal of the American Planning Association* 46, 4: 398–409.

———— and J. Kaufman. 1979. The ethics of contemporary American planners. *Journal of the American Planning Association* 45, 3: 243–255.

Kaufman, J. L. 1979. The planner as interventionist in public policy issues. In *Planning Theory in the 1980s,* edited by R. Burchell and G. Sternlieb. New Brunswick, N.J.: Center for Urban Policy Research, Rutgers University.

———— and H. M. Jacobs. 1987. A public planning perspective on strategic planning. *Journal of the American Planning Association* 53, 1: 21–31.

King, W. R. 1982. Using strategic issue analysis. *Long Range Planning* 15, 4: 45–49.

Klumpp, S. 1986. *Strategic planning booklet for the city of St. Louis Park.* St. Louis Park, Minn.: City of St. Louis Park.

Lindblom, C. E. 1959. The science of muddling through. *Public Administration Review* 19 (Spring): 79–88.

Linneman, R. E. and H. E. Klein. 1983. The use of multiple scenarios by U.S. industrial companies: A comparison study, 1977–1981. *Long Range Planning* 16, 6: 94–101.

Locke, E. A., K. W. Shaw, L. M. Saari, and G. P. Latham. 1981. Goal setting and task performance: 1969–1980. *Psychological Bulletin* 90, 1: 125–152.

Lorange, P. 1980. *Corporate planning: An executive viewpoint.* Englewood Cliffs, N.J.: Prentice-Hall.

————, M. F. S. Morton, and S. Ghoshal. 1986. *Strategic control.* St. Paul, Minn.: West.

MacMillan, I. 1983. Competitive strategies for not-for-profit agencies. *Advances in Strategic Management* 1: 61–82.

McGowan, R. P. and J. M. Stevens. 1983. Local governments initiatives in a climate of uncertainty. *Public Administration Review* 43, 2: 127–136.

Mintzberg, H. and J. A. Waters. 1985. Of strategies, deliberate and emergent. *Strategic Management Journal* 6, 3: 257–272.

Montanari, J. R. and J. S. Bracker. 1986. The strategic management process. *Strategic Management Journal* 7, 3: 251–265.

Olsen, J. B. and D. C. Eadie. 1982. *The game plan: Governance with foresight.* Washington. D.C.: Council of State Planning Agencies.

O'Toole, J. 1985. *Vanguard management.* New York, N. Y.: Doubleday.

Ouchi, W. 1981. *Theory Z: How American business can meet the Japanese challenge.* Reading, Mass.: Addison-Wesley.

Peters, T. J., and R. H. Waterman, Jr. 1982. *In search of excellence: Lessons from America's best-run companies.* New York, N.Y.: Harper and Row.

Pettigrew, A. M. 1977. Strategy formulation as a political process. *International Studies in Management and Organization* 7, 2: 78–87.

Pfeffer, J. and G. R. Salanick. 1978. *The external control of organizations: A resource dependence perspective.* New York, N.Y.: Harper and Row.

Pflaum, A. and T. Delmont. 1987. External scanning—A tool for planners. *Journal of the American Planning Association* 53, 1: 56–67.

Pinchot, G., III. 1985. *Intrapreneuring.* New York, N.Y.: Harper and Row.

Porter, M. 1980. *Competitive strategy.* New York, N.Y.: Free Press.

————. 1985. *Competitive advantage.* New York, N.Y.: Free Press.

Quinn, J. B. 1980. *Strategies for change: Logical incrementalism.* Homewood, Ill.: R. D. Irwin.

Ring P. S. and J. L. Perry. 1985. Strategic management in public and private organizations: Implications of distinctive contexts and constraints. *Academy of Management Review* 10, 2: 276–286.

Rue, L. W. and P. G. Holland. 1986. *Strategic management: Concepts and experiences.* New York, N.Y.: McGraw-Hill.

Savas, E. S. 1982. *Privatizing the public sector.* Chatham, N.J.: Chatham House.

Schon, D. A. 1971. *Beyond the stable state.* London: Temple Smith.

Sorkin, D. L., N. B. Ferris, and J. Hudak. 1984. *Strategies for cities and counties: A strategic planning guide.* Washington, D.C.: Public Technology, Inc.

Stuart, D. G. 1969. Rational urban planning: Problems and prospects. *Urban Affairs Quarterly* 5 (December): 151–182.

Susskind, L. E. and C. Ozawa. 1984. Mediated negotiation in the public sector: The planner as mediator. *Journal of Planning Education and Research* 4, 1: 5–15.

Taylor, B. 1984. Strategic planning—Which style do you need? *Long Range Planning* 17, 3: 51–62.

Thompson, J. D. 1967. *Organizations in action.* New York, N.Y.: McGraw-Hill.

Tomazinis, A. R. 1985. The logic and rationale of strategic planning. Paper presented at the 27th annual conference of the Association of Collegiate Schools of Planning, Atlanta, Georgia. October.

Wildavsky, A. 1979. *The politics of the budgeting process.* 3d ed. Boston, Mass.: Little, Brown.

Wind, Y. and V. Mahajan. 1981. Designing product and business portfolios. *Harvard Business Review* 59, 1: 155–165.

Zaltman, G., D. Florio, and L. Sikorski. 1977. *Dynamic educational change.* New York, N.Y.: Free Press.

3

A Public Planning Perspective on Strategic Planning

Jerome L. Kaufman
Harvey M. Jacobs

Twenty-five years ago, at a planning conference session on the newly minted Community Renewal Program—during which many spoke enthusiastically about the potential of the new program—a skeptic got up and stated bluntly: "The Community Renewal Program is just the latest fad to hit town. Sooner or later it, too, will fade away into oblivion." Whether or not the corporate strategic planning approach to planning in the public sector will prove to have been another passing fad remains to be seen. But there is no doubt that it is the center of a lot of attention nowadays.

In the past five years a rash of articles have called on state and local governments to use the strategic planning approach developed in the corporate world (Olsen and Eadie 1982; Eadie 1983; Boyle 1983; Sorkin, Ferris, and Hudak 1984; Toft 1984; Denhardt 1985; Bryson, Van de Ven, and Roering 1987; Eadie and Steinbacher 1985; Tomazinis 1985). During the same period, strategic plans based on the corporate model have been undertaken for an increasing number of governmental jurisdictions: cities such as San Francisco, San Luis Obispo, and Pasadena, California; Philadelphia, Pennsylvania; Albany, New York; Memphis, Tennessee; and Windsor,

Connecticut; counties such as Hennepin in Minnesota, Dade in Florida, Prince Georges in Maryland, and Prince William in Virginia; and states such as California, Ohio, and Wisconsin. The number of conferences on how to do strategic planning in the public sector is also on the rise. Even the Reagan administration has become a strong supporter of the strategic planning approach for communities. A key section of the administration's 1982 National Urban Policy Report, "Strategies for Cities," reads as if it were taken from a textbook on corporate strategic planning, with its liberal use of terms such as "strategic approach," "external factors," "threats and opportunities," "internal strengths and weaknesses," "comparative advantages," "strategic issues," and the like. The emergence of corporate strategic planning in public planning parallels the rise of economic development in the late 1970s as a focus of local planning. But corporate strategic planning is not limited to economic development planning. It can be and has been applied to transportation, health, environmental, and other functional planning areas. Likewise, it can be and has been applied to planning at the regional and state levels as well as at the city level.

Proponents of corporate strategic planning claim numerous benefits will accrue to communities that follow it. The authors of the *Strategic Planning Guide* funded by the U.S. Department of Housing and Urban Development (Sorkin, Ferris, and Hudak 1984), for example, contend that the approach can result in getting important things accomplished, educating the public, building consensus, developing a shared vision that extends past the next election, positioning a community to seize opportunities, shedding new light on important issues, identifying the most effective uses of resources, and providing a mechanism for public–private cooperation. Some academics contend that, "when done well, strategic planning offers one approach to the revitalization and redirection of governments and the public service" (Bryson, Van de Ven, and Roering 1987).

But there is another side of corporate strategic planning that directly challenges the public planning profession. Some proponents of the approach explicitly or implicitly fault traditional public planning for not having done the job, accusing it of falling short of the mark. They see the corporate strategic planning approach as better suited than more traditional public planning to helping communities cope with changes induced by a dwindling resource base. Given the criticism of traditional public planning approaches and the growing popularity of the corporate strategic planning approach, the field of urban and regional planning may well face crises of both relevance and professional identity.

The purpose of this chapter is to examine strategic planning from a public planning perspective, stressing the application of this approach to communitywide planning, the tradi-

tional focus of public planning. This is distinct from the application of strategic planning to organizations, which might focus on how the city as a public corporation or a single city agency can accomplish its missions more effectively. We first define the corporate strategic planning approach examined in this article. Then we examine the approach in terms of its similarities to and differences from other public planning approaches, based on a review of literature familiar to most public planners. We supplement the literature review with an exploratory study of 15 public sector planners who work in communities where corporate strategic planning is under way, in order to assess practitioners' perspectives on how this approach is similar to and different from other public planning approaches. We close with speculations on how public sector planners might view the advent of strategic planning.

A DEFINITION

Strategic planning originated about 20 years ago in the private sector. Its roots are tied to the need of rapidly changing and growing corporations to plan effectively for and manage their futures, when the future itself appeared increasingly uncertain. By the end of the 1960s, Steiner (1969) estimated, three-quarters of the large industrial corporations in the United States had formal strategic planning in place. By the mid-1980s more than half of the publicly traded companies were using some form of strategic planning (Denhardt 1985).

As it developed, strategic planning began taking a variety of paths. Taylor (1984) identifies five main styles of corporate strategic planning that have emerged in recent years: central control, framework for innovation, strategic management, political planning, and futures research. Bryson, Freeman, and Roering (1986) also distinguish among five models of strategic planning: the Harvard policy, portfolio, industrial economics, stakeholder, and decision process models.

The central features of public sector strategic planning are captured in the acronym *SWOT*, a derivative of the Harvard policy model. In general, a community assesses its strengths, *w*eaknesses, *o*pportunities, and *t*hreats as a basis for devising action strategies to achieve goals and objectives in certain key issue areas. Recognizing that variations are possible in the sequencing of, time spent in, and analytic depth devoted to each phase of the strategic planning process, Sorkin, Ferris, and Hudak (1984) identify the following as the basic steps in strategic planning at the community level:

1. Scan the environment.
2. Select key issues.
3. Set mission statements or broad goals.
4. Undertake external and internal analyses.
5. Develop goals, objectives, and strategies with respect to each issue.
6. Develop an implementation plan to carry out strategic actions.
7. Monitor, update, and scan.

In this conception of corporate strategic planning, opportunities and threats are assessed in step 1 and used as the basis for action in steps 2 and 3. Strengths and weaknesses are developed most pointedly in step 4, but they also serve as the basis for refining decisions in steps 2 and 3 and formulating strategies in steps 5 and 6. Strengths, weaknesses, opportunities, and threats are used together in step 7 to evaluate a plan and determine its continued viability.

For our purpose, we use the above concep- tion as the definition of strategic planning as it is applied in the public sector. Our concern is with the application of strategic planning to communitywide planning, the traditional domain of public planners. Eadie and Steinbacher (1985) and Bryson, Freeman, and Roering (1986) note that strategic planning can be, and has been, applied to both communitywide and line agency planning. The approach outlined above applies broadly to both. The strong history of strategic planning, however, is as a management tool for organizations. It is the proposed application of strategic planning to communitywide issues that is new and raises issues of theory and method for public planners.

THE VIEW FROM THE PLANNING LITERATURE

Consider the following scene: Two rooms adjoin with a door between them. In one room, people are busily at work developing and refining the strategic planning model for use by private corporations. In the other room, a similar intensity of activity goes on as people work at developing and refining planning process models for use in the public sector. No movement, however, takes place between occupants of the two rooms. The door between the rooms is shut tightly.

This metaphor describes what we believe went on from the 1960s to the early 1980s in the respective spheres of corporate strategic planning and public planning. People were hard at work in both spheres, but little or no interaction took place between them. We doubt that more than a handful of corporate strategic planners ever read the articles and books that were cornerstones of reading lists in graduate planning theory courses—for example, Altshuler (1965), Davidoff and Reiner (1962), Etzioni (1967), Meyerson (1956), and Friedmann (1973). Likewise, readings on the corporate strategic planning approach probably were never assigned to students who took planning theory courses before 1980—for instance, the works of Drucker (1954), Chandler (1962), Ansoff (1965), Steiner (1969), and Steiner and Miner (1977).

But in the 1980s the door between the two rooms opened. Some planning academics are walking into the corporate strategic planning room, looking around, and coming to the conclusion that the corporate strategic planning model has applicability for public planning (Bryson, Van de Ven, and Roering 1987; Lang 1986; Tomazinis 1985). Likewise, some proponents of the corporate strategic planning approach (Eadie 1983; Sorkin, Ferris, and Hudak 1984; Toft 1984; Denhardt 1985) are strolling into the public planning room, gazing around, and arriving at a similar conclusion—that the corporate strategic planning approach can be of benefit to communities that public planners traditionally have served.

Some proponents of strategic planning point to significant differences between this approach and the conventional public planning approach. A few are taking some healthy whacks at public planning for its shortcomings. One, for example, says city and regional planning has lost "its flexibility to change dramatically the subject matter of its concerns, the process of its explorations, and the tools of its inquiries" (Tomazinis 1985, 14). Another is even more sweeping and caustic in his criticism: "The history of public planning is replete with tales of overexpectation, underestimation of costs, and disillusionment . . . [It] has proved increasingly less useful" (Eadie 1983, pp. 447–48).

Rather than focus on the harsher criticisms of public planning, we want to look more carefully at the distinctions that proponents of strategic planning draw between that approach and public planning. We want to assess whether these distinctions are real or imagined and, if they are real, whether they are only differences of emphasis or raise truly new points. We will draw on an analysis of the public planning literature with which most graduates of planning schools are familiar.

What, then, are the main distinctions that proponents of the corporate strategic planning approach see between it and conventional public planning?

• Corporate strategic planning is oriented more toward action, results, and implementation;

• it promotes broader and more diverse participation in the planning process;

• it places more emphasis on understanding the community in its external context, determining the opportunities and threats to a community via an environmental scan;

• it embraces competitive behavior on the part of communities; and

• it emphasizes assessing a community's strengths and weaknesses in the context of opportunities and threats.

We believe proponents of corporate strategic planning are essentially correct in contending that their approach differs significantly from conventional planning in those ways, if by public planning they mean long-range comprehensive or master planning. And there is reason to believe that that is the conception many strategic planning proponents hold of public planning (Eadie and Steinbacher 1985; Denhardt 1985; Toft 1984; Eadie 1983; Sorkin, Ferris, and Hudak 1984).

But that conception of public planning has been the subject of long-standing critiques in the planning literature—critiques that have been widely recognized. Several strong strands in the planning literature have moved beyond the notion that public planning should be long-range comprehensive or master planning. Strategic planning proponents may be fixing on a model of public planning that planning authors no longer acknowledge as representative of contemporary planning thought or professional practice. In fact, we contend that most of the principal distinctions that strategic planning proponents draw between their approach and public planning are, as evidenced by contemporary planning literature, much less pronounced or do not exist.

Action and Results Orientation

A major claimed distinction between corporate strategic planning and public planning is that the former is more oriented toward action and results; in other words, it is more relevant for decision making. Yet the call for more decision-relevant planning information and analysis has been the basis of the first important set of critiques of comprehensive planning that began in the 1950s and continue into the present. Walker (1950) raised questions about the organizational position of planners and the independent planning commission and called for a more direct link with decision making and decision makers. Beginning with their groundbreaking study of planning practice (Meyerson and Banfield 1955), Meyerson (1956), Banfield (1959), and then others (e.g., Altshuler 1965; Bolan 1967) began to argue that, even if comprehensive planning was a good idea in theory, it was largely unattainable in the real world of politics and policy.

In his well-known critique, Lindblom (1959) argued that comprehensive planning was an impossible undertaking. It required more intelligence and information than was ever available. Banfield (1959) argued further that in many cases organizations neither wanted to nor could engage in rational comprehensive planning. As a result, these authors and others (e.g., Meyerson 1956; Bolan 1971; Benveniste 1972; Catanese 1974) began to articulate models of more decision-relevant planning that were also more limited in scope, shorter range in time frame, and more sensitive to the decision environment in which planners operate. One of these authors (Meyerson 1956) specifically warned planners that their role could be usurped if they did not move in these directions.

On this one point, then, we contend that planners have long had their attention drawn to the need for being more oriented toward action and results and have been presented various ways of achieving those ends. The abundance of applied policy analysis techniques in planning curriculums, the actual philosophical shift of certain planning schools in that direction, and the support of planners for middle-range, action-oriented programs like the Community Renewal and Model Cities programs suggest that practitioners and academics have gotten the message. We believe the need for policy relevancy has been widely recognized and is, with perhaps only recent dissension (e.g., Isserman 1985; Kreditor 1985), the mainstream of opinion about the appropriate role of planning.

Participation

A second claimed distinction of corporate strategic planning is that it broadens the basis of participation in planning. Denhardt (1985) is an example of a strategic planning proponent who suggests that the constituency for planning is too narrow. Again, as in the above discussion, Denhardt (1985), Eadie (1983), and others seem unaware of the many calls for broadening participation in planning from planning academics (Burke 1968; Friedmann 1973; Rosener 1978) and planning practitioners (AICP Code of Ethics 1981).[1] Advocate and progressive planners, in particular, stress the need to bring people into the planning process who, by design or practice, have not participated (Davidoff 1965; Arnstein 1969; Goodman 1971; Clavel 1983). Like proponents of corporate strategic planning, all these authors argue that diverse participation will lead to more insightful and responsive planning.

So, as with the issue of policy relevancy, the call by strategic planning proponents for more participation in planning is not, in and of itself, a new call to the public planning profession. For more than 20 years we have had vigorous debates on and experiments in participation in planning. What is emphasized more by some strategic planning proponents is the suggestion that we might need greater participation from selected segments of the private business community, although the call for public–private partnership is not absent from the planning literature (Catanese 1974; Branch 1983).

Environmental Scanning

An important contribution that corporate strategic planning has to offer public planning is the idea of scanning the environment. According to Denhardt (1985, p. 175), under strategic planning "the organization is not assumed to exist in a vacuum, but rather both the organization's objectives and steps to achieve those

objectives are seen in the context of the resources and constraints presented by the organization's environment." This environmental sensitivity allows the organization to do smarter, more focused planning and improves its ability to understand the relative risks associated with alternative courses of action. The environmental scan encourages an organization to look beyond itself in space and time.

This basis for planning fits well with the interest in futures studies in general and the work of Naisbitt (1982) in particular. The world is understood to comprise limited resources and certain unchangeable circumstances that need to be accepted and creatively used. Within the context of an environmental scan, an organization then assesses its strengths and weaknesses. That is, strengths and weaknesses are determined relative to opportunities and threats, which are themselves given and essentially unchangeable.

The emphasis on environmental scanning is well developed and, from our perspective, well deserved. However, it also is not entirely new, though it is perhaps less well accepted within the planning community. As far back as the 1920s and 1930s, Lewis Mumford, Benton MacKaye, and their associates in the Regional Planning Association of America wrote plans and developed planning theory that explicitly called for planning within broad social-economic-technological contexts (Stein 1926; MacKaye 1928; Mumford 1938). Under the Roosevelt administration, the work of the National Resource Planning Board, especially in its early years, similarly reflected the importance to planning of broad trend analysis (National Resources Board 1934a; 1934b; National Resources Committee 1937; Clawson 1981).

More recently, planners from many different subfields have stressed the importance of understanding and planning for an organization within a broad context. Environmental planners base much of the justification for their practice on the relation of local activities to broader environmental systems and activities (e.g., McHarg 1969). Planning for air pollution, water pollution, groundwater contamination, farmland preservation, wildlife habitat, and forest management, for example, all require planners to examine resource use and economics regionally, nationally, and even internationally. Likewise, in the field of economic development, planners have available ample literature that stresses the importance of planning for plant location within an understanding of intranational and international changes in population, economics, and technological investment (Perry and Watkins 1977; Bluestone and Harrison 1982). Similarly, in social planning, the definition of key problem areas and target populations for service delivery is commonly based on analysis of broad demographic and economic trends. Etzioni (1967) has formulated an approach to planning in general that stresses what corporate strategic planning proponents call environmental scanning. As noted earlier, Etzioni's work is a source common to graduate planning theory courses, and thus environmental scanning is an idea to which public planners long have been exposed.

Competitive Behavior

Another feature of corporate strategic planning is how it encourages a community to embrace competitive behavior. Its proponents are quite explicit in this regard. For example, Toft argues that "what is called for in most situations... is competitive strategy. A successful community

must view itself as a competitive product." In the 1980s, "governments and community organizations... must be proactive given a more erratic and uncertain environment where there will be winners and losers" (Toft 1984, pp. 6, 7).

That cities, counties, states, and regions are in a competitive position with each other is no news to planners. It is the basis of much of the frustration in planning; to wit, communities searching for an ever-increasing tax base, the related inability to rein in municipal boundaries, the difficulty in managing regional environmental resources, and the companion proposals these frustrations have engendered: tax sharing, councils of governments, and regional and state land use planning reform (Williams 1970; Long 1977; Scott 1975). Practicing planners have long acknowledged the competition of a city with surrounding suburban communities (Catanese and Farmer 1978; Krumholz 1982). Recently, planners have become more acutely aware of interregional and even international competition for jobs and industrial plant location (Perry and Watkins 1977; Bluestone and Harrison 1982).

What is different about corporate strategic planning is not its recognition of competition but its perspective on that competition. The traditional perspective on competition in public planning is to view it as damaging to the economic and social health of a community. Planners and planning theory strove to seek out and foster cooperative, shared solutions. Under strategic planning, competition is seen as inevitable. Communities therefore are exhorted to identify their competitive niche and exploit it or suffer the consequences.

Community Strengths and Weaknesses

The final distinctive feature claimed for corporate strategic planning is the community's critical appraisal of strengths and weaknesses relative to the environmental scan of opportunities and threats and within the parameters of the other features discussed above: action orientation, public involvement process, and competitive perspective on intergovernmental relations. This, too, we conclude, is not an entirely new idea for the planning community, though the exact terms used to describe the exercise and the emphasis accorded this phase of planning may be different under corporate strategic planning.

According to proponents of strategic planning, traditional public planning (i.e., long-range comprehensive or master planning) too often perceives the world around and within as one-dimensional. That is, goals, objectives, and policies that are developed and stated in a plan too often seem to cover all topics of possible concern to the locality and assume that the planning, policy, and administrative units of the government have equal capacity and incentive to act on the plan's recommendations. In contrast, strategic planning is supposed to encourage an honest assessment of a community's capacity to act, seeking to maximize strengths and minimize weaknesses in the context of opportunities and threats. As with the points discussed above, however, this perspective is not entirely new to planning theory or practice, though it may not be as well developed, for reasons that point up one of the main differences in public and private planning.

The discussion of strengths and weaknesses borrows directly from the economic literature on competitive advantage. In fact, it can be seen as nothing more than a shifting of the competitive advantage idea from the market

to the organizational and community sector. At the community level, Tiebout's (1956) formulation of local expenditures and the public choice school of economics has kept the issues of competitive advantage and strengths and weaknesses before the planning community for a long time. Practitioners such as Krumholz (1982; Krumholz, Cogger, and Linner 1975) have shown how planners with particular ethical orientations can pointedly address the strengths and weaknesses of current city planning processes and move an organization toward maximizing its strengths. Likewise, certain traditional and well-regarded plans, such as New York City's (1969), explicitly address the weaknesses of certain city agencies and activities. Other plans we are aware of, such as Chicago's (1966), had similar sections in early drafts that were later edited out to reduce organizational friction and to help generate diverse support for the plans. At one level, identifying strengths and weaknesses, especially the latter, has been a politically unwise and difficult undertaking. But it is not an idea to which planners have been unaccustomed.

Thus, when we examine the planning literature, we find that the components of corporate strategic planning that proponents say are fundamentally different are not really all that different. Many of the implied and explicit criticisms are directed at the comprehensive, long-range, or master planning model. Most of these criticisms are longstanding within the theory and practice of public sector planning. Planners have been told of the need to be more policy relevant, to involve more and different types of people in the planning process, and to do their planning within a realistic assessment of the systems and networks of which they are part. Planners also are aware both of competition and of the idea of identifying and acting on strengths and weaknesses.

What, then, is different about strategic planning from the point of view of the planning literature? We note two differences. The first is the framework of corporate strategic planning, which brings all the above points together. It may be true that the literature has drawn planners' attention to most or all of the points that proponents claim are distinctive about strategic planning. The strategic approach is distinctive, however, in pulling all those elements together into a coherent planning structure. Continuing to highlight the importance of individual elements and stressing their interrelationship may help planners to do better planning.

The second difference is the ideological and programmatic usefulness of corporate strategic planning. By introducing a model of planning that is seen to come out of the private sector, the practice of planning—which nowadays is under attack in some quarters—may be seen as more legitimate. Corporate strategic planning thus may be shifting the debate in public sector planning from *whether* to do it to *how* to do it. In these times, that would be a significant shift.

THE VIEW FROM THE PLANNING TRENCHES

Strategic planning applied to the public sector is a relatively recent development. The preceding analysis of literature indicates that key features of the strategic planning approach, which proponents claim are distinct from the conventional public planning approach, are well ensconced in planning theory and recognized in some of the writings on planning practice. But the exhortations of academics are not necessarily guideposts that all practitioners follow. As we know, the gap between what planning theorists say and what planning practitioners do can be wide (Krueckeberg 1971; Kaufman 1974).

For that reason, we decided to examine how planning practitioners view strategic planning as it has been applied at the communitywide level. We wanted to get firsthand information about how planners steeped in the public planning tradition felt about a planning approach that, although nurtured in the corporate world, is being implanted in the public sector vineyard. Do planners see important differences between strategic planning efforts and the approaches followed in public planning? If so, what are these differences? Are planners' attitudes toward community-based strategic planning ventures enthusiastic? accepting? skeptical? hostile?

To answer these questions, we conducted phone interviews with 15 public planners about their views of strategic planning efforts under way at the communitywide level. Each planner interviewed worked either in a community where a strategic planning program was under way or in one where such a program had been completed recently.[2] These planners represented communities for which strategic planning was far enough along to allow for an informed interview. They could give opinions about the contrast, if any, of the strategic planning process with other, more traditional planning approaches. It was important to the validity of the study that each planner had held his or her position long enough before the introduction of strategic planning that they could discuss its differences and similarities with other forms of public planning in the community. The interview group was small, reflecting the newness of corporate strategic planning. Given the size of the group, we want to stress the exploratory nature of these interviews and to offer these data as the basis for more extensive research in the future.

In a recent paper, Tomazinis (1985, p. 14) said, "Strategic planning has the potential to revitalize public planning...by invigorating the planning agencies, revitalizing the interest in planning of top elected officials, and helping cities and regions rediscover and redefine their crucial problems." We read this positive statement about strategic planning to the group of planners as the opening to our telephone interview, asking whether and why they agreed or disagreed with it.

In general, the planners were divided in their opinions about strategic planning. A few were quite positive about its value. Others were mildly supportive, seeing some benefits but also having some reservations. And some were downright skeptical.

One enthusiast, for example, stated that he unequivocally agreed with the Tomazinis statement. Another supporter saw strategic planning as an opportunity to put planning on a more vigorous footing. Still another commented that the strategic planning program in his community definitely had value in revitalizing elected officials' interest in planning.

Skeptics responded differently to the Tomazinis statement. One said planning in his community was already vigorous, top elected officials already had a strong interest in planning, and crucial problems were being addressed continually by his agency; strategic planning therefore was not really needed. Another said strategic planning "was just an advertising gimmick to sell the old stuff in a new way." Other skeptics saw it as trendy. As one put it,

"Nowadays it's the way to get federal bucks for planning. You have to use the right buzz words to get a share of the dwindling dollars."

Going past these initial reactions, we sensed that a planner's attitude toward strategic planning was conditioned principally by two factors: the planner's educational background and the perceived status of the planning function in the community where the planner worked.

We observed that planners with degrees from planning schools were generally less sanguine about strategic planning than those with degrees in fields other than planning. As one planner with a graduate planning degree said, "I don't see the strategic planning process as significantly different from what I learned in planning school." Another planning school graduate put it this way: "Strategic planning is like pouring old wine into new bottles."

In contrast, a supporter of strategic planning who had a degree in economic geography justified his support by criticizing the planning done in his agency as producing "too many plans that are just damn inventories." He went on to say, "Just as one of Congress' problems is that it has too many lawyers, one of the problems with planning agencies is that they have too many planners." Likewise, an economist who has worked as a planner for many years suggested that "comprehensive plans that planners prepare tend to be too illusionary. The interconnectedness of goals, objectives, and policies is not always clear. Strategic planning avoids these pitfalls."

A crosscutting factor affecting a planner's attitude toward strategic planning was the perceived status of the planning function in the community. Where public planning was perceived to be more vigorous, respected, and involved in community issues, planners viewed strategic planning as unnecessary or redundant. Where the public planning function was perceived to be weak, strategic planning efforts took on a rosier complexion in the planner's view.

The following comments about strategic planning were made by planners who saw their planning programs as strong and healthy:

> In our community, we have an ongoing and lively discussion of issues. Interest in public affairs is high. I don't think we need a strategic planning approach.

> An aggressive planning department like ours is already doing the things that strategic planning proponents are saying strategic planning does. I don't think the strategic planning done by the Chamber of Commerce has much value. It's regarded as a business advocacy plan. It has neither been adopted nor has it had much influence on public policy.

> In our agency, which has lots of professionals who are broadly educated and policy-sensitive, strategic planning is not needed.

This last planner, however, acknowledged that in a community where the planning function is weak, "strategic planning might help to invigorate the planning agency." Likewise, one planner, who admitted he worked for an agency that was not well regarded, saw definite advantages to the strategic planning approach: "It pushes us to be more focused on issues, and it increases our chances of getting things implemented." Another who worked in a community where planning was not considered strong liked the strategic planning approach because it emphasized community strengths as well as weaknesses. He claimed it had led to the realization that "we have some good things going for us in our community,

counteracting the tendency to knock ourselves too much."

Whether they were favorable or unfavorable toward strategic planning, the planners we interviewed agreed that it was *not* fundamentally different from good traditional public planning.

Some skeptics offered these contentions:

> Strategic planning doesn't strike me as much different than the kind of middle-range, policy-sensitive planning we do now in our community.

> We do essentially the same things in our planning program that proponents of corporate strategic planning claim that approach accomplishes.

> Strategic planning doesn't represent much of a change from what we already do. For the last 10 years in our agency we've been taking a strategic approach, looking at strengths and weaknesses of our city, focusing on crucial issues, developing action strategies. Strategic planning is not a new direction.

Even strong supporters of strategic planning saw no fundamental differences:

> Intuitively we were doing strategic planning before. But we didn't have a model that we could specifically cite, like strategic planning, to give a name to what we were doing.

> Although we're doing strategic planning for economic development, the approach is not new; the basis of it isn't any different from what you expect from good comprehensive planning.

Although in agreement that the two planning approaches are not fundamentally different, both the supporters and the skeptics of corporate strategic planning cited differences in emphasis between the two approaches. Both groups seemed to agree that the strategic planning approach tended to be shorter range in focus and targeted on more realistic and feasible proposals. In addition, they were in agreement that strategic planning efforts at the local level emphasized marketing of communities attractively, packaging action proposals in ways designed to excite the public and policymakers, and highlighting the community's competitive advantages—all ideas consistent with the private sector origins of the model. Differences of opinion did surface, however, between the supporters and the skeptics. Whereas supporters tended to assess strategic planning efforts as more analytically rigorous, as involving a broader cross section of the community in planning, and as achieving more implementation success, skeptics—as befitted their label—disagreed with those contentions.

Differences of opinion were sharpest over the limitations of the corporate strategic planning approach. Although supporters acknowledged that strategic planning had some weaknesses (e.g., it can be very time-consuming, it's difficult to maintain the interest level of top decision makers in the process, and it can be a costly undertaking), their criticisms were decidedly tamer than those of the skeptics. The latter were especially blunt in their contentions that strategic planning programs were too narrowly based, reflected too much of a business community agenda, had much less influence on policy decisions than its advocates credited it, and seriously underestimated the problem of implementing priority actions in the decentralized, pluralistic decision-making system of the public sector. Given their contention that their planning agencies were already active both in identifying crucial community issues

and in thinking and acting strategically long before strategic planning came on the scene, one senses that planners who hold strong reservations about strategic planning see little value in it. Quite clearly, their views are not shared by all the planners we interviewed. As we said, a few were quite enthusiastic about the strategic planning efforts under way in their communities, and more who were lukewarm were still positive about some features of the approach.

CONCLUSION

This chapter examines, from a public planning perspective, the adaptation of the corporate strategic planning model to communitywide planning. We have examined five points that proponents of corporate strategic planning put forth as distinguishing it from traditional public planning. We argue that the implied or explicit critique of so-called traditional planning is, at base, a critique of comprehensive, long-range, or master planning; that this is only one mode of planning; and that it is a mode that has long sustained criticism for the very points highlighted by proponents of corporate strategic planning. From the planning literature, we find that the critiques and suggestions embodied in strategic planning are long standing, well developed, and well known. We note, though, that corporate strategic planning is distinctive in bringing these points together into a coherent planning process model.

In addition, we conducted telephone interviews with 15 planners around the United States whose communities have engaged in strategic planning. We found them divided in their assessment of the approach. A few were quite supportive, some had mixed feelings, and still others were decidedly skeptical. All, however, found that strategic planning was not significantly different from good comprehensive planning; it was different in emphasis, they said, but not different in kind.

We are aware of the limitations of the methods used to arrive at the above and subsequent conclusions. Our examination of planning literature, founded in the survey by Klosterman (1981), represents the material we believe is central to debate and development in planning theory. Others whose assessment of the literature is different may find our argument less compelling. In terms of the interviews with practicing planners, the size of the study population was small and necessarily nonrandom. As such our data are exploratory. A more verifiable assessment of what practicing public planners think about strategic planning efforts at the local level would require a larger group of interviewees and a more rigorous interview structure. Nevertheless, we believe the phone interviews provide an accurate snapshot of how selected public planners with exposure to strategic planning view it today. Further, these data provide a basis for developing hypotheses about planners' perceptions of corporate strategic planning and its application in current planning practice.[3]

In the way of general conclusions, we offer the following thoughts. First, recent introspection about corporate strategic planning (e.g., Kiechel 1982; *Business Week* 1984; Hayes 1985) reflects an emerging skepticism toward its application to the management of corporations. Bryson, Van de Ven, and Roering (1987) and Eadie (1983), proponents of corporate strategic planning, show a growing sensitivity to the complexities of transferring this approach to the public sector.

Second, we stress that, at least in the short term, strategic planning will remain an issue in the public sector. Especially in the area of economic development, strategic planning has become an important technique to develop a program of action based on a public–private partnership. As noted earlier, in certain ways we believe that is good for public planning. In a time of fiscal constraint and possible crisis, strategic planning is redefining the nature of the public planning debate. It may be that corporate strategic planning will help turn the discussion from *whether* to do planning to *how* to do planning.

This suggests our third set of thoughts. The public planning community can look at the advent and popularity of corporate-style strategic planning in any of three ways: as a threat, as an opportunity, or as another fad. As a threat, strategic planning seems poised to replace the way public planners have done planning and even the planners themselves (see, for example, Denhardt 1985, p. 175). Even if planners embrace strategic planning, however, it is possible that, although they may become more integrated into decision making, the planning they do may be little different from the management-type planning undertaken by public administrators. Success with strategic planning thus might be bittersweet. Seen in that light, strategic planning is something to be either avoided or fought against so as to preserve the place and style of existing public planning. How successful this posture would be is unclear, especially given the strong support that corporate strategic planning receives from influential members of the private sector and political communities.

On the other hand, strategic planning seems to offer significant opportunities for public planners. If we are correct in our assessment of the components of strategic planning and its relation to existing planning theory, planners already should be well exposed to its concepts and techniques. Even its jargon is becoming familiar to planners. In this case, public planners should be well positioned to play significant roles in strategic planning programs at the community level. They can stress their skills in facilitation, communication, analysis of secondary data, and forecasting. If strategic planning in the future follows the examples of the recent past, substantial amounts of money will be available for such programs. If they look at strategic planning as an opportunity, public planners could be central to deciding how and for what those funds get used. Otherwise, the torch for planning will be carried by other professionals and groups.

Finally, corporate-style strategic planning may be just another passing fad. Like planning-programming-budgeting systems, it may be bursting onto the scene with a great deal of fanfare only to slip into relative obscurity later (So 1984). That is an unknown now, and we attempt no prediction. Instead, we close by noting that, since it is unknown, planners would do well to treat the advent of strategic planning seriously and to view it, in the parlance of the approach, as an opportunity rather than as a threat.

Ultimately public planners will need to wait for more data before making definitive judgments about corporate strategic planning. More strategic plans need to be prepared, and existing strategic plans need to be acted on. Only then will it be known if strategic planning can bring about more effective public planning.

AUTHORS' NOTE

The authors would like to thank the practitioners, academic colleagues, and students who commented on drafts of this chapter. We give special acknowledgment to our colleagues at the University of Wisconsin–Madison, Stephen M. Born and Rosalind J. Greenstein, as well as Raymond J. Burby, John M. Bryson, and Robert C. Einsweiler.

NOTES

1. The American Institute of Certified Planners Code of Ethics (1981) states clearly that planners "must strive to give citizens the opportunity to have meaningful impact on plans and programs." Participation is defined as "broad enough to include people who lack formal organization or influence."

2. Interviews were conducted with top-level planners in San Francisco; the Philadelphia area; the Minneapolis–St. Paul area; Dade County, Florida; Fort Collins, Colorado; Pittsburgh; Madison, Wisconsin; Memphis, Tennessee; Oxford, Ohio; and Albany, New York. For the purposes of this article, the names, titles, and positions of the interviewees are omitted.

3. A broad range of research questions could be pursued with regard to applications of corporate strategic planning in the public sector. For instance, why is strategic planning used in some communities but not in others? Is it a function of leadership, organization, business influence? Who benefits from strategic planning efforts, and how are those benefits realized? Do strategic planning efforts strengthen the planning function? Do strategic planning programs that involve widespread public participation reflect broader consensus or more watered down compromise? Is the idea of regionalism advanced or weakened when communities follow a strategic planning approach that emphasizes competition?

REFERENCES

Altshuler, Alan A. 1965. *The city planning process: A political analysis.* Ithaca, N.Y.: Cornell University Press.

American Institute of Certified Planners. 1981. Code of ethics and professional conduct. Washington, D.C.: AICP.

Ansoff, Igor. 1965. *Corporate strategy: An analytic approach to business policy for growth and expansion.* New York, N.Y.: McGraw-Hill.

Arnstein, Sherry R. 1969. A ladder of citizen participation. *Journal of the American Institute of Planners* 35, 4: 216–224.

Arthur Anderson & Co. n.d. *Guide to public sector strategic planning.* Chicago, Ill.: Arthur Anderson & Co.

Banfield, Edward C. 1959. Ends and means in planning. *International Social Science Journal* 11, 3: 361–68.

Benveniste, Guy. 1972. *The politics of expertise.* Berkeley, Calif.: Glendessary Press.

Bluestone, Barry and Bennett Harrison. 1982. *The deindustrialization of America.* New York, N.Y.: Basic Books.

Bolan, Richard. 1967. Emerging views of planning. *Journal of the American Institute of Planners* 33, 4: 234–246.

———. 1971. The social relations of the planner. *Journal of the American Institute of Planners* 37, 6: 386–395.

Boyle, M. Ross. 1983. The strategic planning process: Assessing a community's economic assets. *Economic Development Commentary* 7, 2: 3–7.

Branch, Melville C. 1983. *Comprehensive planning: General theory and principles.* Pacific Palisades, Calif.: Palisades Publishers.

Bryson, John M., Andrew H. Van de Ven, and William D. Roering. 1987. Strategic planning and the revitalization of the public service. In *Toward a New Public Service* edited by Robert C. Denhardt and Edward Jennings. Columbia, Mo.: University of Missouri Press. In press.

Bryson, John M., R. Edward Freeman, and William D. Roering. 1986. Strategic planning in the public sector: Approaches and future directions. In *Strategic Approaches to Planning Practice,* edited by B. Checkoway. Lexington, Mass.: Lexington Books. Forthcoming.

Burke, Edmund C. 1968. Citizen participation strategies. *Journal of the American Institute of Planners* 34, 5: 287–294.

Business Week. 1984. The new breed of strategic planner. *Business Week* September 17: 62–68.

Catanese, Anthony James. 1974. *Planners and local politics: Impossible dreams.* Beverly Hills, Calif.: Sage Publications.

——— and W. Paul Farmer, eds. 1978. *Personality, politics, and planning.* Beverly Hills, Calif.: Sage Publications.

Chandler, Alfred. 1962. *Strategy and structure.* Boston, Mass.: MIT Press.

Chicago Department of Development and Planning. 1966. *The comprehensive plan of Chicago, Ill.* Chicago, Ill.: CDDP.

Clavel, Pierre. 1983. *Opposition planning in Wales and Appalachia.* Philadelphia, Pa.: Temple University Press.

Clawson, Marion. 1981. *New Deal planning.* Baltimore, Md.: Johns Hopkins University Press.

Davidoff, Paul. 1965. Advocacy and pluralism in planning. *Journal of the American Institute of Planners* 31, 4: 331–38.

——— and Thomas Reiner. 1962. A choice theory of planning. *Journal of the American Institute of Planners* 28, 2: 103–115.

Denhardt, Robert B. 1985. Strategic planning in state and local government. *State and Local Government Review* 17, 1: 174–79.

Drucker, Peter. 1954. *The practice of management.* New York, N.Y.: Harper and Row.

Eadie, Douglas C. 1983. Putting a powerful tool to practical use: The application of strategic planning in the public sector. *Public Administration Review* 43, 5: 447–452.

——— and Roberta Steinbacher. 1985. Strategic agenda management: A marriage of organizational development and strategic planning. *Public Administration Review* 45, 3: 424–430.

Etzioni, Amitai. 1967. Mixed scanning: A 'third' approach to decision-making. *Public Administration Review* 27, 5: 385–392.

Friedmann, John. 1973. *Retracking America: A theory of transactive planning.* New York, N.Y.: Anchor Press/Doubleday.

Goodman, Robert. 1971. *After the planners.* New York, N.Y.: Simon and Schuster.

Hayes, Robert H. 1985. Strategic planning—Forward in reverse? *Harvard Business Review* 63, 6: 111–19.

Isserman, Andrew M. 1985. Dare to plan: An essay on the role of the future in planning practice and education. *Town Planning Review* 56, 4: 483–491.

Kaufman, Jerome L. 1974. Contemporary planning practice: State of the art. In *Planning in America: Learning from Turbulence,* edited by D. Godschalk. Washington, D.C.: American Institute of Planners.

Kiechel, Walter. 1982. Corporate strategists under fire. *Fortune* 106, 13: 34–39.

Klosterman, Richard E. 1981. Contemporary planning theory education: Results of a course survey. *Journal of Planning Education and Research* 1, 1: 1–11.

Kreditor, Alan. 1985. Dilemmas in planning education: Dichotomies between visionary and utilitarian. Paper presented at the annual meeting of the Association of Collegiate Schools of Planning, Atlanta, Georgia. November.

Krueckeberg, Don. 1971. Variations in behavior of planning agencies. *Administrative Science Quarterly* 16, 2: 192–202.

Krumholz, Norman. 1982. A retrospective view of equity planning: Cleveland 1969–1979. *Journal of the American Planning Association* 48, 2: 163–174.

———, Janice M. Cogger, and John H. Linner. 1975. The Cleveland policy planning report. *Journal of the American Institute of Planners* 41, 5: 298–304.

Lang, Reg. 1986. Achieving integration in resource planning. In *Integrated Approaches to Resource Planning and Management,* edited by Reg Lang. Calgary, Alberta: University of Calgary Press. In press.

Lindblom, Charles E. 1959. The science of muddling though. *Public Administration Review* 19, 2: 79–88.

Long, Norton E. 1977. How to help cities become independent. In *How Cities Can Grow Old Gracefully,* prepared for the Subcommittee on the City, Committee on Banking, Finance, and Urban Affairs, U.S. House of Representatives. Washington, D.C.: U.S. Government Printing Office.

MacKaye, Benton. 1928. *The new exploration: A philosophy of regional planning.* New York, N.Y.: Harcourt, Brace and Co.

McHarg, Ian. 1969. *Design with nature.* Garden City, N.Y.: Doubleday and Co.

Meyerson, Martin. 1956. Building the middle-range bridge for comprehensive planning. *Journal of the American Institute of Planners* 22, 2: 58–64.

——— and Edward Banfield. 1955. *Politics, planning and the public interest.* New York, N.Y.: The Free Press.

Mumford, Lewis. 1938. *The culture of cities.* New York, N.Y.: Harcourt Brace Jovanovich.

Naisbitt, John. 1982. *Megatrends.* New York, N.Y.: Warner Books.

National Resources Board. 1934a. *Report of the land planning committee.* Washington, D.C.: U.S. Government Printing Office.

———. 1934b. *Report of the National Resources Board.* Washington, D.C.: U.S. Government Printing Office.

National Resources Committee. 1937. *Our cities: Their role in the national economy.* Washington, D.C.: U.S. Government Printing Office.

New York City Planning Commission. 1969. *Plan for New York City: Critical issues.* New York, N.Y.: NYCPC.

Olsen, John B. and Douglas C. Eadie. 1982. *The game plan: Governance with foresight,* Washington, D.C.: Council of State Planning Agencies.

Perry, David C. and Alfred J. Watkins, eds. 1977. *The rise of the sunbelt cities.* Urban Affairs Annual Reviews, vol. 14. Beverly Hills, Calif.: Sage.

Rosener, Judy. 1978. Matching method to purpose: The challenges of planning citizen-participation activities. In *Citizen Participation in America,* edited by Stuart Langdon. Lexington, Mass.: Lexington Books.

Scott, Mel. 1969. *American city planning since 1890.* Berkeley, Calif.: University of California Press.

Scott, Randall W., ed. 1975. *The management and control of growth.* Vol. 1–3. Washington, D.C.: Urban Land Institute.

So, Frank S. 1984. Strategic planning: Reinventing the wheel? *Planning* 50, 2: 16–21.

Sorkin, Donna L., Nancy B. Ferris, and James Hudak. 1984. *Strategies for cities and counties: A strategic planning guide.* Washington, D.C.: Public Technology, Inc.

Stein, Clarence. 1926. *Report of the New York State Commission of Housing and Regional Planning.* Albany, N.Y.: New York State Legislature.

Steiner, George A. 1969. *Top management planning.* London: Macmillan.

——— and J. B. Miner. 1977. *Management policy and strategy: Text, readings, and cases.* New York, N.Y.: Macmillan.

Taylor, Bernard. 1984. Strategic planning—Which style do you need? *Long Range Planning* 17, 3: 51–62.

Tiebout, Charles M. 1956. A pure theory of local expenditures. *Journal of Political Economy* 64, 5: 416–424.

Toft, Graham S. 1984. Strategic planning for economic and municipal development. *Resources in Review* 6, 6: 6–11.

Tomazinis, Anthony R. 1985. The logic and rationale of strategic planning. Paper presented at the annual meeting of the Association of Collegiate Schools of Planning, Atlanta, Georgia. November.

Walker, Robert. 1950. *The planning function in urban government.* Chicago, Ill.: University of Chicago Press.

Williams, Norman Jr. 1970. The three systems of land use control. *Rutgers Law Review* 25, 1: 80–101.

4

Strategic Public Management

MICHAEL CROW
BARRY BOZEMAN

Strategic management is a field of study presided over by business policy and organization theory scholars and, according to some (Wortman 1979; Steiner and Miner, 1977), the practice of strategic management is the preserve of business management practitioners. However, the strategic planning processes established in the cities of Dallas (1982) and San Francisco (1983), the state of Ohio (1984) and, at the federal level, the Internal Revenue Service (1984), the National Bureau of Standards (1985), and the National Aeronautics and Space Administration (1985) belie the assertion that strategic *public* management is a contradiction in terms.

Public managers' increasing interest in strategic management does not imply that practices and processes employed in government closely resemble those used in business. Particular points of difference between private and public sector strategic management have been suggested (e.g., Wechsler and Backoff 1986; Mazzolini 1981; Steiner 1977; Bozeman 1983; Ring and Perry 1985), but there is no consensus about the particulars or their implications. Ring and Perry (1985) conclude that the context in which public and private sector strategic managers operate is sufficiently different to merit the development of public-oriented strategic management models. In support of this conclusion, a handful of studies (Moffitt

1984; Zif 1981; Ring 1986; Walter and Choate 1984; Denhardt 1985; Eadie 1983; Mazzolini 1980) provide some preliminary models and evaluations of strategic management practices in the public sector. These reviews and case studies indicate a need for generalized theory development so as to put prescriptions on firmer ground.

The conditions that affect the definition of strategic management in the public sector and determine the effect of these conditions on its implementation will be addressed here. Currently, there is no accepted model of strategic public management and substantial confusion exists among both planning and management practitioners and scholars as to exactly how and why public sector organizations might conduct strategic management activities. This is particularly true given documented constraints (Stevens and McGowan 1983; Blumenthal 1979; Bozeman 1984; Wamsley and Zald 1973; Rainey, Backoff, and Levine 1976; Bower 1977, 1983) of public sector management.

STRATEGIC MANAGEMENT: THE NATURE OF THE BEAST

An understanding of the unique features of strategic public management (SPM) requires some agreement as to what private sector strategic management (SM) entails. The problem of making sense of SM is quite different from analysis of SPM. There is a paucity of theory and research in strategic public management, but research, theory, concepts, and definitions of strategic management are abundant (Schendel and Hofer 1979).

One of the most familiar definitions of strategic management is set forth by Chandler (1962, p. 13), who describes strategic management as "the determination of the basic long-term goals and objectives of an enterprise, and the adoption of courses of action and the allocation of resources necessary for carrying out these goals." Some have noted the military origins of the strategy concept. Henderson (1983) points out that strategy in the military, much as in business, relates to concerns with finite resources and their commitment, uncertainty about adversaries' capabilities and intentions, uncertainty about control of the initiative, and the necessity of coordinating action over time *and* distance. In both of these definitions, a key point is that the focus of strategic management is on the development and implementation of a dynamic plan for resource distribution that simultaneously attempts to reduce environmental uncertainty and move the organization into new activity areas. Mintzberg summarizes this point in his conclusion:

> Strategy may be viewed as a mediating force between the organization and its environment. Strategy formulation, therefore, involves the interpretation of the environment and the development of consistent patterns in streams of organizational decisions (strategies) to deal with it. [Mintzberg 1979, p. 106]

This mediation between organization and environment is not unique to the private sector and has been the subject of extensive analysis (Wholey and Britain 1986; Freeman and Boeker 1984). In fact, the literature on the mediation that occurs between the public sector (either as a single organization or in the various manifestations of government) is quite extensive, though often known by other names. Mediation functions in the public sector are often discussed (e.g., Lindblom 1982, 1977; Wilson 1974) in terms of the relationship between external political demand and the subsequent policy (i.e., strategic) response.

It should be clear (Aldrich 1979; Child 1972; Bourgeois 1980) that all organizations, regardless of their ownership, have reasons to be concerned about the strategic management of their external environment and the subsequent changing of organizational behavior. Much of this concern focuses on the linkage between environment, organizational evolution, and survival (Freeman 1984). From this focus, Burgelman (1986) defines organizations as

> opportunity structures motivating strategic behavior on the part of their participants and the strategic process in organizations constitutes an internalized and contrived evolutionary mechanism nested in the external context.

From this perspective, strategic management can be viewed as the processes through which organizations attempt to manage evolution. Thus, strategic public management is the process through which public sector organizations attempt to manage their environment and affect their evolutionary patterns through the implementation of policies, procedures, and plans.

STRATEGY MAKING: PRIVATE VS. PUBLIC

Wheelwright (1984) offers a three-tiered classification of strategy. Corporate strategy involves the selection of business alternatives and the acquisition and allocation of resources. Business strategy clarifies the boundaries and purpose of the business and identifies the competitive advantage to be pursued in the future environment. Finally, functional strategy plans and integrates the new function into the operation of the existing organization. Thus, in this conceptualization, functional strategy is very much akin to what is typically called operational planning, and in contrast to the two higher levels of strategic management, deals with the short term. The three levels make up the process of strategic management.

A related but more precise characterization of strategic management is presented by Hax and Majluf (1984) through their characterization of a five-layered hierarchy of strategic management. These layers include:

1. Corporate-level planning—determining the vision.

2. Share-concern planning—multiple unit planning or multicustomer planning.

3. Shared resource planning—to achieve economies of scale.

4. Business-unit planning—planning competitive behavior.

5. Product-market planning—planning price, product, and services for the environment.

In the Wheelwright conceptualization, layers 1–3 are strategic, layer 4 is tactical and layer 5 is operational. All are a part of the private sector strategic management process. As such, they should serve as a starting point for understanding strategic public management.

As a step toward a model of strategic public management, we suggest that the Wheelwright and the Hax and Majluf levels of strategic management be classified on three levels: strategic, tactical, and operational. In this

generic conceptualization, if strategic deals with the organization's broadest purpose and mission (determining the vision), and operational deals with the day-to-day execution of objectives in pursuit of the environmental adaptation goals of the organization, a third category deals with "middle-level" objectives such as planning competitive behavior. We use the term *tactical* for this category. We argue in a subsequent section that tactical management is especially important for public managers because policymakers (legislators, political executives, elected officials) often play an important role at the strategic level. Table 4–1 provides some perspective by listing typical activities, by sector, categorized as strategic, tactical, and operational management questions.

To further illustrate this conceptualization, Table 4–2 assumes that General Electric is the private sector firm and that NASA is the public sector agency and illustrates the type of activities carried out in strategic management and strategic public management.

It is, of course, a mistake to make too much of artificial distinctions such as categories of management. Clearly, it is possible to disagree on whether any particular issue is strategic or tactical or operational. More to the point, there is wide variation in how organizations interact with their environments and define their goals and activities.

STRATEGY AND CONSTRAINT: COMPARING THE CONDITIONS OF PUBLIC AND PRIVATE STRATEGIC MANAGEMENT

The chief difference between the strategy endeavors of public and private managers is that the government manager more often is subject to a wide array of constraints, not the least

Table 4–1. Strategic, Tactical, and Operational Management Issues (Private vs. Public Organizations)

	Private	Public
Strategic Management	Selecting and acquiring new business opportunities as a means of environmental adaptation.	Shaping new public policy.
Tactical Management	Establishing the boundaries of the business and selecting the competitive advantage; planning competitive behavior.	Designing the program response to the policy action. This includes the establishment of goals and objectives for the long-term implementation of the program.
Operations Management	Integration of new activity into the organization. Operational planning of new business activities; setting price.	Integration of new activity into the agency. Operational planning for new program activities.

Table 4–2. Sample Strategic, Tactical, and Operational Activities (Private vs. Public)

Level of Strategic Management	General Electric (Private)	NASA (Public)
Strategic	In anticipation of future developments and opportunities in the area of advanced space defense systems, GE selects RCA for acquisition. RCA is acquired to fill the need of adjusting to the changing defense market.*	• Jan. 25, 1984. President presents "four great goals to keep America free and secure," including "to build on America's pioneer spirit and develop our next frontier—space." • February–July 1984. Congress modifies and approves national space policy. • August 1984. President approves generalized national space strategy.
Tactical	GE will reshape RCA to take particular advantage of its radar technology data base and advanced satellites. GE will dispose of RCA's consumer electronics division and several other communication groups.	• January–August 1984. NASA prepares national space strategy to implement the national policy for space, including specific objectives, such as the establishment of a manned permanent space station.
Operational	Business integration plans for RCA functions into GE will be developed at this level of SM. Prices will be set, products planned.	• August 1984–1985. NASA prepares 1986 long-range plan providing guidance for the implementation of the objectives detailed at the tactical level and the policy guidance received at the strategic level. These plans include specific milestones that are planned for the period 1986–1991 (NASA, 1985).

*There are several reasons why GE sought and accomplished this merger. The overriding goal was to allow GE an improved market in defense contracting. With the takeover GE moved from sixth to second in defense contracting. GE believes the acquisition also was necessary to obtain an expanded technical data base. GE will benefit from developments in radar innovations and from RCA's long-standing relationship with the Navy. To accomplish the merger, GE stated it was willing to dispose of RCA's consumer electronics division and several RCA-owned radio stations. Items excluded from disposal were GE's aerospace group and RCA's National Broadcasting Co., along with nonconsumer electronics (Ferri 1986).

of which is time. Our approach here is to examine some of the commonly observed differences between public and private management and show how these act to affect the conduct of strategic public management.[1]

For convenience, literature comparing public and private management can be set into four categories: (1) comparisons based on types of authority affecting the organizations, (2) comparisons of tasks and work context, (3) comparisons of organizations and their structure, and (4) comparisons of personnel and personnel systems.[2]

Comparisons of Authority Base

Economic authority is a powerful motivator in virtually every type of organization. Discussions of the role of profit and the bottom line are, in effect, allowances for the different bases of authority for public and private organizations. The market failure and public goods arguments about differences between public and private sectors are familiar (McKie 1970; Wilson 1974) but less useful for comparison of public and private *management* than the property rights theory (Alchian 1965; Alchian and Demsetz 1972; De Alessi 1969, 1980; Demsetz 1967).

According to property rights theorists, the most important distinction between private and government organizations is that government organizations cannot transfer the rights of ownership from one individual or group to another; ownership is nonpersonal and held by the government itself as a legal/rational entity. In this sense, the public sector manager serves as staff to the political representatives of the citizen "owners."

The difference between public and private ownership rights has several important economic implications. It is argued (Alchian and Demsetz 1973; Peltzman 1971) that the ability to exchange ownership is related to economic efficiency. Economists view ownership as a productive input that functions to bear risk and organize managerial activity (Peltzman 1971). In public organizations, risk (at least capital risk) is diffused to such a degree that it virtually ceases to exist.

In contrast, the bedrock of *political* authority is legal and rational legitimacy. The ability of governments to make binding decisions ultimately is traced to individuals' grants of legitimacy, but in most instances political authority is exercised by formally designated policy actors on behalf of the governed. In this conceptualization, the State (city, state, or federal governments) is guided by a general set of system goals that also serve as a source of authority.

The effect of authority base on strategic public management is to alter the character of the environment around the organization from the relatively narrow scope of individual interests to the broader notion of the collective interest. This difference in strategic public management is felt in two important ways. First, the weight and complexity of each strategic decision is greater. Second, the risk resulting from the ultimate strategic decision is so diffuse that it does not manifest itself well at the level of individual decision makers. Thus, the effect of authority base differences between the public and private sector is to diffuse authority (Allison 1983) and thus, decision making. The result, of course, makes strategic public management appear to be a very difficult process indeed.

In contrast, Saunders and Tuggle (1977) would argue that different complexities in private sector strategic management processes are caused by the private character of the organizations involved and make long-range planning efforts very difficult. These include: (1) private managements' tendency to optimize, (2) the relatively low level of environmental uncertainty, (3) organizational predictability, and (4) organizational compartmentalization.

Authority base and ownership does affect the process of strategic management, public or private, and thus, is an important constraint to note when developing an improved model of strategic public management.

Comparisons of Task and Work Context

The most often cited differences between public and private management include the pace of work, the publicness of decision making, and the short time horizons (Rainey, Backoff, and Levine 1976; Bower 1983; Allison 1983; Perry, Rainey, and Bozeman 1985). The public manager usually is more subject to scrutiny from the media and from a wide array of interest groups that have a stake in the public manager's decisions (Blumenthal 1979). The public and the media can easily interpret reflection as inaction and so it often seems better to do something, something visible, than to reflect about strategy. In addition, Bower (1983) has highlighted the significant differences between the efficiency maxim of the private sector and the equity maxim of the public sector.

Probably the most important difference in the time frame of public and private sector managers is related to the political cycles of government. The appropriation process, often an element of strategic public management, generally operates on an annual basis. At the national level, Congress turns over frequently and the presidency is subject to change every four years. This leads to constant pressure to achieve quick results and forces short time frame reevaluations of potential future environments.

The separation of policymaking authority from implementation responsibility and subsequently the separation of strategic public management personnel between strategic and tactical levels, means that public managers more often are reacting to externally imposed change than managing change they have formulated on their own. It is no secret that public managers often have policymaking discretion. Nevertheless, public managers frequently find themselves setting tactics to match the strategies set by the policymakers to whom they report. Government seems more dominated than business by crises. Public managers, like their business counterparts, can sometimes foresee crisis (Billings, Milburn, and Schaalman 1980), but public managers must react to others' perceptions of crises, and in the end have only limited authority to act. In Washington, it is well known that a crisis occurs when Congress says a crisis has occurred (Rosenbaum 1978; Davies and Davies 1975). These crises, real or imagined, have the potential to wreak havoc with the best laid strategic plans of public managers.

These work context differences make the strategic public management process less precise, less based on reliable information, and very fragmented. In sum, strategic public management processes become politicized. The role of various policy actors diminishes the role of any individual manager, thus potentially causing a breakdown between levels in the processes.

Comparisons of Organizations and Their Structures

A number of measurement and theoretical problems intrude (see Perry, Rainey, and Bozeman 1985) in attempts to compare structural attributes of public and private organizations.

Marshall Meyer's (1979, 1972) studies of the structure of state, local, and county finance and comptroller agencies provide a detailed analysis of the structure of government agencies in the United States. The most general conclusion from Meyer's interviews in more than 200 finance agencies is that the Weberian closed bureaucracy stereotype of government agency is inappropriate and "it may be that government agencies are properly more open to external pressures than popular beliefs about them would suggest" (Meyer 1979, p. 14). In another of the more comprehensive government structure analyses, Hood and Dunshire (1981) studied structural attributes of 69 agencies of the British central government and compared results of their findings to a number of related studies (Child 1972; Hage and Aiken 1969) of private sector organizations. Hood and Dunshire are interested in determining the extent to which government-organized structure (e.g., differentiation, hierarchy, specialization, dispersion) could be predicted by technology and environmental variables. They found that these contingency variables were not important determinants of the structure of larger government agencies but did predict the structure of smaller ones.

The differences in structure between sectors are most apparent at the managerial level (Kraemer and Perry 1983) and in the necessity for involvement of the constituency in public sector organizations. The result is that the structures of public sector organizations are internally rigid and externally fluid. The opportunity for interorganizational conflict then is very high. Such conflict can obviously affect strategic public management processes.

Perhaps most important in this discussion is the fact that, as organizational systems, both public and private sector organizations are open systems in the sense that environment is an important variable of structural change. Of course, the environments are different and thus the structures are different, but the nature of the environment/organization interaction is the same.

Personnel and Personnel Systems

Some have argued that differences in personnel systems account for much of the variance in attitudes of public and private employees (Rainey 1979, 1983). The U.S. Civil Service System is unlike any private personnel system in both its contemporary structure and its origins. The Civil Service System was launched in 1883 by the Pendleton Act and was largely a response to the excesses of the spoils system that for decades had dominated government recruitment and advancement. Furthermore, the merit system that evolved in most levels of government after the creation of the U.S. Civil Service is different in important respects from most private personnel systems. Such practices as veterans' preference and "the rule of three" are obvious differences, but the system of grades, examinations, and safeguards on public employee rights and job security have little resemblance to private personnel systems (Shafritz, Hyde, and Rosenbloom 1981).

Another important difference is the limited personnel authority of government managers and, related, the administration of personnel functions by agencies other than the agency to which the employee is assigned. Considering such factors as the disjunction between political and career public employees, the limited ability of public employees to strike, heterogeneous public employee unions (many including managerial personnel), and the standardized pay schedule for government employees, public personnel systems are significantly different from private ones.

The result is that from a strategic public management perspective, public managers have substantial constraints on their ability to effect any organizational change that also requires personnel-type changes. Blumenthal (1979) was very forthcoming about this limitation and its constraining character and indicated that organizational adaptation that required substantial personnel change or control would not be possible.

ANALYSIS OF STRATEGIC PUBLIC MANAGEMENT ACTIVITIES

A brief review of the strategic public management efforts of NASA, IRS, and NBS at the federal level, of several state/local governments, and of literature on strategic management efforts in the private sector indicates several characteristic differences, which are summarized in Table 4–3.

Private sector strategic management efforts, while very difficult to obtain and review, have a number of distinct characteristics that are useful for comparative illustrations. It can be fairly stated that private sector strategic management activities are quantitatively based and are directed toward environmental modification through resource acquisition and disposal efforts. The goal of strategic management is firm survival and adaptation.

The process of strategic management is well articulated and as presented by Hax and Majluf (1984) and Bourgeois (1980) is an integrated process that should include: (1) mission determination, (2) environmental scanning, (3) distinctive competence selections, (4) business strategy formulation, (5) organization design/

optimization, and (6) budgeting. This process is steplike in character and has the potential for significant organizational change.

In contrast, strategic public management efforts, summarized in Table 4–4, are more qualitative in character, tend to be largely focused at the tactical level, and are less directed toward organizational survival. The focus of the strategic public management efforts is on agency adaptation to future environmental settings for enhanced efficiency and service delivery. Agency survival is of course important, but its context is different in the public sector.

In addition, the ability of many public sector organizations to determine mission and budget without substantial influence from political officials is very limited. Thus the strategic public management process, while certainly broad in scope, potentially lacks the ability to be the fully integrated process that strategic management scholars suggest is required.

The agencies whose strategic management activities are reviewed in Table 4–4 are the National Aeronautics and Space Administration (NASA), the National Bureau of Standards (NBS), and the Internal Revenue Service (IRS). Several points are covered for each including their overall purposes for being involved in strategic management activities. Also since public management activities are very much affected by the policy and political process, the level of policy/political influence on strategic public management activities was reviewed and found to vary. In case of NASA, we have very broad objectives being set by the Congress and president in the 1984–1985 national space strategy. For the National Bureau of Standards, the level of management involved in strategic public management activities is primarily agency management with decisions

Table 4–3. Characteristic Differences Between Strategic Management and Strategic Public Management

Strategic Management (Private Sector)	Strategic Public Management
1. Focus of SM is on the control, manipulation and influence of the environment (Fombrun and Astley 1983; Baird and Thomas 1985; Freeman 1984).	1. Focus of SPM is on responding to the policy demands of increasingly complex external environments.
2. Orientation toward asset acquisition and disposal, market share, and growth (Hax and Majluf 1978; 1974; 1984).	2. SPM efforts tend to focus on market failure issues.
3. Basic approaches to SM focus on portfolio development activities (Wheelwright 1984; Ring 1986).	3. SPM efforts are very broad in scope, dealing with systemwide issues at all levels of government. The result is that SPM activities tend to be comprehensive rather than targeted toward particular markets or geographic settings.
4. SM activities are quantitative and analytical in their character. For example, Merrill and Schweppe (1984) review the SM practices used in the electric utilities industry. In each case, the use of advanced quantitative techniques is common practice. Gluck, Kaufman, and Walleck (1982), and Allen (1979), review this fact more generally.	4. SPM efforts tend to build on a base program rather than the acquisition and disposal focus of SM.
	5. Basic approach to SPM focuses on the development of new programs to meet future demand scenarios for public goods and services.
	6. SPM activities are qualitative in character and involve significant forecasting for the general type.
	7. SPM efforts tend toward advocacy.

being mostly tactical in character. For the Internal Revenue Service, strategic public management activities are predominantly tactical and operational in character. Systems issues, or how the strategic public management activities being carried out by the given agency fit into the general context of the role of the agency within society, and the specific objectives of each agency's strategic public management effort are reviewed. Market failure issues leading to the agency's involvement in a particular service delivery function also are reviewed, along with the techniques used by each of the case agencies to carry out strategic public management activities.

An analysis of these characteristics indicate that strategic public management activities conducted in major federal agencies are diverse and dependent on the character of the agency. The IRS and NBS primarily are service agencies with long histories of delivery. Thus, the complexity of the agencies' environments is somewhat diminished and the extent to which political and policy forces influence the strategic management levels of their strategic public management processes is reduced. NASA is a more complicated agency that in many ways has characteristics more like those of a private sector firm. NASA is involved in a competitive arena, in an area of intense policy and political interests. The result is that its strategic public management processes are more elaborate, more influenced by political/policy processes, and in many ways, more characteristic of businesslike strategic management activities.

Although the evaluation of three case studies is certainly far too limited to make any conclusions, it is possible to say that strategic public management efforts are very diverse, dependent upon the character of the agency and

Table 4–4. Characteristics of Strategic Public Management Activities

Public Agency	Purpose of Current SPM Effort	Level of Management and SPM Effort	System Issues	Specific Objectives of SPM Effort	Market Failure Issues	Technique and Format of SPM
NASA	To set the general cause and objective for the post-shuttle space program. To establish space technology and systems development as a national goal.	Objectives set by Congress and President in 1984–85 in the national space strategy were responded to at the tactical level with the development of a 1986–2015 strategic plan.	1. The management of the expanded development of space as a commercial opportunity. 2. The expansion of interplanetary space exploration. 3. Development of space sciences. 4. Generic development of space technology.	1. Develop permanent manned space stations. 2. Expand space commercialization efforts to level of attracting business. 3. Establish model for universal creation. 4. Continue existing program base.	1. Inadequate resources in private sector for systems development. 2. No incentive for large-scale R&D. 3. No incentive for interplanetary exploration.	The strategic plan reviewed is based around program statements and PERT analyses of these goal statements. There are no market analysis efforts. Goal statements review maximum program activities and are not linked to a budget.
NBS	To update the general purpose for the 85-year-old agency, particularly as it relates to new and emerging technologies. To revise the role of the agency to that of a proactive entity in providing for economic growth through technical advance.	This effort reviews the tactical alternatives available for selection by policy decision makers and prescribes the objective scenarios for the NBS.	1. Need for expanded technical infrastructure for society. 2. Need for improved science delivery.	1. Improve technology transfer. 2. Need for improved competitiveness of U.S. firms in international competition.	1. Inappropriability of research results. 2. No incentive for infratechnology development.	Review of NBS role and potential programs in emerging activities in industrial R&D and industrial production. General social and technical variables play an important part of the analysis.
IRS	To establish the general purpose for the transition of the IRS into the twenty-first century.	General goals following mandated mission are established with a tactical and operational management plan.	1. Improve efficiency and effectiveness. 2. Expand services to diverse public. 3. Upgrade entire IRS system for electronic media.	Fifty-five strategic initiatives were identified with specific goals for each.	1. Decreasing incentive for voluntary compliance.	The format is based around the 55 strategic initiatives (SI). Each SI is detailed as to personnel and resources needed and goals. Each SI is also scheduled for implementation.

its programs, highly influenced by policy and political activity, and not necessarily a well-integrated process, as suggested by Hax and Majluf (1984).

CONSTRAINTS AS OPPORTUNITIES: SOME PRESCRIPTIVE PROPOSITIONS ABOUT STRATEGIC PUBLIC MANAGEMENT

Strategic public management not only is possible but is practiced, at least partially, at all levels of government. However, strategic public management labors under a set of conditions different from those encountered by private sector strategic managers. Public managers are constrained by, among other factors: (1) the authority of political executives, particularly with respect to policy and strategy, (2) government personnel systems that protect employee rights but also inhibit managerial discretion, and (3) "governance structures" beginning with the Constitution but also including unique operating procedures accommodating pluralism, government fragmentation, and political cycles.

Each of these factors, and others as well, can be viewed as opportunities and "decision filters," as well as constraints. The prescriptive propositions presented below suggest approaches to possibly turn these conditions to advantage or, when that is not possible, mitigate the effects on the possibilities for strategic public management. The hope is that through the realization of the conditions of the strategic public management environment a more complete strategic management process for public sector application might develop.

Proposition 1. *Strategic public management should seek to exploit (rather than avoid) crises identified by policy actors.* Since it is likely that policymaking and hence public management will

continue to be responsive to crises (real, imagined, or manufactured), strategic public management should seek to turn crisis to advantage. Crises clearly have potential as major disturbances in the flow of policy. However, in at least some instances, policies and plans that appear to be hastily fashioned reactions are in fact carefully thought-out policies that have been on the shelf awaiting an opportune moment of presentation (Smart and Vertinsky 1977; Desai and Crow 1983). Crises are not always agenda wreckers; sometimes they are agenda facilitators.

If it is not possible to exploit crises, then strategic public management should at least retain sufficient flexibility so that strategy will not become rapidly outmoded with changes in the economic or political environment. Consider as an object lesson the case of the strategic plan for the city of Dallas (1983). The Dallas plan was not sufficiently robust to deal with the full range of possible economic environments in which the city might be operating. Consequently, as economic crises developed in the Southwest in the mid 1980s as a result of overbuilding, natural resource price fluctuations, and agricultural problems, Dallas's strategic plan, which failed to consider low-growth or no-growth scenarios, was of limited use. A strategic public management effort that had considered a wider range of future environments could have prescribed behaviors that at least could have provided guidance for tactical and operational management.

Proposition 2. *Public personnel system constraints require "positional" rather than "personal" strategic public management.* The person coordinating a strategic public management effort must plan on the basis of organizational position control rather than attempt to identify and acquire the services of particular individuals or to leverage particular individuals to modify their behavior.

One mechanism that many agencies have found successful as a means of overcoming the constraints suggested here is the extensive use of contractors for a wide range of agency activities. Consider, for example, the strategic plan developed by NASA (1985). NASA assumes that its long-term contractors such as the California Institute of Technology (contractor for the operation of the Jet Propulsion Laboratory) and the North American Rockwell Corporation (contractor for the design and construction of the Space Transportation System) will be more flexible in their personnel activities so as to permit the successful implementation of tactical and operational plans.

This is not to say that public agencies are incapable of overcoming personnel constraints. As indicated in the Internal Revenue Service strategic plan, several of the 55 planned strategic initiatives are directed toward improving the responsiveness of IRS personnel to the changing external environment. This strategic plan calls for initiatives at the operational level in employee physical fitness, employee productivity, improved treatment of managers and executives, improved office environment, and other miscellaneous employee-directed activities.

Proposition 3. *In strategic public management, changing the structure is not the solution.* Research suggests (Zammuto 1982; Meyer 1979) that organizational structure is not a key ingredient in policy effectiveness. The structural configuration of government should be less important to strategic public management participants than the strategic public management process itself. Lindblom (1977) observed that public organizations tend to be geared more toward means attainment than toward ends attainment; as a result, structural change is often an end in itself.

As an example of means and ends reversal, consider the Internal Revenue Service. The IRS's stated goal is to "collect the proper amount of tax revenues at the least cost to the public, and in the manner that warrants the highest degree of public confidence in our integrity, efficiency and fairness" (Internal Revenue Service 1985, p. 1). Despite the straightforward articulation of that goal, the *means* of collecting taxes often supersedes the goal of attaining a high degree of public confidence, efficiency, and fairness. This focus on means shows itself in the complex forms and procedures that often are beyond average taxpayer's abilities and in the agency's orientation not toward building public confidence, but toward simply collecting taxes. A result of this is a subsequent strategic focus on agency design, reorganization, and assessment of organizational efficiency. If the IRS were focused on ends, it would look at taxpayer service standards, the percentage of legal tax revenues collected, and evaluate IRS fairness. Development of a strategic public management effort for an agency like the IRS should include consideration of the potential problems of means–ends reversal and focus less on the structural characteristics of the organization.

Proposition 4. *Implementation of strategic public management requires alternative inducements for public managers.* Because there usually is no pecuniary reward for public managers to participate in strategic public management processes, it is important that alternative incentives be developed to induce participation. This is in contrast to the private sector where successful development and implementation of strategic management activities can result in both career and financial enhancements for those who are involved. Without some type of incentive for involvement and participation in public sector organizations, we can expect that some managers will withhold commitment.

An instructive example comes from the strategic management activities being undertaken by the Internal Revenue Service. As the external environment of the IRS changes from a paper to an electronic media, the IRS also must change its operating procedures and media. Such changes are expensive in terms of personnel changes and potential capital investments and those IRS public managers involved in the transition must take the risk of attempting to acquire the resources for this dramatic organizational change. Unfortunately, within the strategic public management arena, public managers can find themselves on the wrong side of broader based political issues associated with reducing government expenditures or reducing the ability of government to electronically monitor financial transactions. The result is that many managers without other incentives, such as targeted senior executive service bonuses, may decline to participate in a strategic public management process.

Proposition 5. *Strategic public management should highlight the role of the public manager.* Strategic public management implementation efforts should be built around senior career civil servants rather than the political executives who serve the president, governor, or mayor.

In the interest of representativeness, the endorsements and substantive input of legislators and political executives is important, but public managers must flesh out the broad outlines provided by political superiors. The ra-

tionale behind this proposition is that it is the senior public managers who provide the stability to public sector organizations over the long term and it is through these individuals that the institutional memory necessary for successful implementation of strategic management activities will be established. In our conceptualization of strategic public management, the political executives (appointees) who serve in various agencies at all levels of government are not the organization's primary source of managerial leadership and thus should not lead the way in strategic public management. This conclusion is based in part on the necessarily short time horizons of political leaders. It is the political executive's responsibility to assist, by working with career public managers, in developing the broadest assumptions of strategic public management. It is vital that senior public managers play the central role, not only because of their longer time frame, but also because of their implementation responsibility and their bridge to tactical and operational levels. Without strong public manager leadership in strategic public management, it is likely that the processes will be governed by temporal political concerns. In support of this proposition, the IRS plan takes particular care in identifying the lead senior public manager responsible for the implementation of each of the 55 recommended strategic initiatives. In every case, the recommended public official is a career civil servant.

Proposition 6. *Strategic public management should serve as a mechanism for increasing entrepreneurial behavior in public sector organizations.* One of the major criticisms of public sector management activities is the lack of entrepreneurial behavior. Assuming that strategic public management is the integrated process of strategic, tactical, and operational activities outlined in this chapter, there is some opportunity to enhance the entrepreneurial behavior of public managers and overcome the system constraints described earlier. A case in point is the development of the long-range plan by the National Bureau of Standards (NBS) as a principal output of its strategic public management process.

For the past eighty years, the NBS has served the scientific support needs of the United States business community. As that external business community has changed over time, the need for entrepreneurial behavior has increased. In that regard, the NBS's strategic public management process has provided mechanisms for entrepreneurial activities and risk taking. For instance, the charting of a future NBS course with respect to biotechnology is a response to environmental changes in the agricultural research area. The traditional NBS role had been confined to weights and measures standardization and not to new scientific thrusts such as biotechnology. This is entrepreneurial behavior on NBS's part in that it is creatively planning new programs that may enhance the development of a future economic market. This planning is made possible through the integrated process of strategic and tactical management.

Proposition 7. *The psychological and symbolic nature of government and political authority represents strategic public management opportunities.* On January 28, 1986, with the inflight destruction of the space shuttle Challenger, we all became aware that there are substantial emotional attachments not only to people involved in public programs, but to the programs themselves. This is partly due to the symbolic and psychological components of public projects.

Citizens have different and sometimes more stringent expectations of public agencies, but they also have stronger commitments to public agencies than to most private organizations.

Strategic public management, at its highest level, is carried out and communicated largely in the form of broad symbols that are understood as much from an emotional/psychological standpoint as from a technical or rational view. The destruction of Challenger and the reaction of both the government and private citizens indicated that substantial symbolism was attached to the space shuttle activity. This symbolism reflected many of the American ideals concerning technological superiority, scientific interests, and the continuing search for new frontiers.

As a strategic public management opportunity, the emotive power of government can help promote public participation and "investment" in an agency and its missions. Strategic public management must recognize that organizational success and effectiveness is externally defined.

Proposition 8. *Strategic public management should recognize and accommodate political cycles and, specifically, should take into account budget trends.* The budgetary process associated with the acquisition of funds for all government-related activities is well documented and at the same time complex. Strategic public management activities should incorporate budgetary trends and political cycles as part of their basic plan.

At the risk of premature judgment, it is already possible to see problems in the NASA strategic plan, which are associated with the high capitalization costs of a permanent manned space station. While NASA has considered the fact that federal-level budgets are generally incremental and that the trend has been to reduce overall federal spending, the strategic public management activities associated with the space station effort appear to lack careful enough consideration of the extent of the cost unknowns of a project of this magnitude and technical uncertainty. A result is that the deadlines for implementation of the NASA strategic plan, particularly those set for the tactical management level, might prove so unrealistic as to undermine the entire plan.

Proposition 9. *Despite the needs for stability and long-term view, strategic public management should incorporate quick results.* In the development of the strategic plan for a public agency, the relationship between that plan and the political/ policy demands that started the strategic management process should be carefully considered. It is almost always the case that policy demand cycles need quick policy outputs. A result is that the strategic public management processes should include the development of short-term deliverables that can be perceived in the environment as responses to the initiating policy demand.

In the case of the IRS, the objective is to increase the percentage of tax revenue obtained from legal sources. However, the goals for the acquisition of these resources should not be set in a time frame which makes it impossible to measure progress over an extended period. There is a need for the development of deliverables that can be staged over the entire period of the initiative. Policymakers involved in strategic management must have results in the short term in order to satisfy political demands.

Proposition 10. *Within the agency, strategic-level issues should be more modest and play a smaller role than tactical-level issues.* Because of the important role played by policymakers in establishing mandates and limits for the agency, the agency's activities are appropriately centered on tactical rather than strategic issues. The policymaking apparatus of most public sector organizations serves as a buffer between agencies and their environment. While career public managers should play a central role in strategic public management, tactical public management and public management routines inevitably have a dominant role. Strategy dictates purpose and multiorganization activity but not (in most instances) the behavior of individual public agencies. Moreover, without tactical public management, strategic public management could not successfully integrate the activities of the agency with the broader policy arena. The public manager is most critical at the tactical public management level where specific goals and objectives are set based on the direction established at the strategic management level. Therefore, it is at the tactical public management level that the public manager's role is most critical.

SUMMARY

It is clear that the practice of strategic public management will vary from the practice of strategic management in the private sector. Fundamental differences in governance, built-in constraints, and unique features of the public sector make the practice of strategic public management broad and diffuse in character. Our analysis of the practice of strategic public management in several public agencies, as well as a review of public/private managerial differences leads us to the conclusion that strategic public management should be a process of linking policymaking with the tactical management aspects of an agency.

If one views strategic public management as

a linking pin between public policy and intraorganizational management, then the chief difference between the public and private sector's strategic management is manifest: In the public sector, strategic management requires the matching of externally derived goals with organization tactics for achieving those goals; in the private sector, external constraints may be important but external goals need not be. By this view, there is almost inexorably a greater degree of tension in strategic public management as public managers seek to resolve external goals of recognized importance with the internal goals that arise from tactical management. Managing that tension is the meaning and the challenge of strategic public management.

NOTES

1. A similar tack has been taken by Ring and Perry (1985). However, their objective chiefly was to identify differences between public and private organizations' strategic management, and ours is to provide prescriptive propositions about strategic public management. Since our purpose is to use the comparative literature as a point of departure for prescription, the summary presented here is not a comprehensive overview. For a more comprehensive approach, see Rainey, Backoff, and Levine 1976; and Perry, Rainey, and Bozeman 1985; and Bower 1977, 1983.

2. For a complete review of this literature, see B. L. Bozeman, *All Organizations are Public*, San Francisco, Calif.: Josey-Bass, 1987.

REFERENCES

Alchian, Armen, A. 1965. Some economics of property rights. *Il Politico* 3: 816–829.

——— and H. Demsetz. 1972. Production, information costs, and economic organizations. *American Economic Review* 62, 777–779.

———. 1973. The property rights paradigm. *Journal of Economic History* 33, 16–27.

Aldrich, H. E. 1979. *Organizations and environments.* Englewood Cliffs, N.J.: Prentice-Hall.

Allen, M. G. 1979. Diagraming GE's planning for what's watt. In *Corporate Planning: Techniques and Applications,* edited by R. J. Allio and M. W. Pennington. New York, N.Y.: AMACOM.

Allison, G. T. 1983. Public and private management: Are they fundamentally alike in all unimportant respects? In *Public Management: Public and Private Perspectives,* edited by J. L. Perry and K. L. Kramer. Palo Alto, Calif.: Mayfield Publishing Co.

Baird, I. S. and H. Thomas. 1985. Toward a contingency theory of strategic risk taking. *Academy of Management Review,* April.

Billings, R. S., T. W. Milburn, and M. L. Schaalman. 1980. A model of crisis perception: A theoretical and empirical analysis. *Administrative Science Quarterly* June 25, 300–316.

Blumenthal, Michael. 1979. Candid reflections of a businessman in Washington. *Fortune* January 29.

Bolan, Richard S. 1980. The practitioner as theorist: The phenomenology of the professional episode. *Journal of the American Planning Association* 46 (3).

Bower, J. L. 1977. Effective public management. *Harvard Business Review* Vol. 55, No. 2, March–April.

———. 1983. Managing for efficiency, managing for equity. *Harvard Business Review* Vol. 64, No. 4, July–August.

Bourgeois, L. 1980. Strategy and environment: A conceptual integration. *Academy of Management and Review* Vol. 5, No. 1, January.

Bozeman, B. 1983. Strategic public management and productivity: A firehouse theory. *State Government* March, 16–22.

———. 1987. *All organizations are public.* San Francisco, Calif.: Jossey-Bass.

———. 1984. Dimensions of "publicness": An approach to public organization theory. In *New Directions in Public Administration,* edited by Barry Bozeman and Jeffrey Straussman. Monterey, Calif.: Brooks/Cole, 46–62.

Burgelman, R. A. 1986. Organizational ecology and strategic management: An evolutionary process perspective. Research Paper No. 924, Graduate School of Business, Stanford University, November.

Chandler, A. D. 1962. *Strategy and structure.* Cambridge, Mass.: M.I.T. Press.

Child, J. 1972. Organization structure, environment and performance: The role of strategic choice. *Sociology* 6, 1–22.

City of San Francisco. 1983. *San Francisco strategic plan: Making a great city greater.* San Francisco, Calif.: San Francisco Chamber of Commerce.

Davies, J. C. and B. S. Davies. 1975. *The Politics of pollution.* Indianapolis, Ind.: Pegausus.

De Alessi, Louis. 1969. Implications of property rights for government investment choices. *American Economic Review* 59, 13–24.

———. 1980. The economics of property rights: A review of the evidence. In *Research in Law and Economics,* Vol. 2, edited by Richard O. Zerbe, Jr. Greenwich, Conn.: JAI Press, Inc. 1–47.

Demsetz, H. 1967. Toward a theory of property rights. *American Economic Review* 57, 347–59.

Denhardt, R. B. 1985. Strategic planning in state and local government. *State and Local Government Review.* Winter, 17, 1: 174–179.

Desai, U. and M. M. Crow. 1983. Failures of power and intelligence: Use of scientific and technical information in government decision making. *Administration and Society.* Vol. 15, No. 2, August, 185–205.

Eadie, D. C. 1983. Putting a powerful tool to practical use: The application of strategic planning in the public sector. *Public Administration Review.* Vol. 43, September–October, 447.

Freeman, J. and W. Boeker. 1984. The ecological analysis of business strategy. *California Management Review* 26, Spring, 73–86.

Hage, J. T. and M. Aiken. 1969. Routine technology, social structure, and organizational goals. *Administrative Science Quarterly* 14, 366–77.

Hax, A. C. and N. S. Majluf. 1984. The use of growth-share matrix and strategic planning. In *Readings on Strategic Management,* edited by A. C. Hax. Cambridge, Mass.: Ballinger Publishing Company.

Hood, C. and A. Dunshire. 1983. *Bureaumetrics: The quantitative comparison of British central government agencies.* University, Alabama: University of Alabama Press.

Internal Revenue Service, U.S. Department of the Treasury. 1984. *Internal Revenue Service strategic plan,* document 6940, Washington, D.C.: United States Government Printing Office, Department of Treasury, document 6941.

Kraemer, K. L. and J. L. Perry. 1983. Implementation of management science in the public sector. In *Public Management: Public and Private Perspectives,* edited by J. L. Perry and K. L. Kraemer. Palo Alto, Calif.: Mayfield Publishing Co.

Lindblom, C. E. 1977. *Politics and markets,* New York, N.Y.: Basic Books.

———. 1982. The market as prison. *The Journal of Politics* Vol. 44, No. 2, May 324–36.

Mazzolini, R. 1980. The international strategy of state-owned firms: An organizational process and politics perspective. *Strategic Management Journal* Vol. 1.

———. 1981. Strategic decisions in government-controlled enterprises. *Administration and Society* 13, 1: 7–31.

McKie, J. W. 1970. Regulation in the free market: The problem of boundaries. *Bell Journal of Economic and Management Science* Vol. 1, Spring, 9.

Merrill, H. M. and F. C. Schweppe. 1984. Strategic planning for electric utilities: Problems in analytical methods. In *Readings on Strategic Management,* edited by A. C. Hax. Cambridge, Mass.: Ballinger Publishing Company.

Meyer, Marshall W. 1972. *Bureaucratic structure and authority: Coordination and control in 254 government agencies.* New York, N.Y.: Harper and Row.

———. 1979. *Change in public bureaucracies.* London: Cambridge University Press.

Mintzberg, H. 1979. *The Structuring of organizations.* Englewood Cliffs, N.J.: Prentice-Hall.

Moffitt, L. C. 1984. *Strategic management: Public planning at the local level.* Greenwich, Conn.: JAI Press, Inc.

National Bureau of Standards, U.S. Department of Commerce. 1985. *Long-Range Plan of the National Bureau of Standards,* Washington, D.C.: United States Government.

National Aeronautics and Space Administration. 1985. *Strategic plan 1986–1991.* Washington, D.C.

Peltzman, Sam. 1971. Pricing in public and private enterprises: Electric utilities in the United States. *Journal of Law and Economics* 14, 109–148.

Perry, J., H. Rainey, and B. Bozeman. 1985. The public-private distinction in organization theory: A critique and research strategy. Paper presented at the annual meeting of the American Political Science Association, New Orleans, Louisiana., August 28–30.

Rainey, H. G., R. W. Backoff, and C. H. Levine. 1976. Comparing public and private organizations. *Public Administration Review* Vol. 36, No. 2, 233–246.

Rainey, H. G. 1979. Perceptions of incentives in business and government: Implications for civil service reform. *Public Administration Review* Vol. 39, 440–448.

———. 1983. Public agencies and private firms: Incentive structures, goals, and individual roles. *Administration and Society* Vol. 15, No. 2, August, 207–242.

Ring, P. S. and J. L. Perry. 1985. Strategic management in public and private organizations: Implications of distinctive contexts and constraints. *Academy of Management Review* Vol. 10, Number 2, 276–286.

Ring, P. S. 1986. What is the strategic in public sector's strategic management? Paper presented at the Association for Public Policy Analysis and Management, 8th Annual Research Conference, October 30, Austin, Texas.

Rosenbaum, W. A. 1973. *The politics of environmental concern.* New York, N.Y.: Praeger.

Saunders, C. B. and F. D. Tuggle. 1977. Why planners don't. *Long Range Planning* Vol. 10, No. 3, June.

Schendel, D. E. and C. W. Hofer, eds. 1979. *Strategic management: A new view of business policy and planning.* Boston, Mass.: Little, Brown.

Shafritz, J. M., A. C. Hyde, and D. H. Rosenbloom. 1981. *Personnel management in government: Politics and process.* New York: Marcel Dekker, Inc.

Smart, C. and L. Vertinsky. 1977. Designs for crisis decision units. *Administrative Science Quarterly* 22: 640–657.

State of Ohio. 1984. *Toward a working Ohio: A strategic plan for the 80s and beyond.* Columbus, Ohio: State of Ohio.

Steiner, G. P. and J. B. Miner. 1977. *Management policy and strategy.* New York, N.Y.: MacMillan Publishing Company.

Stevens, J. M., and J. R. McGowan. 1983. Managerial strategies in municipal government organizations. *Academy of Management Journal* 26, 527–524.

Walter, S. and D. Choate. 1984. *Thinking strategically: A primer for public leaders,* Washington, D.C.: Council of State Planning Agencies.

Wamsley, G. L. and M. N. Zald. 1973. *The political economy of public organizations.* Lexington, Mass.: D. C. Heath.

Wechsler, B. and R. Backoff. 1986. Dynamics of strategy and public organizations. Paper presented at the American Planning Association conference, Los Angeles, California. April.

Wheelwright, S. C. 1984. Strategy, management, and strategic planning approaches. In *Readings on Strategic Management,* edited by A. C. Hax. Cambridge, Mass.: Ballinger Publishing Company.

Wholey, D. R. and J. W. Britain. 1986. Organizational ecology: Findings and implications. *Academy of Management Review* 11, 513–533.

Wilson, J. Q. 1974. The politics of regulation. In *Social Responsibility of the Business Predicament,* edited by J. W. McKie. Washington, D.C.: The Brookings Institution.

Wortman, M. S., Jr. 1979. Strategic management: Not-for-profit organizations. In *Strategic Managment: A New View of Business Policy and Planning,* edited by D. E. Schendel and C. W. Hofer. Boston, Mass.: Little, Brown.

Zamuto, R. F. 1982. *Assessing organizational effectiveness: Systems change, adaptation and strategy.* Albany, N.Y.: State University of New York Press.

Zif, J. 1981. Managerial strategic behavior in state-owned enterprises—business and political orientations. *Management Science* 27.

Strategic Issues: What Are They and From Where Do They Come?

PETER SMITH RING

With the increasing frequency and complexity of interactions between levels of government, among units of government at the same level, and between government and the private sector, strategic planners in the public sector confront an ever-expanding array of issues. Not all hold the same degree of importance, nor can all of them be addressed. For public sector planners, assessing the strategic nature and relative importance of these issues becomes an increasingly critical task.

One premise underlying this analysis is that the identification of strategic issues is essential to strategic planning processes. In the analysis that follows, two questions germane to this problem are explored: (1) What makes an issue strategic? and (2) Where do you look for strategic issues? The central argument in this chapter is that the means by which these questions can be answered are readily available in models of public policy and business strategy, although these forms or sources may not immediately suggest themselves.

After establishing basic definitions, an approach to identifying the probable sources of strategic issues for public sector planners and a model outlining a process for identifying strategic issues are presented. The five steps in the model are explored at a conceptual level. Practical implications of these steps for strategic planners in the public sector then are discussed. The chapter ends with a brief discussion of additional research on the topic that appears to be warranted.

ASSUMPTIONS UNDERLYING THE ANALYSIS

Our concern is with strategic issues. An issue is "a difficulty or problem that has a significant influence on the way the organization functions or on its ability to achieve a desired future, for which there is no agreed-on response. Issues can be internal or external to an organization, or both" (Nutt and Backoff 1987, p. 47). An issue is assumed to be strategic if planners perceive it will involve decisions and actions related to changes in "the basic long-term goals and objectives of an [organization], and the adoption of courses of action and the allocation of resources necessary for carrying out these [changed] goals" (Chandler 1962, p. 13). The discussion that follows is based on an assumption that the strategy process is dynamic, evolutionary, and emergent (Mintzberg 1978) rather than static. Thus, the identification of strategic issues must involve a process or set of processes that are ongoing.

There is a significant debate as to what makes an issue "strategic." Evered (1983) provides a thoughtful review of the literature that has explored the concept and concludes that strategy has a number of common features. Among those most relevant for public sector planners are:

- Strategy is a continuous process.
- The focus is on what needs to be done and why.
- Strategy looks at the whole, not the parts.
- It involves value judgments, and is oriented toward assessing change and consciously generating change.
- It has a future orientation.
- It is "resource mobilizing."

For purposes of this analysis, an issue becomes more strategic as it takes on these elements.

Finally, because the terms *planner* and *public sector organization* have multiple meanings it may be helpful to understand how they are used here. It is difficult to speak simply of a public sector organization. The reasons why there are public sector organizations, and the tasks in which they become involved, vary greatly across levels of government. Answers to the questions explored in this analysis will be contingent on the kind of agency, the level of government, and the set of goals an organization is pursuing. When the word *planner* is used it refers to practitioners involved in strategic planning; i.e., those people who focus on the basic goals and objectives of an organi-

zation or the way in which they will be implemented, regardless of formal job titles.

IDENTIFICATION OF STRATEGIC ISSUES

Identifying sources from which strategic issues might emerge provides some guidance to a planner asking the question, "Where do strategic issues come from?" Answering this question is the first step in the process of strategic issue identification set forth in this chapter (see Table 5–1).

Step One: Identifying Sources of Strategic Issues

A good first step in the process of identifying strategic issues is knowing where to look for them. An argument is made here that strategic issues have three sources: environmental, structural, and processual. There can be various environmental sources, including internal, external, and operating conditions with which the planner must work. Structural sources of strategic issues are derived from the enduring patterns of governmental relationships or enduring patterns in relationships between government and other sectors of the economy or of society. Processual sources refer to changes in these patterns or in policies or procedures being dealt with within structural relationships. These sources of strategic issues are briefly examined in the sections that follow. Table 5–2 outlines sample sources of strategic issues. A busy planner will not be able to scan all sources of strategic issues. When forced to choose between environmental, structural, and processual sources, planners are likely to find an initial focus on processual sources more effective because they have significantly more control of the policies of their agencies than the formal structures of government. To fully explain the

Table 5–1. Strategic Issue Identification Process

STEP 1 Identify Sources of Strategic Issues	STEP 2 Identify Contexts of Strategic Issues	STEP 3 Complete Information Sorting	STEP 4 Employ Analytical Tools	STEP 5 Strategic Issues Identified
See Table 5–2	Issue Characteristics Agenda Processes (Characteristics) Phase in Cycle of Attention	Actor Focus Agency Focus Problem Focus	Stakeholder Analysis SWOT/7-S Analysis Portfolio Analysis	

model, however, all three sources are treated illustratively in the discussion that follows.

Thomas (1974, p. 28) identifies three generic environments from which strategic issues might arise. These environmental sources are generic because they can be applied with ease to public, private, or so-called third-sector organizations. The first of these he describes as the general environment, which encompasses "the national and global context of social, political, regulatory, economic, and technological conditions...." Thomas's term general will be designated as *institutional* here because it is a term with which we believe public sector planners may be more familiar. A second generic environment is the *operating* environment: "The set of suppliers and other interest groups with which the firm deals." Dill (1958) has referred to this as the task environment. The third generic source of strategic issues described by Thomas is the *internal* environment, or those things "within the firm's official jurisdiction."

For the public sector, the institutional environment entails geopolitical or intergovernmental issues. The operating environment will be contingent on the level of government at which a planner is employed. A regional planner's operating environment, for example, will involve state agencies, local agencies, other regional agencies, as well as a myriad of com-

munity and business interest groups. The internal environment, regardless of the level of government, generally can be defined as within the organization's boundaries.

The Institutional Environment. Within the institutional environment, two examples of structural sources of strategic issues are suggested: (1) the overall organization of government, and (2) fundamental differences between the public and private sectors of the economy. These two sources of potential strategic issues are examined below, as are some examples of structural or processual sources associated with each of them.

Our federal set of political institutions is more complex and more fragmented than those of any other nation state in the modern era. Issues of strategic importance may arise from *federalism*—the formal sharing of power by state and national governments. Wright (1978, p. 8) observes, however, that there are aspects of public sector relationships that are not captured by the concept of federalism:

> Whereas federalism emphasizes national–state relationships with occasional attention to interstate relations, the concept of *intergovernmental relations* [IGR] recognizes not only national–state and interstate relations, but also national–local, state–local, national–state–local, and interlocal relations. In short, IGR encompasses all

Table 5–2. Illustrative Sources of Strategic Issues

Environmental Sources	Structural Sources	Processual Sources	Strategic Issues
Institutional Environment	Organization of government, e.g., federalism, intergovernmental relations. Public–private sector differences.	Ill-defined public policy. Openness of the organization. Diverse publics. Artificial time constraints. Shaky coalitions.	Who decides plant locations? Who funds primary/secondary education? What is Orange County transit plan? What does NASA tell the public? Who are police stakeholders? What do we do in first term? How do we keep labor on board?
Operating Environment	Public–private sector interaction, e.g., economic regulation, social regulation, industrial policy. Policy source, e.g., legislative, judicial, executive.	Policy types, e.g., distributive policies, redistributive policies, regulatory policies, constituency policies.	Open state to out-of-state banks? Impose quotas for fire hiring? Support enterprise zones? Should buses take wheelchairs? Do tax reductions trickle down? Exempt Ford/GM from m.p.g. regulations? Home ports for battleships?
Internal Environment	Organizational structure Civil service systems.	Policy formation. Policy goals and objectives. Resource allocation processes. Policy implementation. Tractability of problem (e.g., technical difficulty). Extent to which policy vehicle structures implementation (e.g., decision rules). Nonstatutory variables (e.g., public support). Policy evaluation. Performance measures.	Do we want safe streets? Selective vs. across-the-board service cuts? Does pyrolysis solve our waste disposal problem? When do we decide we have spent enough experimenting on pyrolysis? "Combat" zones for adult theater? When are streets safe?

the permutations and combinations of relations among the units of government in our system.

Three examples of these kinds of relationships are: (1) layer cakes (Grodzins 1966), (2) picket fences (Wright 1978), and (3) marble cakes (Grodzins 1966).[1]

Government relationships structured in layer cake form might create strategic issues related to boundaries. A planner in a local police department must be concerned about how federal law enforcement agencies will react to her plan to crack down on prostitution by providing prostitutes with the choice between a jail term and a bus ticket out of town. Organization by program, an inherent aspect of a picket fence structure, creates strategic issues related to coordination, overlapping responsibility, and the sharing of resources. Health, education, or social service planners will often see strategic issues of this sort. The marble cake theory implies that strategic issues could crop up in connection with the identification of responsibility, programmatic focuses, or diffusion of effort.

Another structural source of strategic issues results from fundamental differences between organizations located in the public and private sectors of the economy. Ring and Perry (1985) highlight five fundamental differences between the two sectors.[2] These differences may be a source of strategic issues which are processual in nature. For example, Ring and Perry note that coalitions required to get a program of strategic initiatives enacted and implemented may come apart without warning. Thus, the design and long-term management of these coalitions could be a strategic issue, and economic development planners may have to decide which interest groups should be included when

building a coalition designed to bring new industry to a community.

The Operating Environment. While some strategic issues inevitably will arise from the institutional environment, more relevant issues for public sector planners are likely to stem from sources associated with the organization's operating environment.

Interactions between private and public organizations may generate strategic issues. The various ways in which these interactions occur cannot be adequately treated here (see, e.g., Fritschler and Ross 1980), but the examples that follow are illustrative of structural interactions.

• *Regulation.* The regulation of the activities of business might create strategic issues for agencies at all levels of government. Deciding among the competing interests involved in the need to bring new medical techniques or drugs to market against the need to protect the public's health is likely to be a strategic issue source for the Food and Drug Administration.[3] In the current business environment, strategic planners for state banking regulators must determine the degree of competition they want to foster among commercial banks. At the local level, planners may be confronted with a host of strategic issues regarding health and environmental regulation of industries that produce toxic wastes.

• *Industrial policy.* Development and protection of American business, in the form of so-called industrial policy, also produces significant public–private interactions. Thus, the International Trade Commission must decide whether foreign producers of steel, textiles, cars, shoes, and microprocessor chips ought to be investigated for dumping their products in U.S. markets. At the same time, the Commerce Department may have to make strategic decisions about providing government subsidies to certain industries or firms.

At the state level, increasing competition for the jobs and revenues generated by plant location decisions, such as the competition engendered by General Motors in search of a site for its Saturn plant, creates a host of potentially strategic issues. For example, should the state compete for the plant site? How will existing businesses react? If the state does compete, what incentives, if any, should it offer?

Similar issues arise for local governments. For an airport commission planner, a strategic issue may involve deciding the criteria for the allocation of landing slots among competing airlines, or whether to impose additional regulations designed to further suppress takeoff and landing noise. A local economic development planner may have to determine whether more jobs can be created by designating areas of the community as enterprise zones, or by seeking long-term tax breaks for firms that relocate to the community.

• *Policy.* In itself policy is a structural source of strategic issues. It may be a creature of any of the three branches of government, and in each case is likely to be quite different in its design and objectives. As Ring and Perry (1985) have suggested, legislatively based policy tends to be ambiguous, a fact which itself may give rise to strategic issues. Policy that results from judicial decree, in contrast, tends to be much more specific and is likely to narrow the potential range of strategic issues.

The type of policy with which a planner has to deal thus becomes a processual source of strategic issues. Lowi (1964) identifies four categories of policy: *distributive* (policies that produce real results—e.g., ramps instead of stairs for the physically disabled), *redistributive* (policies such

as those advocated by the Reagan administration designed to shift government spending from social programs to defense), *regulatory* (such as the FCC's stance on the Fairness Doctrine), and *constituency* (Lyndon Johnson's decision that NASA would have a presence in Texas). We expect that distributive policies would generate a different array of strategic issues than would regulatory policies. In the former case, the strategic issue for a planner might involve the best means of accomplishing the task of providing access to public facilities to the physically disabled, while in the latter the issue might be whether these same standards will be applied to private sector organizations.

The Internal Environment. The internal environment of an organization itself will be a source of strategic issues for that organization's planners. Designing the organization's structure may create strategic issues; for instance, how much autonomy should be given to patrol officers in investigating criminal acts? Formalized civil service systems are another structural source of potential strategic issues. As illustrated in Table 5–2, strategic issues related to the internal environment may also arise out of the processes of policy formation, implementation, and evaluation.

Setting goals and objectives for a public organization is a task that involves actors at different constitutional levels of government, within different constitutional branches and of differing status, such as political appointees versus career civil servants. Thus, one strategic issue will be related to the question of "who" should be involved in policy formulation in some organizations.

Table 5–2 points to implementation as a possible source of strategic issues. Mazmanian and Sabatier (1983) propose a model of implementation that suggests three likely sources of strategic issues. One element of their model is the tractability of the problem. Answering this question will raise strategic issues such as "What stakeholder groups are we attempting to satisfy with our program and how will they react to our proposal?" In addition to tractability, Mazmanian and Sabatier argue that the statute (or other policy structure) can affect the course of implementation. Using their model, a planner can identify seven factors, each of which could give rise to, or in fact may be, a strategic issue. Restated in the form of questions, the seven factors include:

1. Are our objectives clear and consistent?
2. Have we incorporated adequate causal theory in our planning?
3. What allocation of financial resources will we initially employ?
4. What degree of hierarchical integration within and among competing institutions is needed to achieve our objectives?
5. What decision rules will we employ?
6. How will we recruit implementing officials?
7. How much formal access will outsiders have to the processes of implementation?

Mazmanian and Sabatier also identify a set of nonstatutory variables related to implementation, all of which are relevant to the question of the sources of strategic issues. As an example, they include public support among the nonstatutory variables. For a transit planner who knows that the public is strongly opposed to a light rail concept, a strategic issue might be: How do we sell the most cost-effective way to move people to a public that won't "buy" the solution?

In evaluating policy outcomes, strategic issues may also be generated in deciding on evaluative criteria. The choice of evaluators may become strategic. Similarly, for those employed to do policy evaluation, deciding who is the real audience of a report is likely to be a strategic issue, as is the format used in presenting the findings (see, for example, Patton 1978; Weiss 1977).

To this point in the discussion, potential sources of strategic issues have been identified without regard to a particular context. Planners, however, are captives of context. In the section that follows, the role of context is introduced into our model of strategic issue identification processes.

Step Two: Identifying Issue Contexts

Table 5–1, step 2, lists three sets of context factors that should help public sector planners make decisions about the strategic nature of a particular issue. The first set relates to *characteristics of an issue*. Cobb and Elder (1972) provide three guideposts that a planner can use in the process of identifying strategic issues. First, the more concrete the issue, the more likely it is to be strategic. The threat or opportunity it creates for an agency is more clearly defined for the planner. Second, an issue's social significance is an important factor. Dealing with AIDS clearly is strategic in San Francisco, but that probably is not so to the same degree in Butte, Montana. Finally, the planner may ask, how fundamentally enduring is an issue? In New York City, criminal justice planners since at least 1970 have been debating a total merger of the New York City Police Department and the Transit Police. One suspects that the issue of merger is strategic for Transit Police planners.

A second context is provided by *agenda* processes. Cobb and Elder (1972) identify two types of agendas: systemic and institutional.[4]

The systemic agenda "consists of all issues that are commonly perceived by members of the political community as meriting public attention and as involving matters within the legitimate jurisdiction of existing governmental authority" (1972, p. 85). The institutional agenda is "that set of items explicitly up for active and serious consideration of authoritative decision makers" (1972, p. 85). That an issue makes its way to either type of agenda can be viewed as evidence that it is potentially strategic. Between the two types of agenda, strategic issues are more likely to be found on the institutional agenda. This does not mean, however, that all issues on the institutional agenda automatically are strategic. Still, when an issue related to changing the whole of an organization's goals or major resource reallocations has reached the point where formal action is required, it seems reasonable to assume that it is strategic.

A final set of issue context factors can be derived from the *cycle of issue attention* (Downs 1972). The cycle involves five phases. An issue that remains in phase one—the preproblem state—is not likely to be strategic. A mesh between initiators and triggering devices (Cobb and Elder 1972), however, may push the issue to a second phase, that of "alarmed discovery and euphoric enthusiasm." If the initiators gain access to an institutional gatekeeper—an important legislator, for instance—then the stage in which benefits and costs are traded off, phase three, or the period of "a realization of the cost of significant progress," may produce action. If not, phase four, the period of "gradual decline in public interest," follows, and the issue is likely to lose its strategic importance. People give up hope that the problem will be solved, or they become bored, or

their attention shifts to other issues. This fifth phase of the process, the post-problem stage, is associated with almost universal lack of interest in the issue, although occasionally interest will flare up among the truly dedicated.

Issues will assume greater or lesser strategic importance at each of the five phases. For example, in the first stage (the preproblem phase) deciding on a course of action for the management of public attention and the gaining of "good currency" for the issue (e.g., Bryson, Van de Ven, and Roering 1985; Schon 1971) will involve strategic planning. In the second phase of Downs's cycle, strategic planning will require framing the issue in a policy perspective that is actionable. Thus, the strategic issue is not "What works?" but "What works for the three-person coalition that controls the council?"

Step Three: Information Sorting

The models of the policy process discussed here suggest practical ways planners can begin to identify strategic issues. Other models can serve the same purpose. However, use of such models alone will not enable a planner to identify a strategic issue, because they will supply too much information. To counter this problem, the information should be further sorted. The models of the policy process just discussed also provide *three distinct sets of focuses* within which potentially strategic issues can be grouped: actor, agency, and problem. *Actors* include those individuals, interest groups, and other organizations with an interest in an issue. *Agency* is defined exclusively in terms of the governmental organization that is attempting to identify strategic issues. *Problem* focuses include those human or natural events that may be the sources of strategic issues.

Tools of strategic planning initially conceived in private sector contexts are presented in the fourth step of the model, and are used to provide *analytical filters* that enable a planner to identify strategic issues within these three sets of focuses. Some of these tools are addressed in the discussion of step four that follows.

Step Four: Employing Analytical Tools[5]

Bryson, Freeman, and Roering (1985) synthesize the literature and identify five schools of thought or models of strategic planning, including: (1) the Harvard policy model, (2) portfolio models, (3) industrial economics models, (4) stakeholder models, and (5) decision process models. They note, however, that *"most do not tell the user how to identify strategic issues"* (1985, p. 24, emphasis added).

In the section that follows, some of these models are explored in greater detail. The tools illustrated were chosen because they directly relate to the three information-sorting screens briefly outlined in step three.

Stakeholder Analysis. This tool can be used in identifying strategic issues related to actors. There are a number of approaches to this kind of analysis, for example, King and Cleland 1978; Freeman 1984. The Freeman model, which mandates consideration of a broad array of individuals, groups, or organizations in the planning process, is used in the following example. Stakeholders are individuals, groups, or organizations whose actions can have an impact on a focal organization, or who are affected by the actions of that organization. Freeman thus captures in his analytical framework those with illegitimate as well as legitimate stakes in the organization. In addition, his model requires the analyst to consider the values of the stakeholders and the effects those

values might have on their actions or on the focal organization.

The model is readily identifiable with a pluralistic approach to politics or the policy process (see, for example, Dahl 1984). A criminal justice planner will find stakeholder analysis particularly useful in determining who might be adversely affected by a plan to increase unsupervised release for minor offenders, and, most importantly, the intensity of their response to the plan and the reasons underlying that response. This last piece of information is derived from the required analysis of the values of the various stakeholder groups affected by the plan. If a significant number of major stakeholders are adversely affected by the plan, then one strategic issue may be how to change their views. Another one might be whether to go ahead with the plan at all.

SWOT/7-S Models/Organizational Analysis. When the focus is on the agency, many models can be used in analyzing its strengths and weaknesses. Two are briefly described here: the SWOT model and the so-called 7-S model. The SWOT model is a component of the Harvard policy model and the 7-S model is the brainchild of Waterman et al. (1979). The SWOT model contrasts an organization's strengths and weaknesses with the threats and opportunities arising out of its external environment. While the model is not explicit in defining areas of inquiry related to organizational strengths and weaknesses, the tradition has been to focus on functional aspects of the organization (that is, production, sales).

The 7-S model has a much more explicit focus. Each of seven interrelated categories is viewed as a source of strengths and weaknesses for an organization. The categories include: strategy, structure, staff, skills, systems, style, and superordinate goals (or shared values). Strategy and structure are self-explanatory. Staff refers to all the people employed by the organization, while skills defines the organization's distinctive competences. Style refers to the overriding management style (for example, open-door style), while superordinate goals or shared values are synonyms for organizational culture.

Successfully employed—an accomplishment that demands significant organizational soul-searching—these tools can identify a variety of strategic issues for public sector planners. Initially, they will force decision makers to ask questions such as: "What is our strategy?" and "What are our overarching goals?" Beyond that, the strategic nature of issues raised by these forms of organizational analysis will depend on the context within which an issue is embedded. A personnel planner, for example, will find the 7-S model extremely helpful in identifying strategic issues associated with a merit pay proposal. Its use will force the planner to consider the proposal's impact not only on staff, but also on the other six S's and across agencies. Such an analysis is likely to reveal instances in which merit pay may be inconsistent with other objectives of an organization.

Portfolio Analysis. In the private sector, portfolio analysis is typically used as a planning tool in determining if the various businesses of a diversified firm continue to fit the firm's strategy. Portfolio analysis also is used as an analytical tool in making capital investment decisions in the diversified firm.

A number of approaches are available to the planner, including those developed by the Boston Consulting Group (BCG) and General Electric (see, for example, Bryson et al. 1985 for a more detailed description). The BCG technique is used here for illustrative purposes. The model is set forth in Figure 5-1 and modified for our purposes in Figure 5-2.

The BCG model requires the analyst to look at the growth of an industry and his firm's growth relative (to the industry leader's) market share in that industry. If the firm is the market share leader then it will be placed in the left-hand side of the horizontal axis. If the industry is experiencing high growth (an arbitrary figure is used, usually 10 percent) then the firm is placed in the upper quadrants of the vertical axis. In managing the portfolio, the objectives are to use the excess revenues generated by the cash cows to fund growth by the stars and some of the question marks. The usual prescription for dogs is to harvest or divest.

Using the modified model,[6] a public sector planner would look at the relative tractability of the various problems confronting his or her agency and the relative degree of public support for each of the problems. Those problems falling in the lower left quadrant will generate different strategic issues for the agency than those in the upper right. In the latter case, one objective might be to generate public interest in the issue as a means to demonstrate the agency's effectiveness, since the problem is more easily solved. Support for the agency caused by it being able to cope effectively with issues in the upper left quadrant could be used to gain time while solutions are sought for problems associated with the lower left quadrant. Problems in the lower right quadrant would be "managed" so as not to inadvertently stir up public awareness.

CONCLUSIONS

The model discussed here only scratches the surface of the relevant research. Table 5-1

Figure 5–1. The BCG Portfolio Model

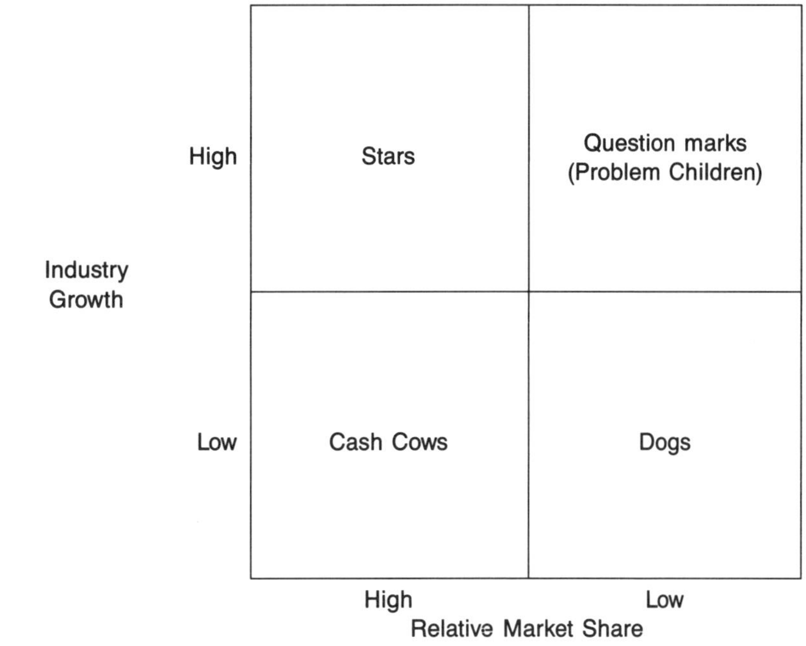

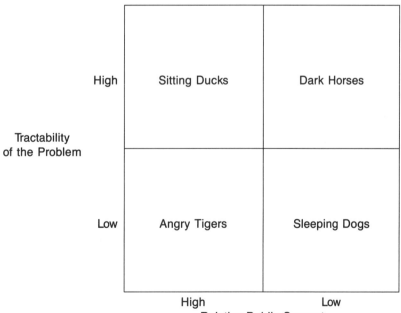

	High	Stars	Question marks (Problem Children)
Industry Growth			
	Low	Cash Cows	Dogs
		High	Low

Relative Market Share

Figure 5–2. The Issue/Problem Portfolio (Modified BCG Model)

	High	Sitting Ducks	Dark Horses
Tractability of the Problem			
	Low	Angry Tigers	Sleeping Dogs
		High	Low

Relative Public Support

illustrates a model designed to help planners in public sector organizations identify strategic issues. Step one suggests that potential sources of strategic issues first be identified. Illustrations of some of these sources are outlined in Table 5–2.

The planner is urged in step two to consider the context within which a strategic issue arises and in step three to sort the information derived in the actor, agency, and problem categories. Step four suggests the planner then apply analytical models as an aid to the identification of strategic issues related to actors, agencies, or problems.

What conclusions can a strategic planner in the public sector draw from the preceding discussion? First, the sources of strategic issues are so great that comprehensive efforts to identify the full range are likely to be futile. A more productive strategy might be to review carefully the sources of the strategic issues with which the organization has had to deal over the past three to five years. It is probable that some patterns will emerge from this analysis, and that one or two sources will emerge as having produced a significant number of the strategic issues the agency has confronted. The utility of Figure 5–2 is that it provides the planner with a classification scheme that can be used in sorting through the strategic issues being analyzed. In this way, their contexts ought to become more apparent to the planner.

Assuming that a limited number of sources have provided the majority of the strategic issues with which planners have had to deal, a second course of action is for the planner to evaluate the processes by which the organization scans the environments associated with those sources. Is the scanning done on a regular basis? Is it done by someone within the or-

ganization or by outsiders? Available research (for example, Norman 1971) suggests that if the scanning is done by insiders it will be accorded greater credibility while outsiders are thought to provide more objective assessments.

As suggested in the chapter, this limited scanning of the sources of strategic issues is likely to produce too much information for an individual planner to process. Steps 2 and 3, as outlined in Table 5–1, can provide the planner with additional information screens. However, the planner should resist this kind of information screening during the environmental scanning process. Unless the planner has taught the scanner the strategic implications that are embedded in the information being sorted and screened in steps 2 and 3, the analysis undertaken by the planner in step 4 probably will be incomplete.

Planners also may want to consider the extent to which their own operating assumptions define context for them. In large measure, steps 3 and 4 are intended to challenge these (usually) unstated assumptions.

In the course of employing analytical models such as the stakeholder, SWOT, 7-S and portfolio analysis models illustrated in step 4, a strategic planner must keep two thoughts in mind. First, the models can only provide data for the decision-making process; they do not make decisions. Second, the planner must control for the fact that these models originally were designed for use in private sector contexts. To the extent that they are based on assumptions that are not valid in public sector contexts, the planner may have to modify their application. For example, the 7-S model assumes that in an organization there will be one dominant management style. In a public sector organization, however, the styles of political managers may be very different from those of career managers.

Planners may also want to consider the frequency with which a single strategic issue is defined solely in terms of an actor, agency, or problem. One suspects that this occurrence is rare. As a consequence, the processes of identifying strategic issues, of necessity, will be more complex than the model outlined in Table 5-1 implies. The value of the model is not in simplifying reality, but in making explicit the elements of its complexity.

A final conclusion drawn from the analysis is that a basic problem in previous efforts to specify models of processes for identifying strategic issues has been a failure to offer public sector planners a useful analytical framework. A solid body of existing research clearly provides public sector planners with substantial guidance on the questions raised at the outset. Combining analytical tools developed in private sector contexts (such as portfolio analysis) with appropriate public sector models (such as policy types) may be extremely helpful in identifying the source and nature of issues of strategic importance to public sector organizations. However, we need to know more about the approaches that public sector planners are using to identify strategic issues and the perceived value of those approaches. There very well may be a number in use that are better suited to the task than the one proposed here.

In the final analysis, questions such as those raised in this chapter and elsewhere in the book must be pursued in a way that will produce useful prescriptions for strategic planners. We do not need a set of research findings ten years from now similar in content to those for the private sector of Fahey and King (1977) or Utterback (1979): that public sector planners

recognize the importance of understanding where strategic issues come from and what they are, but despair of finding techniques helpful to them in accomplishing those tasks.

NOTES

1. Wright (1974) attributes the term to Joseph McLean during the 1940s.

2. Perry and Kraemer (1983) and Rainey, Backoff, and Levine (1976) provide the interested reader with comprehensive analyses of these issues.

3. The reader should understand that throughout this analysis deciding to do nothing is considered a decision. The decision to do nothing may very well involve strategic issues. I am thankful to a reviewer for highlighting this point.

4. Reviewers of earlier drafts have suggested that Cobb and Elder's model may not apply as directly to smaller local governments. This may be the case for the model as they described its use. However, I believe that the elements of the model can be used by planners at all levels of government in assessing the strategic nature of issues destined for whatever agenda processes govern action in a community.

5. Space limitations do not permit adequate development of the value to the public sector of the full range of private sector models of strategic planning. However, planners are urged to consider "dialectic" and "devil's advocate" models (for example, Mitroff and Emshoff 1979; Crosier in press). Williamson's (1985) transactions cost analysis also offers a useful economic approach to the identification of strategic issues. The literature on strategic issue management (e.g., Ansoff 1980; King 1982; Chase 1984) provides a further vehicle for the identification of strategic issues.

6. For a fuller explication of the modified model, the reader is directed to Ring (1986).

REFERENCES

Ansoff, Igor H. 1980. Strategic issue management. *Strategic Management Journal* 3, 131–148.

Bardach, Eugene. 1977. *The implementation game.* Cambridge, Mass.: MIT Press.

Bryson, John, R. Edward Freeman, and William Roering. 1985. Strategic planning in the public sector: Approaches and future directions. Discussion Paper #37.

Minneapolis, Minn.: Strategic Management Research Center.

Bryson, John, Andrew Van de Ven, and William Roering. 1985. Strategic planning and the revitalization of the public service. Discussion paper #39. Minneapolis, Minn.: Strategic Management Research Center.

Chandler, Alfred D., Jr. 1962. *Strategy and structure: Chapters in the history of the American industrial enterprise.* Cambridge, Mass.: MIT Press.

Chase, W. Howard. 1984. *Issue management: Origins of the future.* Stamford, Conn.: IAP.

Checkoway, Barry, ed. 1985. *Strategic perspectives on planning practice.* Lexington, Mass.: Lexington Books.

Cobb, Roger W. and Charles D. Elder. 1972. *Participants in American politics: The dynamics of agenda building.* Boston, Mass.: Allyn and Bacon.

Crosier, Richard. In press. Methods for improving the strategic decision: Dialectic versus the devil's advocate. *Strategic Management Journal.*

Dahl, Robert. 1984. *Modern political analysis.* (Fourth edition.) Englewood Cliffs, N.J.: Prentice-Hall.

Downs, Anthony. 1972. Up and down with ecology—the "issue attention cycle." *The Public Interest* Summer, 38–50.

Evered, R. 1983. So what is strategy? *Long Range Planning* 16, 57–72.

Fahey, Liam and William R. King. 1977. Environmental scanning for corporate planning. *Business Horizons* 20, 61–71.

Freeman, R. Edward. 1984. *Strategic management: A stakeholder approach.* Boston, Mass.: Pittman Press.

Fritschler, A. Lee and Bernard H. Ross. 1980. *Business regulation and government decision-making.* Boston, Mass.: Little, Brown.

Grodzins, Morton. 1966. *The American system.* Chicago, Ill.: Rand-McNally.

King, William R. 1982. Using strategic issue analysis. *Long Range Planning* 15, 45–49.

———— and D. I. Cleland. 1978. *Strategic planning and policy.* New York, N.Y.: Van Nostrand Reinhold.

Lowi, Theodore J. 1964. American business, public policy, case-studies, and political theory. *World Politics* 677–715.

Mazmanian, Daniel A. and Paul A. Sabatier. 1983. *Implementation and public policy.* Glenview, Ill.: Scott, Foresman and Company.

Mintzberg, Henry. 1978. Patterns in strategy formulation. *Management Science* 24, 960–971.

Mitroff, Ian and James R. Emshoff. 1979. On strategic assumption-making: A dialectical approach to policy and planning. *Academy of Management Review* 4(1), 1–12.

Norman, R. 1971. Organizational innovativeness: Product variation and re-orientation. *Administrative Science Quarterly* 16, 203–215.

Nutt, P. C. and R. W. Backoff. 1987. A strategic management process for public and third-sector organizations. *Journal of the American Planning Association* 53(1): 44–57.

Patton, Michael. 1978. *Utilization-focused evaluation.* Beverly Hills, Calif.: Sage.

Perry, James L. and Kenneth Kraemer, eds. 1983. *Public and private perspectives.* Palo Alto, Calif.: Mayfield.

Peters, Thomas J. and Robert H. Waterman. 1982. *In search of excellence: Lessons from America's best-run companies.* New York, N.Y.: Harper & Row.

Porter, Michael E. 1981. The contributions of industrial organization to strategic management. *Academy of Management Review* 6(4), 609–620.

Porter, Michael E. 1980. *Competitive strategies.* New York, N.Y.: The Free Press.

Pressman, Jeffery and Aaron Wildavsky. 1973. *Implementation.* Berkeley, Calif.: University of California Press.

Rainey, Hal, Robert Backoff, and Charles Levine. 1975. Comparing public and private organizations. *Public Administration Review* 36, 233–244.

Ring, P. S. 1986. What is the strategic in public sector's strategic management? Papers presented at the Association for Public Policy Analysis and Management, 8th Annual Research Conference, October 30, Austin, Texas.

Ring, Peter S. and James L. Perry. 1985. Strategic management in public and private organizations: Implications of distinctive contexts and constraints. *Academy of Management Review* 10(2), 276–286.

Schendel, Dan E. and Charles W. Hofer, eds. 1979. *Strategic management: A new view of business policy and planning.* Boston, Mass.: Little, Brown.

Schon, Donald. 1971. *Beyond the stable state.* New York, N.Y.: Norton.

Thomas, Philip S. 1974. Environmental analysis for corporate planning. *Business Horizons* 17(5), 27–38.

Utterback, James M. 1979. Environmental analysis and forecasting. In *Strategic Management: A New View of Business Policy and Planning,* edited by Dan. E. Schendel and Charles W. Hofer. Boston, Mass.: Little, Brown.

Van Meter, Donald S. and Carl E. Van Horn. 1975. The policy implementation process: A conceptual framework. *Administration and Society* 6(4), 445–481.

Waterman, Robert H., Thomas J. Peters, and Julien R. Phillips. 1980. Structure is not organization. *Business Horizons* 23(4): 14–29.

Weiss, Carol H. 1977. *Using social science research in public policy making.* Lexington, Mass.: Lexington Books.

Williamson, Oliver E. 1985. *The economic institutions of capitalism.* New York, N.Y.: Free Press.

Wolin, Sheldon S. 1960. *Politics and visions.* Boston, Mass.: Little Brown.

Wright, Deil S. 1978. *Understanding intergovernmental relations.* North Scituate, Mass.: Duxbury Press.

———. 1974. Intergovernmental relations: An analytical overview. *The Annals of the American Academy of Political Science* 416, 1–19.

6

Sagas, Ventures, Quests, and Parlays: A Typology of Strategies in the Public Sector

MICHAEL S. RUBIN

The application of strategic planning techniques in public organizations over the past decade has raised a wide variety of questions about the nature of strategy and strategic planning (Bryson et al. 1985a; MacMillan 1983; Christensen 1985; Cartwright 1973). Techniques developed in the corporate sector that do not "fit" the public sector and the multiple objectives and environmental complexities of public organizations have spurred expansion of both the conceptual foundations and specific techniques of strategy formulation and implementation (Wechsler and Backoff 1986; Nutt 1982).

The proliferation of alternative constructs and processual structures has, in turn, created the need for ordering principles which align types of strategy with particular external and internal parameters. These typologies unfortunately have been nearly as various as the strategies they describe, ranging widely in terms of the parameters and patterns chosen to provide an order or classification of strategies (for example, Mintzberg and Waters 1985; Glueck and Willis 1979).

Originally, the goal of this chapter was to develop a "metatypology" that would provide a more cohesive framework through which to interrelate a wide variety of these constructs and procedures. However, in the course of our investigation we became dubious about the prospects for such a scheme. The reasons for doubt centered on three issues.

First, despite the attention directed to definitions of strategy, and its distinction from policy (read: normative planning) or tactics (read: operational planning), there is still considerable confusion over whether or not "strategy" represents a technology, a process, or a way of organizing (Quinn 1980). Thus, it was often like comparing apples (i.e., techniques) to oranges (i.e., orientations).

Second, our review of the literature raised concern about the contradiction of an expressed regard for the differences between the public and private sectors and a lack of appreciation for how the meaning of strategy changes from one context to the next. It appears that the transformation of strategic concepts from the private to the public sector often has been treated as if it were equivalent to a technological transfer from one culture to another. By such a view, strategy is reduced to a set of alternative techniques, requiring only sensitive adjustments as it is shifted from one environment to the next. Put another way, it appears that a syntax of strategy has been developed without an equivalent concern for a semantics of strategic action. A result is that strategic concepts and methods often are inappropriately transposed from one context to another (Guth 1971; Hall 1973; Mintzberg 1979).

Third, there was little discussion on the range of presenting situations that tend to initiate strategic planning efforts in the public sector. It seemed that too often small sets of case studies had been used to delineate different types of strategies or strategic orientations. A contextually grounded typology would require the identification of a full range of these situations in order to assess the match between structural circumstances and strategic approaches. (Wechsler and Backoff [1986] have begun this important task in their longitudinal studies of strategic planning in Ohio State governmental agencies.)

Given these three issues, it was difficult to locate a starting place from which a metatypology might be developed. Starting with a catalog of current techniques and processes would run aground in integrating different logical types (that is, orientations versus techniques). Beginning with the contextual distinctions between the private and public sectors might be informative, but would ultimately founder due to the fact that the majority of current techniques have in fact been borrowed from the corporate world.

To avoid a spurious integration of diverse ideas, we turned our attention to a reconsider-ation of the most elemental aspects of strategic behavior. What was needed was an "archetypal typology" of strategic action—a framework that was elemental enough to apply to any context. Through such a framework insights might be gained into the ways in which particular strategic approaches applied to distinct contexts and situations.

A CONTEXTUAL REAPPRECIATION: STRATEGY AS METAPHOR

A review of the management literature suggests that strategic planning comprises a set of techniques and processes that were developed in the private sector—designed to advance the competitive position of an organization through the targeting of ends and the judicious selections of means—and recently have been adapted to address problems in the public realm (Quinn 1980; Lorange 1983; Ansoff 1972). Acceptance of such a view promotes the image of strategy as a set of generic techniques with readily identifiable elements in which alternative strategic approaches simply represent an array of variations. It appears that until quite recently this was the dominant account of the emergence of strategic planning—that of an evolving set of management tools that came into use in the 1950s and gradually became routinized into a sequence of organized steps and phases, presumably at companies such as General Electric and Shell Oil (Ansoff 1965; Boston Consulting Group 1968; Cannon 1968).

Quinn (1980) has noted that strategy has a far more ancient history than this literature suggests. He further argues that business strategies could be improved through an appreciation of the axioms of classical military strategy (Sun Tzu, Napoleon, Van Clausewitz,

Foch, Hart, Montgomery).[1] While a general understanding of strategy might benefit from an appreciation of earlier military concepts, we also would argue that with each shift in context the *meaning* and therefore the *structure* of strategy changes. As Schon (1980) and Mitroff (1976) have noted, the process of "metaphoric construal" obstructs a contextual appreciation of strategy. A brief discussion is in order in this regard.

The term strategy is derived directly from the Greek *strategos,* which meant a general set of maneuvers or a scheme exercised to take advantage of an enemy in combat, and literally is translated as "generalship." The term later was adopted in the political realm, and at the time of Machiavelli was extended to mean the planned exercise of power and influence to achieve the political ends of the state (Machiavelli 1950).

While having specific meanings in war, military terms such as combat, enemy, generalship, attack, and battle became metaphors in the political arena. Thus, an enemy slaughtered in battle might very well have been dismembered, but an enemy crushed in a political battle was more likely to have received considerably less support for his position than an opponent. This is not to say that strategic efforts in one quarter were any less significant than in the other, but rather that the modalities and intermediate objectives in each environment were quite distinct. The objective in military strategy has been to win or secure territory, while the end of political strategy has been to influence or garner support for a position, policy, or platform. The modalities of the modern military include battles, campaigns, front lines, charges, and pincer movements. The modalities in the political environ-

ment may include constituencies, elections, votes, debates, and lobbying. This is useful to keep in mind when considering the more recent emergence of strategic planning in the corporate sector.

Thus, while a number of the tools of military strategy developed during World War II subsequently were employed in the private sector (i.e., operations research) the objectives and environmental context of the corporation must be understood as distinct—market share is only metaphorically equivalent to territory. More to the point, the goal of the military is to secure the sovereignty of the state through a territorial monopoly, while antitrust regulations prohibit corporations in the United States from monopolizing their markets.

The use of the word strategy to describe the various maneuvers designed to achieve specific objectives within the private sector must therefore also be appreciated in metaphoric terms. Certainly the success of applied operations research, research and development techniques, and complex decision support systems in World War II led to the desire to transfer these technologies to the private sector—to make business at once more efficient and capable of achieving its goals (Drucker 1954). However, the application of these discrete management techniques was somewhat problematic. The corporate environment was more complex in many respects than the military; goals were multiple rather than singular, and the battle was continuous, without termination (Gore 1964; Henderson 1979). Strategy thus became associated with the advancement of a variety of ends, while at the same time an extended range of environmental parameters was incorporated into its formulation. Strategy in the corporate sector became focused on the relation between particular temporal horizons (i.e., goals, contingencies, opportunities) and the contextual forces that constrained or facilitated their realization (i.e., economic, political, technological). In the corporate world, strategy became associated with the image of a *competitive environment*, in which organizations sought to "capture" market share or a comparative advantage over other firms in the same industrial subsector or region (Porter 1979). Strategy was only metaphorically related to those strategies enacted on the battlefield where the context was one of armed conflict. Nevertheless, the terms used by corporate strategists clearly connoted the military campaign by suggesting the defeat of an enemy through the "capturing of a territory," "advancing one's mission," or "securing a positional advantage" (Porter 1980). The problem with this transposition of terms is that it led to an underestimation of the environmental and organizational complexities inherent within the private sector, and supported the spurious notion that strategic planning was a technological procedure, derivative of actions on the battlefield and as objectively clear in its ends as a game of chess. However, as Mintzberg (1984) has shown to the contrary, the richness of the contextual environment, the range of organizational cultures, and the diversity of situational parameters in the private sector has in fact led to a wide array of strategies and an equally diverse range of strategists.

Caution therefore is in order when considering the more recent transposition of strategic thinking from the private sector to the public realm. That is to say, ends in public sector organizations are difficult and often more complex than those in corporate organizations, and the relevant environmental parameters are generally more numerous (Bryson, Van de Ven, Roering 1985b; Wechsler and Backoff 1986). Therefore, the application of the term must once again be recognized as at least partly metaphoric. That is to say, governmental organizations usually do not actually compete in a market place—even when attempting to attract a firm to a particular locale—and it is hoped that they are as concerned with issues of equity as with questions of enhanced efficiency. Yet strategic planning in the public sector has largely been discussed in terms that apply to a competitive market, such as position, advantage, targets, and share.

To get at this problem of metamorphic construal requires going beyond a reappreciation of the contextual shifts in the meaning of strategy. It is also essential to expand what is meant by strategy, and how the concept is applied both in describing and prescribing action. In so doing, there may be more awareness of the metaphors that obstruct a contextual understanding of the concept, by recognizing the diversity of settings in which actors attempt to direct their efforts to realize preferred outcomes (Schon 1980).

The first problem that must be confronted here concerns the general depiction in management literature of strategic planning as a sequence of steps and stages, or a cyclical pattern of reiterative steps, that moves from the selection of goals through assessments of the external environment and internal capacities of the organization to the evaluation of alternative means and implementation options. This procedural rigor, whatever its merits as an instrumental template, downplays the context within which strategies are created, the situational dynamics which constrain or support these processes, the roles played by leadership and various dramatis personae, institutional and regulatory forces, organizational structures and cultures, and the particular incidents or events leading up to the initiation of a strategic planning effort (Bolan 1980). Strategies clearly do not arise in a vacuum, but are instead motivated by specific incidents and intentions. As Mintzberg and Waters (1985) have noted, strategies are shaped by the particular generative situations that led to their initiation.

Recognizing that the meaning of strategy can vary from one context to the next places a new burden on understanding the concept. More specifically the concern in this chapter will be in developing a typology that respects both the unique contextual circumstances of the public sector and the more fundamental orientations that would underlie strategy formulation in any context.

STRATEGY: FOUR ARCHETYPES

Schon (1981) has noted that while metaphors can be used effectively to make a discordant set of circumstances appear more sensible, there also is a tendency to underestimate the richness of the contextual surround when these apperceptive devices are applied. Given the human propensity for metaphoric reasoning in circumstances of complexity, he recommends discursive awareness of metaphors by recognizing the "generic" or "archetypal" constructs that undergird them. Following this advice, we searched for distinctive patterns in the organization of strategic action that could be used as the basis for identifying a set of archetypes.

First, in its most elemental form, a strategy is a pattern of action through which actors propose to achieve desired goals, modify current circumstances, and/or realize latent opportunities (Miller, Galanter, Pribram 1960; Oxford Abridged 1984). A strategy is similar in this regard to a plot, in transforming a discordant, unordered set of events into a patterned sequence (Ricoeur 1984). Most significantly, a strategy serves to create a temporal relation between the past, present, and future. A well-developed strategy redirects the material and human resources of an organization in conjunction with a new temporal order, in which changes in the contextual environment, internally directed objectives, and action sequences are developed into a cohesive whole.

With this elemental definition, we turned our attention to the range of temporal orientations through which a course of strategic action might be developed. The question of temporal orientation has, of course, been at the root of some of the fundamental debates about the nature of planning and human action (Ozbekhan 1971; Habermas 1979; Krieger 1984). Formal strategic planning, for example, has been premised on an orientation in which a distant mission and long-term objectives direct strategic action. In this model a *future horizon* is central for organizing a sequence of action steps and setting intermediate goals. Arguing against this orientation, logical incrementalists such as Quinn (1980) have promoted the advantages of a process in which the *present* figures more heavily in directing strategic action. Adding to this debate, two public policy scholars recently have suggested that strategists have made insufficient use of history, and proposed that the use of the *past* has clear advantages over the application of current circumstances or projected events in orienting strategic decisions (Neustadt and May 1986).

Ackoff's (1981) typology of planning approaches was useful in distinguishing these orientations. Ackoff maintains that there are four dominant attitudes to planning that are shaped by an actor's or organization's perception of its past, present, and future. In Ackoff's scheme, four strategists are used to describe these orientations: the reactivist, the preactivist, the inactivist, and the interactivist. Ackoff's reactive strategist is one who looks unfavorably both on contemporary conditions and the anticipated future. The reactive strategist prefers a previous (imagined?) state, the recreation of which becomes the basis for directing action. The characteristics or qualities that are presumed to have led to the earlier state become the subject of considerable concern, as do the current constraints that are perceived to be obstructing the reconstitution of such a state.

The inactive strategist, by contrast, places a high value on the present. The complexities of the future are seen as largely outside the control of human agency, and the past is seen in particularist terms—far removed from the present contextual surround and therefore hardly applicable to contemporary affairs. The inactivist focuses on piecemeal shifts and incremental tactics, with the intention of making "moves" as situations present themselves.

A preactive strategist is defined as one who emphasizes the relative value of the future over the present and past. As Ackoff notes, preactivism represents the dominant attitude toward strategic planning in the corporate sector. It is premised on taking advantage of opportunities and mitigating against emergent problems by accurately assessing trends and predicting future conditions through forecasts and related analytic techniques. Preactivism is based on a predict-and-prepare mentality, in which it is supposed that a strategic advantage will be gained by those organizations that accurately perceive key trends and thereby ready themselves to capture emergent opportunities before their competitors.

Ackoff reserves the term interactivism (or more commonly proactivism) to describe a temporal orientation in which the future is seen as potentially subject to control or redirection through the articulation of a desired end. Through the design of a desirable future, the interactivist can test and initiate a range of moves to both advance and further assess this potential end. These temporal attitudes are summarized in Table 6–1, in accord with Ackoff (1981, p. 53).

Table 6–1. Temporal Orientations in Planning (after Ackoff 1981)

Orientation	Past	Present	Future
Reactive	(+)	(−)	(−)
Inactive	(−)	(+)	(−)
Preactive	(−)	(−)	(+)
Interactive	(+/−)	(+/−)	(+/−)

(+) = Favorable attitude
(−) = Unfavorable attitude

Ackoff has argued persuasively for the relative merits of the interactive orientation, but has also submitted that the other three temporal orientations may have their place in given situations (Ackoff 1985, p. 53). Here, on the other hand, the decision was to start with the assumption that all four temporal orientations were equally valid for organizing strategies, depending on the particular types of generative situations and the particular contexts within which they were formulated.

It also was necessary to fully appreciate that any form of strategic action was likely to be *perceived as dramatic*—if not by consultants and academics, then certainly by the actors engaged in those efforts. That is to say, these events are characterized by risk and opportunity, and often involve such archetypal elements as heroes, adversaries, challenges, encounters, victories, losses, and so forth. What was needed was a language that would adequately convey the dramatic quality of the four orientations and would displace any preferences for one stratagem over another.

THE SAGA

The term *saga* was chosen to describe here the temporal orientation in which an organization's past becomes the focus for strategic action. Literally speaking, a saga is an often recounted tale of heroic exploits that serves to bind a group's identity through a shared past. Here, saga describes those situations in which actors sense that a set of core values has been lost or is in imminent danger of being lost due to changes in the external environment, growing institutional inadequacies, emerging value shifts, or the appearance of deep conflicts within the organization. The saga is thus a strategy configured to regain or protect a position or set of values perceived to be threatened by major external or internal change. It is not intended that the saga is simply a reactionary or reconstructivist stance in which actors attempt to recreate a lost past. To the contrary, this stratagem allows actors consciously to consider how to reestablish a set of core values in recognition of a new or emergent set of conditions. Thus the vision which drives the saga is not a restoration of the past, but rather a recreation or repositioning of a core mission.

The civil rights movement of the late 1950s and early 1960s serves as an example of the sagalike pattern. The strategy of the civil rights

activists (which developed over a six-year period), focused on testing individual rights of access in a variety of public settings through direct confrontations, resulting in a combination of court cases and political contests. The source and vision for the heroes of the civil rights movement were the Constitution and the Bill of Rights, the core precedents of which, they argued, had never been fully realized and were in danger of being lost.

Mintzberg and Waters (1985) described a similar type of action pattern which they termed an ideological strategy:

> When members of an organization share a vision and identify so strongly with it that they pursue it as an ideology, then they are bound to exhibit patterns of behavior, so that clear realized strategies can be identified. These may be called *Ideological Strategies.* [Mintzberg and Waters 1985, p. 262]

Mintzberg suggests that the vision that inspires such a strategy is rooted in a set of historic core values, often emanating out of the institutionalization of the vision of a charismatic leader. This vision is generally sketchy and open to interpretation, however, so the intentions that underlie it may be adapted or modified in relation to changes in the organization or its environment. According to Mintzberg, such a strategy is ultimately directly related to a specific historic mandate or doctrine that guides an organization or institution through its life. True, such an internally driven pattern may direct the strategy of an organization, but the saga can be seen in broader terms. That is to say, it seems just as likely that an external event may cause an organization to actively search for a past or discover a precedent set of values to guide it in developing goals or a vision of the future. The ideological strategy may therefore be but one example of this broader archetypal pattern in which the past is used to guide actors in articulating a desired future.

The view of this chapter is that the time horizon of the saga is an extended one, involving a long-term commitment to change. The environmental conditions that would support such a strategem would generally involve disturbing, widespread changes that finally have come to a head after a protracted period. The internal circumstances that might lead to this pattern would include a major transition in leadership structure or a deep conflict between key members or factions within the organization.

THE QUEST

The term *quest* is used here to describe the temporal orientation that characterizes the attitude of the interactive strategist. Here, actors organize their efforts around a vision or mission for the future, which derives from a desire to make fundamental change in the current operations, priorities, or values of the organization. A quest is defined as a search for something of great material or spiritual value (e.g., the Holy Grail), often involving adventure and tests of courage (Oxford Abridged 1984; Webster's Collegiate seventh ed.). The quest generally requires the presence of a strong or inspired leader who instills a sense of destiny and purpose among the members of an organization. The quest involves leaps in creativity and faith, where established perspectives about the present and future are reinterpreted and replaced by a new vision. Situations that would encourage such bold initiatives would be of two types: (1) those in which a new leader (or leadership structure) feels impelled

to alter the core mission of the organization due to a perceived mismatch between its mandate and changing environmental conditions, and (2) situations in which belief in the purposes of the organization is brought into serious question through conflicts, failures, or the anticipation of a major crisis. Indeed, situations of the latter type may represent the preconditions that lead to the call for new leadership.

In some sense, the quest bears a closer similarity to the saga than one might expect, given the interactivist and reactivist attitudes from which they were derived. In fact, the expectation would be that the saga often follows from a quest, in which the original vision of a charismatic leader (read: a quest) is reembraced by a later generation of organizational actors who reinterpret and reactivate this vision as the basis for a recommitment to certain core values (read: a saga).

Using another example from the public arena of the 1960s, President John F. Kennedy's inspiring vision of putting an American on the moon involved an obvious leap of faith at that time and entailed a fundamental reorientation of national priorities and commitments to the future. On the other hand, Lyndon Johnson's failed vision of the Great Society illustrates that the success of a quest depends on a widespread belief that the search for something truly valuable justifies the risks of shifting priorities and surrendering institutional traditions (Giddens 1984).

Mintzberg (1985) has used a schema in which he distinguishes strategies according to the degree to which they are deliberate (i.e., organizationally directed) or emergent (i.e., environmentally driven). The quest is an archetypal stratagem that would clearly undergird the most deliberate of strategies. While we do not feel completely congenial to this schema, we do agree that a successful quest involves either considerable control over the environment or a remarkable match between an organization's purposes and evolving contextual circumstances. In the public sector such circumstances are present when the environment (e.g., regulatory, legislative, etc.) is at least partially subject to imposed conditions. In the private sector, such conditions are likely to be present only when an organization has great influence over a particular market. This, of course, harkens back to the point that strategies conceived within the context of a market will vary substantively from those formulated within the context of a polity. However, the majority of situational circumstances in the public sector are those in which environmental uncertainties clearly outweigh the competence or capacity of organizations to undertake long-term strategies. The following two temporal orientations are ones that we propose drive strategic action in situations in which environmental forces outpace organizational controls.

THE VENTURE

The term *venture* is used here to describe a pattern of action that focuses on either perceived opportunities or emergent problems. The predominant temporal orientation underlying this stratagem is one in which the present and near future are seen as filled with opportunities and risks. A venture is defined as an undertaking involving calculated risk, speculation, and uncertainty (*New Century*, Vol. II). A strategic venture is pursued in situations in which environmental forces are somewhat patterned, which allows actors to assess, albeit imperfectly, evolving trends. Perceived problems or latent

opportunities can serve equally well as the motivation for such actions.

While this archetypal stratagem bears a close resemblance to the predict-and-prepare attitude that characterizes the preactive orientation, a distinction needs to be made. Actors pursuing a venture recognize the limitations of their perceptions of the future and the inherent risks involved in their efforts. In fact, it is an explicit appreciation of these risks that provides the undertone of drama in this stratagem.

Ventures appear not only to focus on the emergent, but also on the divergent. That is to say, ambiguous or complex problems affecting organizational performance may lead actors to undertake a venture in which optional courses of action are pursued. These actions are in effect short-term experiments conducted in situations in which no clear resolution is evident. Finally, the venture may also be the preferred strategic orientation in situations involving collaboration among diverse interests. In such situations, the long-term goals of various interests may be inconsistent or unclear, while interim goals may provide a point of convergence.

THE PARLAY

The fourth archetypal stratagem evolves in situations of extreme turbulence (Emery and Trist 1971) where no clear trends or historic patterns can be discerned with any degree of confidence. The term *parlay* is used here to describe this pattern of strategic action. A parlay literally means to make a move in order to leverage or advance one's position through a second move. The term derives from games of chance in which an original wager and its winnings are subsequently bet on a second race or contest. More generally, parlay has come to mean the exploitation of an opportunity or

Figure 6–1. Matrix of Archetypal Strategies

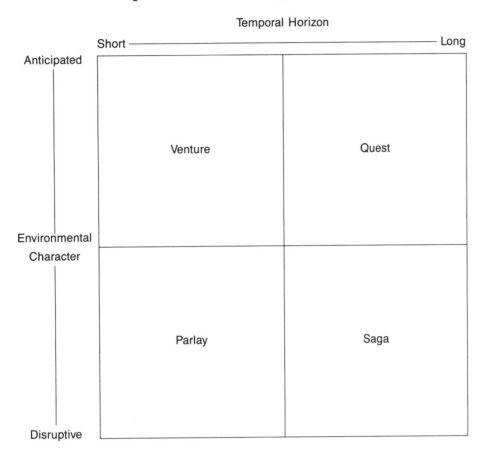

resource in order to reposition one's self for further and greater opportunities, as in: "Parlaying one's inheritance into real estate to create a fortune" (*New Century*, Vol. I; *Oxford*, abridged 1984).

The temporal orientation underlying the parlay centers on the present. Like the inactivist attitude described earlier, this stratagem is premised on the belief that changes in the contextual environment are far too complex to be subject to control or intervention, and that one can only act strategically by proceeding through piecemeal moves. Unlike the inactive orientation, however, parlaying assumes each incre-

mental move leads to a better strategic position through consistent leveraging.

The four archetypal stratagems can be organized into a simple two-by-two matrix by differentiating them according to the degree of environmental turbulence and the length of the temporal horizon that characterizes them. See Figure 6-1.

GENERIC SITUATIONS AND PUBLIC SECTOR STRATEGY FORMULATION

The four archetypal stratagems describe the basic underlying patterns of strategic action that evolve in any organizational context—

military, political, corporate, nonprofit, governmental—resulting in a typology that might best be thought of as *protocontextual*. The terms used here, which do not reveal a preference for one orientation over another but do connote the dramatic dimensions of each, are meant to reinforce the idea that the relevance of a strategy can best be assessed against particular generating situations within distinct contextual circumstances.

To explore this assertion, a list of various "generic situations" which appeared to serve as the impetus for strategic planning efforts in the public sector was developed. This list comprised recollections of the typical presenting circumstances about which public sector clients sought advice or consultation, and a range of situations that were discussed in a year-long roundtable on strategic planning held in 1984 at the University of Pennsylvania.[2] The list, which is not intended to be encyclopedic, consists of seventeen typical situations:

1. Sudden Crisis
2. Gradual or Anticipated Crisis
3. Conflict Between Interests
4. Leadership Transition
5. Operational Ambiguity
6. Goal Divergence (intra-agency)
7. Authority Gaps
8. Goal Conflicts Between Interests/Constituents
9. Media Problems
10. Organizational-based Pathologies
11. External Pressure/Influence
12. Regulatory and Legislative Demands
13. Budgetary Uncertainty
14. Contingencies beyond Administrative Tenure
15. Intergovernmental Conflicts/Ambiguities
16. New Opportunity/Initiative
17. Initiating Public–Private Partnerships, Ventures, Contracts

Each of these situations was reviewed in relation to the four archetypal stratagems in an effort to map them onto the simple two-by-two matrix. Figure 6–2 depicts the results of this mapping exercise. We do not pretend that these matches involve exclusive relationships, but would propose that it is more likely that the given situation would foster the strategic orientation with which it is matched than it would the other three orientations.

General Examples

Examples may help clarify these relationships. We often are asked to advise organizations in which key decisions, operations, or project initiatives are logjammed due to a lack of clarity about responsibilities and roles within the agency (i.e., operational ambiguity, authority gaps). In these situations it is common for organizational members to be deeply frustrated with the current condition of the organization and to have difficulty generating either agreement or alternative visions about its long-term future. The concerns of the organization in these situations tend to focus on missed opportunities and emergent problems that are seen to be the consequence of a lack of organization, inadequate capacity, poor communication, and the like. In such circumstances, actors often use a new initiative as the impetus to reorganize, implicitly recognizing that such efforts raise the risk of identifying hidden conflicts, exposing incompetent personnel, and revealing fundamental problems in the management of the agency. The strategy for organizational change here thus takes the form of a venture, in which the rewards for engaging in the effort are to be realized in the near

Figure 6–2. Presenting Situations in the Public Sector

Temporal Horizon

Short ◄─────────────────────────────► Long

Venture Pattern Operational Ambiguity Organizational Pathologies Authority Gaps Opportunity (Initiative) Public–Private Collaboration	**Quest Pattern** Leadership Transition (Transformative) Regulatory & Legislative Demands Public–Private Conflict Gradual or Anticipated Crisis Goal Divergence (Intergovernmental) Goal Divergence (Among Interests)
Parlay Sudden Crisis Media Problems Budgetary Uncertainty Contingencies External Pressure/Influence	**Saga Pattern** Conflict Between Interests Intergovernmental Conflicts Leadership Transition (Reformative)

Anticipated ↑

Environmental Character

Disruptive ↓

term—usually at the conclusion of the initiative. For other reasons the same pattern generally arises in situations in which the public and private sectors attempt to collaborate on an initiative. This may not be particularly surprising since such collaborative efforts usually involve large-scale projects or programs with risks that neither party wishes to incur alone. Less apparent is the fact that the short temporal horizon chosen for such initiatives has a great deal to do with the tenure of the public and private leaders involved. It is indeed rare to see projects of this type which extend beyond seven years—at least by intention (see Hall 1980).

In situations characterized by extreme turbulence and rapid change, such as budgetary debates, media problems, or a sudden crisis, we see strategic behaviors that resemble the parlay. For example, an agency competing for limited allocations during a period of retrenchment is unlikely to be forthcoming about its priorities and long-term goals. Instead, the agency will attempt to reprioritize services or identify points of leverage that can be used in negotiating with legislators. Similarly, a sudden crisis rarely provides the moment for establishing a new mission. Far more often, these events provide the opportunity to advance a neglected program or target an area for special attention. For example, the sudden collapse of a bridge might provide the leverage a governor needs to reallocate funds from community development to infrastructure renewal. Likewise, a flood-ravaged town might use the disaster to secure economic development assistance that had formerly eluded it. These strategies are piecemeal moves meant to seize an opportunity of the moment and use it to further advance one's position or interest.

Quests tend to evolve out of situations characterized either by deep and apparently intractable conflicts or by transitional events. The occasion of a dynamic leader taking over an organization represents the type of situation with which we have the most experience. Under such conditions, an opportunity is present to reconsider the organization's mission and to develop a new vision of the future. The second most common situation in which this strategic pattern seems to predominate follows from deep-seated conflicts between organizational members. In such cases, the resolution of differences between interests seems to depend on the articulation of distant goals that everyone can agree on. This often requires stepping outside of the immediate and near-term objectives of the conflicting parties, and using the long-term future to agree on a set of ends that works to realign these interests.

The saga is a pattern that bears a curious relationship to the quest. In both cases the vision of a long-term future serves to organize strategic actions; in the saga, however, the source of this inspiration derives from the past. Hence, the presenting situations matched to the saga closely resemble those we associated with the quest. The major difference was that using an organization's past to direct its future

seems to arise in environments that are turbulent or unstable. Thus, a leadership transition following a period of corruption and indictments is more likely to inspire a reformative vision than an image of transformation.

TOWARDS A CONTEXTUALLY GROUNDED TYPOLOGY

Having described the four archetypal patterns in relation to typical initiating situations in the public sector, exploring whether we could shift to a more "prescriptive framework" came next. That is to say, rather than recounting when one temporal orientation seemed to be preferred over another we hoped to suggest a range of substrategies that could be used to advance each of the archetypal orientations.

To develop this array, cases collected in developing the seventeen generic situations were used. Nearly 60 cases and engagements having mixed levels of information were involved. Some cases were quite reliable and detailed, others were rather fragmentary. The focus was put on those cases of which we had personal knowledge or reliable information on the organizations and the approaches pursued (a total of 27 cases). The goal was to identify distinctive strategies within each cell of the matrix.[3] A result of this effort was a list of 12 strategies, three matched to each of the four orientations. While clearly a bit too pat numerically and far in excess of a degrees of freedom test, the array was interesting enough to report, if only to indicate how the archetypal framework might be transformed into a contextually grounded typology. These strategies are reviewed briefly in the following section.

Ventures

Venture strategies were most common in the

cases we reviewed (11 of 27), suggesting that situations characterized by emergent problems and rather short temporal horizons may drive a majority of strategic planning initiatives in the public sector. We subsequently distinguished three venturelike strategies which we referred to as *targets, trials,* and *compacts.*

Targets. The target is a familiar strategic concept. Through this strategy, organizational and financial resources become concentrated on a particular initiative, which is intended to resolve an emergent problem or capture a latent opportunity. This venturelike strategy closely approximates the market-driven targeting that often directs private sector planning. However, in the public sector, targeting appears to be as much an effort to address problems of organizational capacity as it is directed to taking advantage of trends in the external environment. For example, in a quasi-public organization we recently consulted it was the lack of experience of key staff that led the agency to turn *from* diversifying its services *to* targeting projects that would take advantage of the core skills of its professional staff.

Trials. The trial is a second form of strategic venture, in which a situation viewed as intractable is addressed with a short-term experiment or temporary arrangement. This strategy may take the form of an alternative procedure, the assignation of temporary roles and responsibilities, the introduction of new incentives for a period of time, various stopgap measures, and/or temporary organizational realignments. The intentions of strategists during a trial are not directed to ultimately resolving what is recognized as a deep-seated structural problem, but rather to relieving the situation or "moving it" somewhat (Schon 1983). For example, in a large metropolitan human services agency in which client demand greatly exceeded intake and treatment capacities, temporary liaisons and referral arrangements were created with the city's health department and housing agency. It was understood from the outset that this interdepartmental venture was an experiment, and at the very least would have to be redesigned to meet state compliance regulations.

Compacts. The compact represents a third form of venture we felt could be distinguished as a strategic type. This strategy involves short-term agreements between levels of government, between operating departments, or between public and private sector organizations. The compact does not involve a specific project (target) or experiment (trial) but rather is directed toward establishing a temporary relationship between two or more bodies. In the cases reviewed, situations involving authority gaps and operational ambiguities, in which organizations had either overlapping responsibilities or ambiguous relationships, often resulted in such agreements. We were also surprised to find a number of public–private ventures that were organized around general agreements rather than specific project initiatives. For example, a major regional public-private development consortium with which we work, first agreed on the interorganizational procedures and relationships that would guide them over their first year of operation before explicitly discussing any of the projects, programs, or priorities that they would pursue. The first year of operation was treated as a venture focused on the goal of establishing a comfort level and working relationships between the key actors.

Quests

Seven of the cases we reviewed closely followed the quest pattern. We termed the three strategic variations we distinguished as *the new agenda, the grand vision,* and *the alternative course.* What these strategies had in common was that they were organized around a rather distant end which was to be advanced through a variety of intermediate and short-range objectives.

The New Agenda. In a leadership transition or in the launching of a new organization there is a critical tension that exists between establishing new priorities and mitigating against the short-term objectives of established or opposing interests. The agenda is a strategic tool ideally suited for balancing such tensions and deflecting opposition. The structure of the agenda allows the chief executive to protect key initiatives that might otherwise be opposed by packaging them with other projects that draw in opposing interests or by differentiating subinitiatives that draw in a wider range of constituents. Of course, the politics of agenda formation has been a major topic of discussion in the literature on power theory (Bacharach and Baratz 1962, 1963), but to our knowledge the concept has received little attention in the strategic planning literature. While bearing some structural resemblance to portfolio strategies, an agenda is organized around a personal sense of mission and a calculated estimate of constituent and oppositional interests. Agendas are thus designed for coalition building, rather than for gaining a comparative advantage over one's competitors. Also, unlike portfolios, agendas seem to require linkage to a long-range time frame for their legitimacy. That is, while certain initiatives are to be accomplished within the tenure of the leader, the agenda itself is meant to advance some public purpose of extended value.

For example, in a state health agency we recently consulted, the newly appointed commissioner developed an agenda of seven strategic initiatives, all of which were intended to advance the quality of health care in the state by the twenty-first century. While a number of these initiatives were somewhat controversial, each tended to attract different bases of support creating a critical mass of supporters that began to buy into the more general transformative goal of quality health. While there were many different interpretations of what quality health meant—ranging from statewide AIDS prevention programs to downsizing overbedded hospital facilities—this seven-initiative concept served as the glue that bonded a diverse set of interests around a mixed agenda.

The Grand Vision. We supposed that questlike strategies would also emerge in situations of deep conflict, since an image of the future that extended well beyond the temporal horizon of the controversy might provide the only basis of compromise or agreement between opposing interests. Such an image would, of course, need to be either embracive or diversely supported, and also probably would have to overcome more immediate obstructions to cooperation.

The term *grand vision* is used to describe questlike strategies that are organized around a provocative image of the future. The essential difficulty with this strategy in the public sector is that it depends on a vision that can cohere a wide range of diverse interests. Nevertheless, the relevance of this type of quest is evidenced by the incredible variety of alternative future projects undertaken in cities and states in the past decade (e.g., Chatanooga Venture, Seattle 2000, Cleveland Tomorrow, Philadelphia: Past, Present & Future, Los Angeles 2000+20).

It has often been claimed that Philadelphia's economic development strategy between 1950 and 1980 centered on a physical vision of a revitalized city center, an image that is credited with guiding development decisions for more than two decades. But grand visions clearly do not have to be physical. A more recent vision that centered on transforming Philadelphia from a regional center to an international city served as the impetus for initiatives among the region's health services industries, educational institutions, arts and cultural organizations, and public and private sectors.

The Alternative Course. The third questlike strategy we distinguished as an illustrative type appears to be most closely linked to situations of gradual or anticipated crisis. In such situations there is a pervasive preoccupation with the impending event, which consequently prevents strategists from considering a broad range of possible futures. Instead the quest becomes directly focused on the anticipated occurrence, and the envisioned future is conceptualized in direct opposition to it.

We use the term *the alternative course* to describe this type of quest. The most common instances of this strategy occur when major service programs appear to be failing and the underlying policy assumptions are perceived to be misguided. For example, the urban renewal policy of the 1960s served as the animus against which a new vision of neighborhood revitalization was forged.

Only one of the cases with which we are familiar seemed to follow this pattern. In this case, a consortium of human service and health agencies was organized with the goal of developing a strategy to address the needs of the homeless mentally ill and mentally retarded in a large northeastern city. The alternative course there was conceived in direct opposition to the state's long-term policy of deinstitutionalization, a position which was seen as a major contributing cause to the current problem.

Sagas

Six of the reviewed cases we considered to be sagas in orientation. This was a surprise because we expected that the majority of cases would fall into this category. This expectation was probably related in part to the fact that we recalled these cases most vividly (for reasons we are not quite sure of). However, the major reasons for this assumption was our belief that impending crises or conflicts were the events that most often initiated strategic planning efforts in the public sector (Bryson 1981).

The cases reviewed led us to suggest three sagalike strategies that we termed *restorative, reformative,* and *conservatory.* The distinctions between these strategies may appear somewhat subtle, but could affect an organization's actions significantly.

Restorative strategies. The goal of recapturing a lost quality or position through the design of new policies or the reorientation of organizational mandates is the base of restorative strategies. For example, in the early 1980s a number of North Atlantic Port organizations attempted to reposition themselves in the face of continuing declines in export trade activity through ambitious retrofitting projects (e.g., channel dredging and construction of container facilities) and through equally agressive diversification strategies (e.g., waterside real estate development, landside industrial development). The motivation underlying these ambitious undertakings was that maritime trade had been the engine of economic development for these port cities and had to be restored to a place of preeminence to curtail wider patterns of decline.

Reformative strategies. On the other hand, reformative strategies center on the modification of existing governmental policies or regulations that are seen as either archaic or corrupt, relative to perceptions of the quality of governance in an earlier era. For example, recently in Philadelphia a special committee was formed to solicit proposals for a strategy to reform the city's charter. This document, which sets the relationships and parameters of authority for all the city's operating departments and executive functions, has been viewed as outdated and unresponsive to current needs for services. Interestingly, the charter was an artifact of a major reform effort of the 1950s to reestablish "good government" in Philadelphia.

Conservatory Strategies. The objective to preserve a set of values, an institution, or other resources that appear to be threatened by contextual shifts, external forces, or internal conflicts characterizes conservatory strategies. For example, the passage of Gramm-Rudman-Hollings in 1986 led a wide variety of cities to develop alternative financing strategies in order to carry out valued capital projects and maintain key community development programs.

Parlays

While the parlay is probably the strategic behavior most commonly referred to in descriptions of public management, the fewest number of our cases followed this pattern. It may be that in these circumstances a consultant is rarely called for advice, or that public managers consider these moves as something other than

strategic. Nevertheless, we could produce only three cases that fit this pattern, all of which came from efforts public managers told us about. It is important to note that generally this pattern of action has either been critiqued as a nonstrategic form of "muddling through" or alternately commended as an incremental maneuver suited to situations of rapid change or deep ambiguity. To the contrary, we see the parlay as an important *type of strategy*, particularly suited to situations in which current events are full of uncertainty. We were not able to clearly delineate types of parlays from the cases, but felt that generally speaking one could parlay by *hedging, leveraging,* or *advancing* toward a preferred position—while mitigating against unacceptable levels of risk.

Hedging. The term hedging is used to refer to a parlay in which the strategist is primarily concerned with counterbalancing risks. For example, in situations in which multiple contingencies are anticipated, hedging could be a particularly productive strategy. Returning to the example of the port organizations, the recognition that transshipment technologies and trading patterns would continue to change unpredictably over the next decade led many of these agencies to retreat from long-term capital commitments and invest in a mix of short-term operations and facilities. Hedging also may provide a productive strategy for public agencies in periods of budgetary or resource uncertainty. By balancing a number of programs in their budget proposals rather than prioritizing key initiatives, executive or legislative decisions on program cuts may be buffered or redistributed by the agency's management.

Leveraging. The term leveraging is used to describe a parlay in which the strategist uses an event or relationship to increase his or her influence over an area of strategic concern or a longer range objective. For example, when the state of New Jersey required municipalities to provide certified emergency medical technicians by a per capita formula, many townships responded by adding these responsibilities to the duties of their fire departments. A good number of municipal fire chiefs, after agreeing to this new area of community service, used their expanded influence to negotiate for pay increases, additional personnel, new equipment, training funds, and modified work schedules. In the best of circumstances, the longer term goal of professionalizing fire and emergency services served as the object of these leveraging strategies.

Advancing. The term advancing is used for a third type of parlay where the strategist reduces risk by using an unexpected opportunity or situation to advance toward a particular goal. Unlike hedging, the strategist is concerned with a single objective rather than a range of acceptable outcomes and unlike leveraging, the situation does not facilitate the extension of the organization's control or influence over a particular area of strategic concern. For example, a state-funded center for technology development which we advise recently

Figure 6–3. Array of Public Sector Strategies

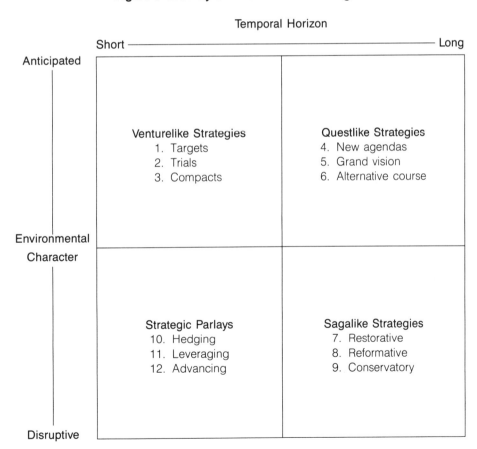

used a one-time increase in the state's annual grant to develop a monitoring system to check on the performance of its projects in the area of human resource development. The center's long-term goal to enhance the quality and performance of projects in this otherwise neglected area was thus "advanced" through the situation. The risks associated with otherwise fuzzy projects in this area were substantially reduced during this period, encouraging the state to provide continued support for the center's monitoring efforts.

Figure 6–3 depicts the 12 types of public sector strategies discussed within the four-cell matrix.

CONCLUSIONS

A new appreciation of strategy formulation is in order. Until quite recently, strategic planning has been depicted as monotypic technology—a sequence of analytic steps, which if followed with rigor and deliberation would increase the competence of an organization to achieve its goals. Experience in developing strategies outside the corporate sector has led a number of academics, administrators, and consultants to question the predominant view of strategy and to begin the search for alternative conceptions. In part this has led to a rediscovery of the military origins of strategy with its emphasis on situational sensitivity (Quinn 1980). In part, these inquiries have led to concerns about whether the *meaning* and, therefore, the *structure* of strategy can in fact be applied from one sector to the next (Mintzberg and Waters 1985).

This chapter attempts to contribute to this call for a more situationally sensitive and contextually grounded understanding of strategy. An archetypal typology of four strategic orientations was proposed, which we claim is ba-

sic to any context and is in effect protocontextual. Each of these orientations was described in terms intended to connote a sense of texture, situation, and drama. Strategy always is dramatic for the actors involved, entailing considerable risks and uncertainties.

With the identification of these archetypal stratagems, we believe the problem of misapplying the techniques and the meanings of strategy from one context to the next can be mitigated. Mapping a range of seventeen characteristic "presenting situations" onto the archetypal framework helped in the consideration of a variety of meanings and approaches to strategy formulation in the public sector. Delineating 12 types of strategies helped suggest the variety of approaches that one could expect to uncover through more comprehensive and rigorous case analysis. Seven key points have been made in the course of this discussion.

1. The meaning or semantics of strategy changes from one context to the next, because the objectives and rules of each context are distinct. This recognition is critical in avoiding what Schon (1980) has called metaphoric construal—the transposition of terms and meanings from one context which become metaphors in another context.

2. To obviate the problem of metaphoric construal, a set of archetypal stratagems were proposed. These patterns of action were considered basic enough to apply to any context representing what we called a protocontextual framework.

3. The archetypal stratagems were largely based on four *temporal orientations*. This set up the limiting conditions on the number of core strategies we were willing to consider. The quest relates to an emphasis on the long-term future, the saga is based on a concern with a previous position or state, the venture relates to the near term, and the parlay is focused on the immediate. Recognizing that temporal orientations are themselves conditioned by perceptions of the environment, we organized the stratagems into a simple two-by-two matrix to reflect both of these dimensions.

4. The archetypal typology was used to interpret a range of strategies that might be employed in public sector settings. This required grounding the archetypal orientations against the *characteristic situations* that lead to strategic planning efforts in the public sector. In taking this tack we depended on a combination of our knowledge and experience in 27 engagements.

5. The situation-based approach led us to propose 12 strategic variations of the four archetypal orientations. We proposed this array simply as a suggestive range, recognizing that a greater number of cases and more rigorous method of evaluation would be required to more adequately delineate types of strategy in the public sector, as well as in other contextual settings.

6. We emphasize that strategy must be understood from the perspective of the actors engaged in these efforts, and not strictly from the viewpoint of academics and consultants. This principle has of course been recognized by ethnographers for some time, but has not been sufficiently emphasized in the management literature despite the recent appreciation of culture and context. For this reason, we used terms that suggested the inherent drama in each of the orientations.

7. A contextually grounded, situationally based approach to strategy promotes an alternative view to the predominant perspective of strategy as technique. In addition, the long-standing arguments between incremental and synoptic, and short-term versus long-term approaches are somewhat displaced by this view. The appropriateness of strategy is conditioned by context and situation, and as the latter changes so should strategic orientations and techniques.

The perspective we have presented opens the way to an episodic approach to strategy formulation and implementation. Strategy is neither technique nor processual structure by this view, but the application of technique and process to particular situations in distinct contextual settings. The range of strategic orientations is hardly limitless; to the contrary, we suggest that a small number of possible orientations shape the nature of strategic episodes.

Episodes are defined as "distinct undertakings within a longer course or journey."[4] As we see it, strategy is episodic in that distinct undertakings conditioned by particular situations are pursued in recognition of a longer course of objectives, values, and aspirations. While strategic episodes are conditioned by situation and context, they are created events that may have an impact on the surrounding circumstances and the culture of the organization. Thus, an organization may launch a strategy with a quest, reaffirm its intentions years later through a saga, steer a steady course through ventures and parlays, and still later alter its core mission through yet another quest. This perspective, we believe, can contribute to a more realistic account of organizational strategy as a dynamic and dramatic activity shaped by context, situation, and intention.

NOTES

1. Quinn suggests that corporate models of strategic planning might be enriched by classical concepts of military strategy:

> Executives are generally intrigued by the insights the classical strategists offer. . . . Yet I find little specific reference to classical principles in the management literature, and I repeatedly see formally developed business strategies that ignore basic strategic axioms to the point of embarrassment. . . [Quinn 1980, pp. 6, 7].

2. Between September 1984 and April 1985, three research centers at the University of Pennsylvania held a series of roundtables with 20 high-level public administrators during which case presentations on strategic planning efforts in the public sector were presented and analyzed. The results of this project were reported in an unpublished volume entitled "Governance with Foresight." The author acted as a cochair of this project, with Professors Thomas Gilmore and Seymour Mandelbaum, of the Wharton School and the Department of City and Regional Planning at the University of Pennsylvania, respectively. The project was supported through a grant from the United Parcel Service Public Policy Initiatives Fund.

3. The author is grateful to colleagues at the Fels Center, the Wharton Center for Applied Research, and graduate interns in the Masters of Government Administration program at Fels for their assistance in developing the case material. In addition, Michael Ferreri of Booz Allen Hamilton, Ron Jonash of Arther D. Little, Bob Guzek of Coopers & Lybrand, and Jim Hudak of Arthur Anderson provided case material that was of fundamental importance for the concept of strategy formulation presented here.

4. For a more complete treatment of strategic episodes see M. S. Rubin (1986), *Towards a Concept of Mediated Development: An Episodic Model of Purposeful Systems Development*, unpublished doctoral dissertation, Ann Arbor, Mich.: University Microfilms International. Episode is derived from the Greek where it came to mean a distinctive passage in a dramatic work, and more recently has been used by Weick (1972), Bolan (1980), Schon (1980), and others to describe strategic events and interventions.

REFERENCES

Ackoff, R. L., 1981. *Creating the corporate future*. New York, N.Y.: Wiley.

——— 1985. *Management in small doses*. New York, N.Y.: Wiley.

Ansoff, H. I. 1972. The concept of strategic management. *Journal of Business Policy* Summer, 2–7.

——— 1972. *Corporate strategy: An analytic approach to business policy for growth and expansion*. New York: McGraw-Hill.

Bacharach, P. and M. S. Baratz. 1962. Two faces of power. *American Political Science Review* Vol. 56, 947–952.

——— 1963. Decisions and nondecisions: An analytic framework. *American Political Science Review* Vol. 57, 632–642.

Bolan, Richard S. 1980. The practitioner as theorist: The phenomenology of the professional episode. *Journal of the American Planning Association* 46: 261-274.

Boston Consulting Group. 1968. *Perspectives on corporate strategy*. Boston, Mass.: BCG.

Bryson, John M. 1981. A perspective on planning and crises in the public sector. *Strategic Management Journal* 2: 181–196.

Bryson, John M., R. Edward Freeman, and William D. Roering. 1985. Discussion Paper #37. The Strategic Management Research Center. University of Minnesota.

Bryson, John M., Andrew H. Van de Ven, and William D. Roering. 1985b. Discussion Paper #39. The Strategic Management Research Center, University of Minnesota.

Cannon, J. T. 1968. *Business strategy and policy*. New York, N.Y.: Harcourt, Brace and World.

Cartwright, Timothy J. 1973. Problems, solutions, strategies. *Journal of the American Institute of Planners* 39, 3, May, 179–187.

Christensen, Karen S. 1985. Coping with uncertainty in planning. *American Planning Association Journal* Winter, 63–73.

Drucker, P. F. 1954. *The practice of management*. New York, N.Y.: Harper & Row.

Emery, F. E. and E. Trist. 1971. *Towards a social ecology*. London: Plenum.

Giddens, A. 1984. *The constitution of society*. Berkeley, Calif.: University of California Press.

Glueck, W. F. and R. Willis. 1979. Documentary sources and strategic management research. *Academy of Management Review* Spring, 127–137.

Gore, W. J. 1964. *Administrative decision-making: A heuristic model*. New York, N.Y.: John Wiley & Sons.

Guth, W. D. 1971. Formulating organizational objectives and strategy: A systematic approach. *Journal of Business Policy* Autumn, 24–31.

Habermas, J. 1979. *Communication and the evolution of society.* Boston, Mass.: Beacon Press.

Hall, W. K. 1972. Strategic planning models: Are top managers really finding them useful? *Journal of Business Policy* Winter, 33–42.

Henderson, B. D. 1979. *Henderson on corporate strategy.* Cambridge, Mass.: Abt Books.

———— 1979. *The non-logical strategy.* Boston, Mass.: The Boston Consulting Group.

Krieger, M. H. 1981. *Advice and planning.* Philadelphia, Penn.: Temple University.

Lorange, P. 1983. *Implementation of strategic planning.* Englewood Cliffs, N.J.: Prentice Hall.

Machiavelli, N. 1950. *The prince, and the discourses.* New York, N.Y.: Modern Library.

MacMillan, I. C. 1983. Competitive strategies for not-for-profit agencies. *Agencies in Strategic Management* Vol. 1, 61–82.

Miller, G. A., E. Galanter, and K. H. Pribram. 1960. *Plans and the structure of behavior.* New York, N.Y.: Holt.

Mintzberg, H. 1979. *The structuring of organizations.* Englewood Cliffs, N.J.: Prentice-Hall.

———— 1984. *Power in and around organizations.* Englewood Cliffs, N.J.: Prentice-Hall.

Mintzberg, Henry and James A. Waters. 1985. Of strategies, deliberate and emergent. *Strategic Management Journal* Vol. 6, 257–272.

Mitroff, I. I. and R. H. Kilman, 1976. On organization stories: An approach to design and analysis of organizations through myths and stories. In R. H. Kilman et al. *The Management of Organization Design* Vol. I. New York, N.Y.: North-Holland.

Neustadt, R. E. and E. R. May. 1986. *Thinking in time.* New York, N.Y.: MacMillan.

Nutt, Paul C., 1984. A strategic planning network for nonprofit organizations. *Strategic Management Journal* Vol. 5, 57–75.

Ozebekhan, H. 1971. Planning and human action. In *Hierarchically Organized Systems in Theory and Practice,* edited by P. Weiss. New York, N.Y.: Hafner.

Porter, M. E. 1979. How competitive forces shape strategy. *Harvard Business Review* March.

Quinn, James Bryant. 1980. *Strategies for change: Logical incrementalism.* Homewood, Ill.: Richard D. Irwin.

Ricoeur, P. 1984. *Time and narrative.* Vol. I. Chicago, Ill.: University of Chicago.

Ring, P. S. See Chapter 5.

Schon, D. A. 1980. Framing and reframing the problems of cities. In *Making Cities Work,* edited by David Morley, Stuart Proudfoot, and Thomas Burns. Boulder, Colo.: Westview Press.

———— 1983. Organizational learning. In *Beyond Method: Strategies for Social Research.* Beverly Hills, Calif.: Sage Publications.

Wechsler, B. and R. B. Backoff. See Chapter 7.

The Dynamics of Strategy in Public Organizations

Public agencies, like other complex organizations, operate in turbulent environments that impose numerous, rapidly changing demands, requiring substantial adaptive capacity (Ansoff 1985; Emery and Trist 1963). In order to manage the future course of the organization and to establish the most viable strategy for achieving organizational goals, leaders must understand the dynamics of strategy in public organizations.

The concept of strategy has both a lengthy history and a well-known usage (Bracker 1980). An organization's strategy can be found in the pattern of major, nonroutine decisions, choices, and actions that set its direction into the future. This pattern can be seen in the way an agency pursues a variety of activities, including formal planning and goal setting, policy adoption and implementation, development of programs or changes in the relative emphasis among them, reorganization of internal structure, alteration of service delivery systems, and searches for new sources of funding and external support. Factors such as the political goals of elected officials, demands of powerful constituents, judicial mandates, budgetary constraints, the organization's capacities and resources, and its cooperative and competitive relationships with other organizations—both public and private—powerfully influence agency strategies. Thus, the strategies of public agencies and the way those strategies change over time result largely from the interaction of organizational intention and capacity with the external environment.

In this chapter we examine the dynamics of strategy in public organizations by attempting to detail and account for the evolution of strategy in three Ohio government agencies. In the first section we review some of the literature on strategic planning and management and present the conceptual framework for our study. We discuss the Ohio studies in section 2 and present our findings in section 3. In section 4 we employ our conceptual framework to analyze the dynamics of strategy in the three agencies. Finally, we discuss our conclusions and their implications for organizational strategists and planners.

CONCEPTUAL FOUNDATIONS

In much of the management literature, strategy is presented from a *process* perspective, focusing on systematic analysis, comprehensive planning and strategy formulation, and purposeful choice and action by strategic managers and planners (Ackoff 1970, 1981; Ansoff 1965, 1979, 1985; Lorange 1980; Nutt 1984; Schendel and Hofer 1979; Thompson and Strickland 1980). In a separate stream of research, the *content* approach has emphasized understanding the specific pattern of forces both inside and outside that produce strategy and set direction for the organization (Miles and Snow 1978; Miller and Friesen 1978; Mintzberg 1978). Regardless of orientation (process or content), theories of strategy and strategic management generally have been concerned with private business organizations, not with public organizations.

In fact, students of public policymaking and administration have begun only recently to explore the process and content of strategy in public organizations (Bragaw 1980; Bryson and Boal 1983; Eadie and Steinbacher 1985; Levine 1985; Ring and Perry 1985; Wechsler and Backoff 1986). Extending lines of inquiry in political science, public administration, and planning as well as in business management, this newly emerging literature holds that the strategies of public organizations arise within a governmental authority system (Lindblom 1977). That is, rather than being formed in response to the requirements of markets, the strategies actually carried out by public organizations are products of complex processes and interactions set in the context of constitutional government.

Dimensions of Strategy

In the business literature, strategies have been characterized in a variety of ways (Miles and Snow 1978; Miller and Friesen 1978; Mintzberg 1978). Unfortunately, none of those frameworks is easily applied to public sector organizations (Rainey, Backoff, and Levine 1976). In order to describe and analyze the patterns of strategy found in the Ohio agencies, we de-veloped a conceptual framework based on the following eight dimensions.

1. *Strength of external influence* means the extent to which external demands and pressures influence the strategy of an agency (Bolan 1969; Easton 1979; Pfeffer and Salancik 1978). It is the level of influence exerted by those who have stakes in the outcome of the strategy—such as government officials, clients, and constituents—to control policy and program direction, resource allocation, and service delivery.

2. *Strategy impetus* indicates how an agency develops its strategy, whether in an active or reactive fashion (Ackoff 1981; Harmon 1981; Miles and Snow 1978; Miller and Friesen 1978). Active strategies anticipate situations and events, with the intention of acting on them before they act on the organization. Reactive strategies cede the impetus to situations and events, leaving planners and strategists in a purely responsive mode.

3. *Strategy orientation* refers to the objectives emphasized by an agency's strategy (Bower 1983; Clark and Shrode 1979; Wechsler and Backoff 1986). Some strategies emphasize the political interests of elected officials, external constituents, or members of the organization (*politically oriented* strategies). Others aim to add resources, improve performance, control internal operations, and/or develop capacity (*organizationally oriented* strategies). Strategies that have a *policy orientation* are formed in response to actors, both internal and external, who identify with a particular policy community, such as those organized around environmental and human service issues.

4. *Attitude toward change* refers to the agency's intentions with regard to itself and its environment (Braybrooke and Lindblom 1963; March and Simon 1958). For example, strategies may be designed to produce fundamental change in programs, organizational structure, service delivery systems, or relationships with external actors. Conversely, strategies may be designed to maintain the status quo both inside the organization and in its external relations.

5. *Scope of strategy* refers to the range of concerns addressed by the agency's strategy (Hofer and Schendel 1978). The scope of strategic choice and action for a specific agency may be broad or narrow, focusing on a relatively comprehensive or a relatively limited set of issues and concerns.

6. *Level of activity* means the amount of attention an agency gives to achieving its strategic objectives (Osgood, Suci, and Tannenbaum 1957). An organization that has a high level of strategic activity is one that pays significant attention to specific strategic issues and makes substantial efforts to achieve preferred outcomes. An agency with a low level of activity does not devote much attention or energy to a strategic agenda and may appear to be passively drifting.

7. *Target of strategy* refers to the direction of an agency's strategy (Miles 1980; Wamsley and Zald 1973). Strategy can be directed internally to achieve control over operations, more efficient use of resources, or increased organizational capacity; it can be aimed externally as a means of responding to or transforming the environment; or it can have mixed (internal and external) targets.

8. *Locus of control* reflects the balance between external (political, legal, and economic) demands and pressures and internal (organizational) intentions and capacities

(Pfeffer and Salancik 1978; Rotter, Seeman, and Liverant 1962; Wechsler and Backoff 1986). This dimension indicates whether an agency's strategy is controlled by external forces and actors or by internal strategists and planners.

A Framework for Understanding Strategy Formation

To aid us in examining how public organizations develop strategies, we have developed a conceptual framework for the process (see Figure 7-1). The framework has four main sections. The *strategy environment* consists of external (political, economic, and legal) and internal (organizational) factors. External factors in the strategy environment include constraints on resources, the preferences of various stakeholders, the political agenda, the level of public support for the agency's program, government budget conditions, the balance of power among constituents, and various legal mandates and judicial orders (Bolan 1969). Among the internal factors in the strategy environment are the strength of leadership, intensity of the formal planning effort, the organization's capacity for performance, the degree of internal policy consensus, the amount of discretion allowed strategists and planners, the availability of autonomous funding sources, and the type of policy for which the agency is responsible.

Interaction of the dimensions described above determines the character of the second section of the framework. Tension between external demands and pressures and strategic intentions and capacities determines to what extent the organization determines its own strategy. If the agency has an internal locus of control, then its strategy will reflect more

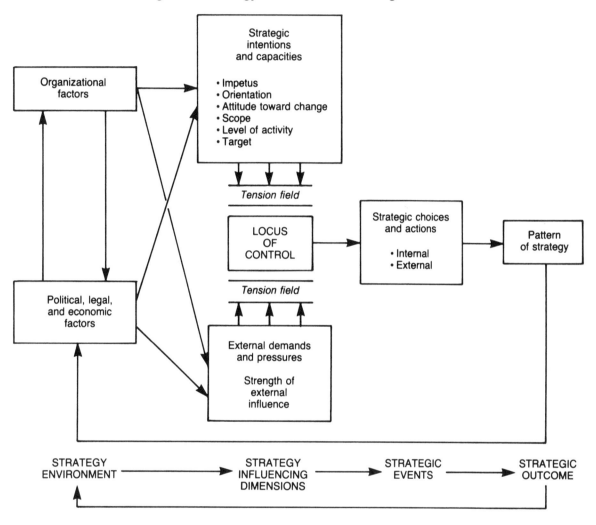

Figure 7–1. Strategy Formation in Public Organizations

closely the intentions of its strategists and planners. Conversely, if its locus of control is external, then the agency's planning efforts will be far less relevant and its strategies will arise from environmental circumstance instead of from plans (Mintzberg 1978). *Strategic events* include specific choices and actions, both within and outside the organization, that result in major organizational commitments, set direction for the organization as a whole, and establish its

character and purpose. Examples include legislative and judicial mandates, decisions about budget allocation, changes in structural arrangements and service delivery networks, changes in agency leadership, program and policy decisions, and development of management systems. From an agency's specific choices and actions emerges a specific pattern of strategy. This pattern, reflecting the *strategic outcome* of the strategy formation process, captures the essential theme of the agency's actual or realized strategy. While planners and strategists act in ways that are "intendedly" rational (March and Simon 1958), actual patterns of strategy are more emergent and may be the result of more nearly random "garbage can" processes (Cohen, March, and Olsen 1972).

We identified several patterns of strategy in the Ohio cases described below. Although these patterns are characteristic of the strategies of public organizations, they do not necessarily exhaust all possible strategies. The strategies have been labeled *developmental, political,* and *protective.*

Strategists and planners explicitly choose *developmental* strategies to enhance the organization's status, capacity, resources, and influence and to produce a new and better future for the organization. Strategic actions, designed to employ existing resources to build capacity for future action, often are guided by formal planning processes.

Political strategies come in two types. One type emerges from changing environmental conditions and aims simply to accommodate the balance of power among external forces. An organization's planners and strategists have some control over this type of strategy, but they remain generally reactive rather than active. The second type of political strategy conceives of the organization as an instrument of partisan politics and as a means of rewarding supporters and key constituents. This type of strategy often is associated with changes in regime and frequently results in changes in staffing, structure, and policy and program emphases.

A hostile and potentially threatening environment, combined with limited organizational capacity for planning and strategic action, produces the *protective* strategy. This type of strategy attempts to accommodate strong external pressures while maintaining the organizational status quo. Although commonly guided by an organizational or policy orientation, the protective strategy is often played out in political terms. Strategic decisions are made and actions taken in reaction to and controlled by external actors, causing internal observers to question management capacity and commitment.

In the remainder of the chapter we employ these concepts to explore the dynamics of strategy in three Ohio agencies.

THE OHIO STUDIES

Our research is based on a series of intensive field studies in three state government agencies in Ohio: the Department of Natural Resources, the Department of Public Welfare, and the Public Utilities Commission of Ohio. We studied the development and evolution of each agency's strategy from 1974 to 1984. During that period, Ohio state government experienced deteriorating economic circumstances, demands for new and different programs and forms of service delivery, new institutional and legal arrangements, organizational restructuring, and, very important, transition from the Republican administration of Governor James Rhodes (1974–1982) to the first-term Democratic administration of Governor Richard Celeste (1982–1987). For those reasons the period seemed to offer an excellent opportunity to examine strategic planning and management in state government and to investigate the factors contributing to the evolution of agency strategies.

Research Methods

Our research team conducted intensive interviews with 38 informants in the three agencies, including directors, deputy directors, division and program heads, and others who were directly involved in strategic planning and management. We also interviewed important external stakeholders from government and constituent groups (e.g., staff members in the governor's office, legislators, representatives of advocacy and lobbyist groups, and public and private service providers). In addition, we systematically collected and analyzed annual reports, budgets, and other documents from the agencies, the State of Ohio Archives, and other sources.

From those data we developed extensive accounts of agency strategy and strategic management (Wechsler 1985). Then we analyzed those accounts in terms of the dimensions described above and tested hypotheses about the factors that account for strategic change in public organizations. This process involved the authors as well as several other faculty members and graduate students. Using the accounts of each agency, researchers independently rated each of the dimensions and factors. These ratings were discussed among the researchers and led to a tentative consensus. In later stages of the research we tested initial decisions about the ratings with informants. (For a more detailed discussion of the methodological approach see Wechsler 1986.)

STRATEGIC MANAGEMENT AND PLANNING IN THE OHIO AGENCIES

The following sketches briefly describe the strategies of each of the Ohio agencies. While much shorter than the original accounts (Wechsler 1985), they capture the essential character of the agency's strategy.

Department of Natural Resources

The Ohio Department of Natural Resources (DNR) is responsible for the management, de-velopment, protection, and recreational use of Ohio's natural areas and resources. DNR engages in facility management, long-range land use planning, water management and soil conservation, environmental regulation, licensing and enforcement, and public education. The department serves a large number of constituencies, including hunters and fishermen, farmers, recreational boaters and campers, conservationists, and developers. Those constituencies often take divergent positions regarding natural resource protection, management, and development and have very different preferences for policies, programs, and services.

During the Rhodes administration the department added programs, facilities, and services, built a highly qualified professional staff, established an agencywide planning process, generated support among its competing constituents, secured independent sources of funding, and created an organizational culture emphasizing high performance. Each of these actions was chosen as part of a deliberate strategy designed to develop the organization's capacity—a *developmental* strategy.

DNR's strategists deliberately sought to improve the agency's political position, secure more independent bases of funding, and increase the capacity of its personnel and management systems so as to increase its overall capacity for continued development (Lenz 1980). Internal factors driving this strategy included the leadership of Director Robert Teater, the presence of professional expertise within the department, preferences about the organization's future shared among many of its employees, and substantial managerial discretion. External factors included relative freedom from resource constraints, strong support from the general public, and balanced power among constituents, which diffused the strength of external claims on the agency.

In the first years of the Celeste administration, DNR's strategic management became subject to more control from political officials and interest groups. Strategic objectives were generally *political* in character, related to satisfying and rewarding a few favored constituent groups and to gaining top management control over the department's internal operations in order to further political objectives. Structural arrangements and control mechanisms also reflected a political orientation. A key manifestation of this approach was a plan for reorganization that segmented program lines, reduced divisional autonomy, and centralized control over policy and program direction. Appointments, which had been made on a nonpartisan, professional basis during the Teater years, were similarly politicized (Shein 1983). These actions were explicitly designed to centralize control of the organization, to reduce competition among programs and units, and to direct departmental operations toward achievement of political objectives.

Thus DNR's pattern of strategy had become almost exclusively *political*. Its intended strategic program was aimed at securing internal operational control, staffing positions with political loyalists, and rewarding favored constituents (e.g., environmental groups). These efforts were consistent with partisan political objectives as well as gubernatorial policy preferences. An influential actor in the politicization of the department was Director Myrl Shoemaker, who, while serving concurrently as lieutenant governor of Ohio, pursued a personal agenda heavily influenced by his extensive legislative experience and continuing political career.

This substantial change in strategy between administrations (from developmental to political) can be explained in terms of changes in the strategy environment of DNR. The growing influence of political interest groups, combined with structural and staffing changes inside the department, moved the locus of control outside the organization. The orientation of the administration and senior management within the agency led to a pattern of strategic choice and action designed to achieve political outcomes.

Department of Public Welfare

The public welfare system in Ohio is operated by county welfare departments and children's services boards. The role of the Ohio Department of Public Welfare (DPW) is to supervise the welfare system, ensuring that individuals and families in need of social services, medical care, and/or emergency financial aid receive appropriate assistance. DPW serves as a source and conduit of funds and as a monitor of local government performance, rather than as a provider of direct services to clients.

During the Rhodes administration, DPW was confronted with (1) poor relationships with legislators, local government and private welfare providers, and the news media; (2) increased demands from clients for program services; (3) decreased funding; (4) changes in federal policy and program requirements; and (5) poor organizational performance and morale. In combination, these situations produce a strategy environment that was perceived as hostile and threatening to the department, its programs, and its clients. In response, the senior management sought to "bring peace to the place and get it out of the newspapers" (Creasy 1984).

For the most part, DPW was able only to *protect* its core programs and prevent substantial reductions in benefits. Given the politics of the

Rhodes administration, efforts to protect programs, benefits, and service levels were not guaranteed success. Realization of those objectives required that DPW reestablish good relationships with the Ohio General Assembly, lower its public profile, and impose tight controls over internal operations. In addition, the senior management established a highly politicized internal environment. Not surprisingly, both strategy and operations were guided largely by the need to accommodate legislative overseers and the news media.

Because the Celeste administration had a greater commitment to human services and experienced less of a budgetary crisis, DPW was able to adopt a substantially different strategic approach. Less driven by the need to mend political fences (with legislators, news media, and welfare advocates), DPW's leadership was able to establish a strategy guided by organizational intentions and capacity. Building on the management experience and policy preferences of the director and his senior staff, the management focused its strategic agenda internally, aiming to mobilize an agency that had been "asleep for eight years" (Cuddy 1984). As a result, various initiatives were undertaken to enhance the department's capacity and improve its performance. Implementation of a *developmental* strategy led to the creation of new management systems, computerization of operations, and development of training programs. Through those efforts the department not only improved its operations but also gained more external credibility and support.

This case illustrates how the interaction between internal and external factors can contribute to changes in organizational strategy. During the Rhodes administration, DPW was essentially protective; its internal management was concerned with pacifying hostile forces in its environment. With the election of Governor Celeste and Democratic majorities in both houses of the legislature, hostility toward the department and its portfolio of programs decreased. This change in the political context allowed DPW to direct its attention internally and to use the skills of the new senior management team to rebuild organizational competence and capacity. Strategic managers in DPW saw this as necessary if the department were to regain external credibility and set new policy direction. The combination of a changed external climate and different internal intentions and capacity resulted in DPW's movement from a protective to a developmental strategy.

Public Utilities Commission of Ohio

The Public Utilities Commission of Ohio (PUCO) regulates companies that provide public utilities, telecommunications, and transportation in Ohio. No regulated company can begin, end, or change a service, increase the rates it charges for providing services, or modify its service area without the approval of PUCO. The commission is required by Ohio statute to ensure that consumers receive adequate services from providers at reasonable cost and, at the same time, that the regulated companies have the opportunity to earn a fair rate of return on investment. During most of PUCO's history, these regulatory activities involved mostly technical questions related to the rate base and to the appropriate rate of return on investment. Because of improvements in technology, economies of scale, and the availability of low-cost energy, utilities in the post–World War II period were able to maintain or even reduce the cost of their services (Kelly 1983). In this relatively benign environment, it was not difficult for PUCO to satisfy both producers and consumers.

Events in the past decade have resulted in a fundamentally different climate of regulation. Changes in the Ohio statutes governing regulation of public utilities, establishment of the Office of Consumers' Counsel, and growing politicization of utility-related issues destabilized the regulatory environment. Beginning in the late 1970s, PUCO came under intense pressure to modify its traditional approach, which many constituents began to see as unduly favoring the regulated companies.

Because of these pressures, the strategy that emerged in PUCO was very much the product of external influence. Over time, important new external actors and forces gained influence, grew in strength, and changed the nature of the demands on the commission. As required by law, members of the commission attempted to weigh and balance the interests of competing claimants. As the outcomes of its traditional strategy became less acceptable and external pressures increased, however, PUCO and its staff came to be guided by a *political* strategy, while maintaining a rhetorical commitment to the underlying logic of balancing. In both administrations, regulatory decisions and activities reflected the commission's increased responsiveness to public opinion and to pressures from legislators and other political actors. With the election of Governor Celeste, additional pressure was exerted on PUCO to be more active in protecting consumer interests (Liebman 1984). Not only did the governor appoint new commissioners who were more sympathetic to consumer interests, but he and his staff directly intervened to establish regulatory direction. The commission's capacity to resist these moves was minimal, largely because of rapid turnover

on the commission and increasingly burdened technical resources (Borrows 1984).

In the case of PUCO, the actual pattern of strategy resulted largely from changes in the environment. Consumer demands for lower utility rates, the politicization of regulatory issues, changes in Ohio statutes, and the creation of the Office of Consumers' Counsel pressured the commission to adopt a new regulatory approach favoring consumers over producers. Throughout this period (from 1974 to 1982), PUCO moved further and further away from a legal-technical approach to one that took account of the political environment. The advent of the Celeste administration served not only to intensify this political orientation but also to shift it from a reactive, accommodating mode to a more intended, active political strategy.

DYNAMICS OF STRATEGY

As shown above, there is considerable diversity in the strategies of the Ohio agencies within administrations and relatively consistent change in strategies across administrations (see Table 7–1 for a summary of the research in terms of the framework described above). In this section we identify the factors that shaped the evolution of strategic planning and management in the three agencies, then discuss the dynamics of strategy in public organizations.

Factors Influencing the Strategies

As hypothesized, significant sources for change in the strategies of the Ohio agencies can be found in the external (political, economic, and legal) and internal (organizational) factors discussed above. Table 7–2 arrays these hypothesized factors across agencies and administrations and indicates whether their pres-

Table 7–1. Change in Strategic Dimensions from Rhodes Administration to Celeste Administration

Dimensions	Department of Natural Resources	Department of Public Welfare	Public Utilities Commission of Ohio
	Developmental → Political	Protective → Developmental	Political
Strength of external influence	Weak ————→ Strong	Strong ————→ Weak	Moderate ————→ Strong
Strategy impetus	Active ————→ Reactive	Reactive ————→ Active	Reactive ————→ Active
Strategy orientation	Organization ——→ Political	Political ——→ Organization	Political ——→ Political
Attitude toward change	Incremental—→ Incremental	Status quo ——→ Incremental	Incremental—→ Fundamental
Scope	Broad ————→ Moderate	Narrow ————→ Moderate	Narrow ————→ Moderate
Level of activity	High ————→ Moderate	Low ————→ High	Low ————→ Moderate
Target of strategic action	Mixed ————→ Mixed	Mixed ————→ Mixed	Mixed ————→ External
Locus of control	Internal ————→ External	External ————→ Internal	Internal ————→ External

Table 7–2. Factors Influencing Strategies in the Ohio Agencies

Factor	Rhodes administration			Celeste administration		
	DNR	DPW	PUCO	DNR	DPW	PUCO
External						
Resource constraints	A	P				
Stakeholder preferences				P	P	P
Political agenda		P	P	P	P	P
Public support	P	A			A	
Budget conditions		P			P	
Balance of power	P		P	A		P
Legal mandates		P				P
Internal						
Leadership	P	A	A		P	A
Formal planning	P	A	A			A
Capacity	P	A	A	A	P	A
Policy consensus	P			A	P	
Discretion	P				P	
Autonomous funding	P					
Policy type		P	P		P	P

P = Presence of factor influenced strategy.
A = Absence of factor influenced strategy.
Blank = No effect on strategy.

ence or absence influenced the agency's strategy. The presence of a formal strategic planning process was a significant factor only in DNR (under Rhodes). The absence of planning capacity, however, influenced the strategies of both DPW (under Rhodes) and PUCO.

These findings suggest that changes in the strategy environment produced changes in the pattern of strategy found in a particular agency. For example, leadership, capacity for performance, and internal policy consensus changed as strategy evolved in both DNR and DPW.

Changes in these factors from the Rhodes to the Celeste administration contributed to DNR's shift from a *developmental* to a *political* strategy. In contrast, the emergence of these factors in DPW led to the adoption of a *developmental* strategy. In the case of PUCO, changes in stakeholders' preferences and in the balance of constituents' power were significant factors in the emergence of a *political* strategy intended only to accommodate environmental pressures. As these factors intensified during the Celeste administration, PUCO adopted a deliberate strategy designed to meet the political objectives of the administration and the demands of consumers.

Explaining Strategic Evolution

The strategies of public organizations, unlike business strategies, are produced in response to a variety of competing signals that emanate not from markets but from complex political, economic, legal, and organizational structures, processes, and relationships. Externally these signals may take the form of demands from clients and constituents, instructions from political officials, or legal mandates. How the organization responds to external signals is a function of its internal strategic intentions and capacity. Organization members have preferences about strategic posture and direction and about specific policies and programs. Those preferences are both influenced by and competitive with external sources of agency strategy. In addition, strategy depends on an agency's capacity for performance. Personnel, finances, physical capital, and management systems are the resources that are available for implementation of an agency's strategic plans and programs (Lenz 1980).

At any time, the prevailing balance of internal and external forces influences the agency's strategy. Processes are frequently at work, moreover, that have the effect of undoing that balance. In the long run, making choices and acting on them leads to changes in the organization and its primary environment. Every effort to align internal forces with external ones changes the balance between them (Thompson 1967). This disequilibrium produces a new cycle of strategic choices and actions, and, potentially, a new pattern of strategy. Similarly, changes that occur in the environment but are beyond the scope of organizational action can produce both direct and indirect pressures for changes in internal-external balance (Emery and Trist 1963). Thus, patterns of strategic choices and actions may evolve in response to events and conditions beyond the boundaries of the organization or the intentions of its strategists. Finally, assessments of external pressure, strategy preferences, capacity for performance, and specific choices and actions are products of the way the organization's planners and strategists perceive and interpret the world. Changes in the membership of the strategic planning and management group as well as changes in political administration can affect the strategy of an agency by altering the way the strategy environment is interpreted and acted on.

CONCLUSIONS AND IMPLICATIONS

We have described and analyzed the strategies of three Ohio agencies and demonstrated the dynamic quality of their strategies over time. The diversity of strategies found within administrations and the changes in agency strategies across administrations are interesting and significant findings. Both result from multiple forces in the strategy environment of the agency.

Under certain conditions, strategy is largely a matter of organizational intention. When clear and widely shared organizational objectives, substantial capacity for performance, extensive amounts of discretion, and adequate resources are found in opposition to a weak or divided external influence field, an agency's pattern of strategy is likely to coincide with its intentions and plans. In contrast, when external forces are strong relative to internal intention and capacity, the actual pattern of strategy may diverge from the intentions of agency strategists and planners (Mintzberg and Waters 1983). Similarly, the diversity of strategies within a single administration reinforces the notion of segmented, pluralistic demands and pressures affecting organizational choice and action rather than monolithic preferences and patterns of authority (Dahl 1961). Agencies operate in distinctive strategy environments, so strategies may be different from those desired or intended by elected officials and policymakers. An administration may plan for a singular jurisdictionwide strategy across agencies, but it is unlikely to realize that intention.

From the Ohio findings it appears that an administration must come to accept multiple strategies among agencies. The pattern of changes in strategy across administrations provides additional support for this argument and for the claim that agency planners and strategists are generally responsive to changes in political control. In each of the Ohio cases, newly emergent strategies were consistent with the political goals of the administration and politically relevant stakeholders.

The Ohio studies have several important implications for organizational planners and strategists. One concerns the identity and roles of planners in the strategic planning and man-agement process. Our research shows that the work of strategic planning and management typically engages general managers rather than staff planners. Where planners and formal planning processes were significant factors in the actual strategy (as in the Department of Natural Resources under Governor Rhodes), it was because of a participative management style that encouraged involvement in the strategic management process by a variety of actors. In other agencies, planners and plans were often irrelevant to the determination of agency strategy. If planners are to play a significant role, it will be usually in support of general managers rather than as strategists themselves. Our research also suggests the kinds of contingencies and constraints to which the planner must attend in supporting strategic management activity. As described above, elements of the political, economic, and legal environment are significant factors in an agency's actual strategy. Although many of these elements are beyond the control of the organization and its strategists, continuing assessment and surveillance of the strategy environment by planners seems crucial to the organization's performance and effectiveness.

The strategy environment of a public organization not only influences the actual strategy of the agency but also determines the feasibility of various approaches that might be taken to strategic planning and management. Comprehensive agency strategic planning and management is feasible only in certain strategy environments. Internal capacity is required, but the external environment also must support internal aspirations and preferences. In the absence of capacity and reinforcing support from the environment, strategies necessarily will be more limited and incremental. From this perspective, effective strategies are those that adopt the most feasible approach, not the most comprehensive and elegant planning system.

Finally, although our discussion has focused on actual rather than intended strategy, we recognize that leaders of agencies seek to choose and direct the future course of their organizations. While the realized strategy represents a viable accommodation of internal and external dimensions, strategists and planners may want to alter these patterns so as to better realize their strategic intentions. Since strategies reflect the existing balance of internal and external forces, change efforts must aim at affecting that balance (Lewin 1951). Thus, leaders may seek to remove restraining forces in the environment (e.g., build better relationships with the legislature and other stakeholders, secure new sources of funding, seek changes in legislative or judicial mandates, or establish more favorable media relations). Similarly, leaders may seek to enhance organizational capacity, either by building on strengths or overcoming weaknesses (e.g., develop new management systems, establish training programs, or redirect slack resources to more critical needs). These maneuvers not only affect the balance between internal and external forces but also tend to shift the locus of control toward organizational leaders. As demonstrated in several of the Ohio cases, the organization can take actions that create for itself a cycle of increasing capacity for intended, self-directed action.

REFERENCES

Ackoff, R. L. 1970. *A concept of corporate planning.* New York, N.Y.: John Wiley and Sons.

———. 1981. *Creating the corporate future.* New York, N.Y.: John Wiley and Sons.

Ansoff, H. I. 1965. *Corporate strategy.* New York, N.Y.: McGraw-Hill.

———. 1979. *Strategic management.* New York, N.Y.: John Wiley and Sons.

———. 1985. *Implanting strategic management.* Englewood Cliffs, N.J.: Prentice-Hall International.

Bolan, R. S. 1969. Community decision behavior: The culture of planning. *Journal of the American Institute of Planners* 35 (September): 301–310.

Borrows, J. 1984. (Director, Public Utilities Commission of Ohio) Personal interview.

Bower, J. L. 1983. *The two faces of management.* Boston, Mass.: Houghton Mifflin.

Bracker, J. 1980. The historical development of the strategic management concept. *Academy of Management Review* 5 (April): 219–224.

Bragaw, L. K. 1980. *Managing a federal agency: The hidden stimulus.* Baltimore: Johns Hopkins University Press.

Braybrooke, D. and C. E. Lindblom. 1963. *A strategy of decision.* New York, N.Y.: Free Press.

Bryson, J. M. and K. B. Boal. 1983. Strategic management in a metropolitan area. *Proceedings of the Academy of Management* 43: 332–336.

Clark, T. D., Jr. and W. A. Shrode. 1979. Public sector decision structures: An empirically based description. *Public Administration Review* 39 (July/August): 343–354.

Cohen, M., J. G. March, and J. P. Olsen. 1972. A garbage can model of organizational choice. *Administrative Science Quarterly* 17 (March): 1–25.

Creasy, K. 1984. (Director, Ohio Department of Public Welfare, 1977–82) Personal interview. July.

Cuddy, J. 1984. (Director, Ohio Department of Public Welfare, 1983–84) Personal interview. July.

Dahl, R. A. 1961. *Who governs?* New Haven, Conn.: Yale University Press.

Eadie, D. and R. Steinbacher. 1985. Strategic agenda management: A marriage of organizational development and strategic planning. *Public Administration Review* 45: 424–430.

Easton, D. A. 1979. *A framework for political analysis.* Chicago, Ill.: University of Chicago Press.

Emery, F. and E. Trist. 1963. The causal texture of organizational environments. *Human Relations* 18: 12–32.

Harmon, M. 1981. *Action theory for public administration.* New York, N.Y.: Longman.

Hofer, C. W. and D. E. Schendel. 1978. *Strategy formulation: Analytical concepts.* St. Paul, Minn.: West.

Kelly, J. 1983. (Chairman, Public Utilities Commission of Ohio, 1980–82) Personal interview. February.

Levine, C. H. 1985. Police management in the 1980s: From

decrementalism to strategic thinking. *Public Administration Review* 45, special issue (November): 691–99.

Lewin, K. 1951. *Field theory in social relations.* New York, N.Y.: Harper and Row.

Liebman, H. 1984. (Director, Legal Department, Public Utilities Commission of Ohio, 1982–present) Personal interview. February.

Lindblom, C. E. 1977. *Politics and markets.* New York, N.Y.: Basic Books.

Lorange, P. 1980. *Corporate planning.* Englewood Cliffs, N.J.: Prentice-Hall.

March, J. G. and H. A. Simon. 1958. *Organizations.* New York, N.Y.: John Wiley and Sons.

Miles, R. E. and C. Snow. 1980. *Organizational strategy: Structure and process.* New York, N.Y.: McGraw-Hill.

Miles, R. H. 1980. *Macro organization behavior.* Santa Monica, Calif.: Goodyear Publishing Co.

Miller, D. and P. Friesen. 1978. Archetypes of strategy formulation. *Management Science* 24 (May): 921–933.

Mintzberg, H. 1978. Patterns of strategy formation. *Management Science* 24 (May): 934–948.

——— and J. A. Waters. 1983. The mind of the strategist(s). In *Executive Mind: New Insights on Managerial Thought and Action*, edited by S. Srivastva. San Francisco, Calif.: Jossey-Bass.

Nutt, P. C. 1984. Types of organizational decision processes. *Administrative Science Quarterly* 29 (September): 414–450.

Osgood, C. E., G. J. Suci, and P. H. Tannenbaum. 1957 *The measurement of meaning.* Urbana, Ill.: University of Illinois Press.

Pfeffer, J. and G. R. Salancik. 1978. *The external control of organizations.* New York, N.Y.: Harper and Row.

Rainey, H. C., R. W. Backoff, and C. H. Levine. 1976.

Comparing public and private organizations. *Public Administration Review* 36 (March–April): 233–244.

Ring, P. S. and J. L. Perry. 1985. Strategic management in public and private organizations: Implications of distinctive contexts and constraints. *Academy of Management Review* 10 (April): 276–286.

Rotter, J. B., M. Seeman, and S. Liverant. 1962. Internal vs. external control of reinforcements: A major variable in behavior theory. In *Decisions, Values and Groups*, Vol. 2, edited by N. E. Washburne. London: Pergamon Press.

Shein, R. 1983. Personal interview. February.

Schendel, D. E. and C. W. Hofer, eds. 1979. *Strategic management.* Boston, Mass.: Little, Brown.

Thompson, A. A., Jr. and A. J. Strickland III. 1980. *Strategy formulation and implementation.* Plano, Texas: Business Publications, Inc.

Thompson, J. D. 1967. *Organizations in action.* New York, N.Y.: McGraw-Hill.

Wamsley, G. A. and M. N. Zald. 1973. *The political economy of public organizations.* Lexington, Mass.: D. C. Heath.

Wechsler, B. 1985. Strategic management of public organizations: Studies of public policy making and administration in Ohio. Doctoral dissertation. Columbus, Ohio: Ohio State University.

———. 1986. Logic of inquiry for strategic management research: Standards of good practice from the qualitative tradition. *New Directions in Public Administration Research* 1 (Spring).

——— and R. W. Backoff. 1986. Policy making and administration in state agencies: Strategic management approaches. *Public Administration Review* 46 (July/August): 321–27.

A Process for Strategic Management with Specific Application for the Nonprofit Organization

ROBERT W. BACKOFF

PAUL C. NUTT

The efficient and effective provision of services by government, health, charitable, and cultural organizations is central to our life-style expectations (Hatten 1982). A strategy for providing services identifies, among other things, program and service profiles and aims, such as growth and stability. For example, a strategy in a mental health center might aim for steady growth in the number of clients served in the next five years, with emphasis on providing care to adults, children, and the severely mentally disabled through outpatient, day treatment, and residential care programs. Public and third-sector (private, nonprofit, or not-for-profit) organizations have critical needs to articulate, evaluate, and manage the evolution of their strategies. Strategists often overlook the unique problems of those organizations (Bryson, Freeman, and Roering 1985).

This chapter offers a new process to address these unique problems. We call the process *strategic management*, broadening the traditional notions of strategic planning to include implementation as well as formulation and acting as well as thinking. Strategic management merges short- and long-term planning by seeking immediate actions that simultaneously address short- and long-range issues in a dynamic, evolving environment. The process integrates planning with the ongoing management of an organization by removing barriers that treat planning as a staff function, insulated from managerial action.

Public and third-sector organizations face problems that are quite different from those faced by firms. Two of the more important distinctions stem from goals and operating environments. In the business firm, the strategic planner or manager can assume a profit goal. Most strategic planning methods use some form of profit measurement to select among courses of action (e.g., Porter 1985). In nonprofit organizations goals are often ambiguous. When attempting to sweep away this ambiguity two related situations can arise: (1) "goal mania," which can lead to (2) continuing the current, implicit strategy. Goal mania results when the difficulty of goal setting supersedes the development of strategic options. Goal-setting processes that become ends in themselves stymie action. Leaving goals implicit makes it difficult to modify or even evaluate current practices. Without some concept of the organization's intentions, all change becomes contentious and the organization's strategy tends to stay rooted in past practices and conventional wisdom.

A second distinction stems from the operating environments of public and third-sector organizations, which differ from those of business firms (Rainey, Backoff, and Levine 1976). The firm sets strategy for its lines of business by selecting markets or market segments in the industry (e.g., steel) in which it is located. Strategic managers can test the appropriateness of specific strategies by obtaining feedback on profitability from sales to customers in the marketplace. Public and third-sector organizations, however, must be responsive to oversight by external political authority as well as to their clients in the provision of services. Their strategic emphasis, therefore, shifts from simple marketplace dependence to a more complex set of political, economic, and legal considerations. Typically, the political oversight function in governmental and third-sector organizations is vested in elected officials and appointed boards. Strategic management in such organizations must include the building of *joint* commitments to carry out new strategies. Strategists must take into account all parties who either affect or who are affected by the organization's

strategies—called stakeholders—by including them directly in the process, by consulting them, or by considering their views (Mason and Mitroff 1981). Given the political authority system in which such organizations operate, many parties can have stakes in their strategies. These stakes will be communicated not only by client demands (similar to market-based exchanges) but also by political mandates, voting, bargaining, budgeting, and judicial renderings. A business firm's stakeholders are its stockholders, which leads the firm to cater to the short-term profit maximization demands of the managers of retirement and mutual funds that hold most of its stock.

Our strategic management approach is designed to aid the managers of public and third-sector organizations as they steer their organizations toward ambiguous goals in the context of political authority systems and the claims of multiple stakeholders. In the sections that follow we illustrate the approach, using as a case example the strategic management of a not-for-profit community mental health center. This particular center was under the general direction and oversight of a multicounty volunteer board. The board received its revenues from federal and state block grants, local levies, and some limited fees for services. A politically appointed "648 board"[1] contracts with the center for the delivery of the mental health services.

The center's interest in using a strategic management process was triggered by the termination of federal funding for mental health centers, increased competition from hospitals and other providers, and shifts in sources of revenues. Those considerations prompted the center's leaders to establish a more dynamic, anticipatory approach to planning. They sought to supplement their annual planning activities with a long-range, action-centered process. The center operated on a $4 million budget with a 120-member staff including psychiatrists, psychologists, social workers, counselors, and technicians. Through five clinics, about 2,700 clients were being served. The center offered a range of services including aftercare, adult outpatient care, day treatment, children's residential care, consultation and education, emergency services, and substance abuse treatment. The center is similar to several other organizations that have used our strategic management approach. The case should give the reader a straightforward example of how the approach works in practice and serve as a vehicle to discuss the conceptual underpinnings of the process.

In the following sections we describe our approach, identify the principal participants in it, outline the six stages of the process and the three steps for each stage, and suggest guidelines to select techniques appropriate to each step. Finally, we offer ways to improve the results of strategic management.

THE STRATEGIC MANAGEMENT PROCESS

Our approach calls for the strategic management process to be carried out by a strategic management group, hereafter termed the SMG, composed of 5 to 15 key members of the organization. Typically, the chief executive officer, the senior staff, and up to three levels of management responsibility are involved. It is not unusual for representatives of oversight boards or strong stakeholder groups to participate. In the mental health center case, the 14 participants all came from within the center and included its director. Outside stakeholders were involved in legitimizing the process at the beginning and became involved again during the formulation and implementation of strategies. Outside consultants helped establish the strategic management process by holding seven four-hour meetings with the SMG. During this start-up phase, an SMG engages in a series of activities to launch the strategic management process and develop the task force as a strategic management team.

The strategic management group moves through a process that has six stages. Individual stages depict the organization's historical context in terms of its environmental trends, its overall direction, and its normative ideals; assess the immediate situation it faces in terms of current strengths and weaknesses and future opportunities and threats; develop an agenda of current strategic issues to be managed; design strategic options for managing priority issues; assess the options in terms of stakeholders affected and resources required; and implement high-priority strategies by mobilizing resources and managing stakeholders. Once the process is under way for at least one issue and one strategy to manage the issue, the stages of the process may be repeated in whole or in part.

Within each of the stages, the SMG engages in three basic steps. In the first step, a *search* for information and ideas is conducted. The group carries out the second or *synthesis* step to seek generalizations, patterns, or themes in the pool of information and ideas. In the final step, *selection*, the group applies criteria to determine priorities for action as the process moves from one stage to the next. As we will discuss in a later section, different planning techniques are required for each of these steps. The process stages and steps are shown in Table 8–1.

Table 8–1. The Strategic Management Process

Stages	Steps		
	Search for:	Synthesis of:	Selection of:
1. Historical context (a) Trends and events (b) Directions (c) Ideals			
2. Situational assessment (a) Strengths (b) Weaknesses (c) Opportunities (d) Threats	[Techniques to carry out the stages and the steps for each stage are explained later in the chapter.]		
3. Strategic issue agenda			
4. Strategic options (a) Action sets (b) Strategic themes			
5. Feasibility assessment (a) Stakeholder analysis (internal and external) (b) Resource analysis			
6. Implementation (a) Resource mobilization (b) Stakeholder management			

Stage 1: Historical Context

In the first stage, the strategic management group (for convenience, "SMG") identifies trends and critical events, directions, and ideals that characterize the historical context of the organization. The further back in time a stream of events can be recalled, the longer into the future a potential action and event stream can be projected (Weick 1979). During stage 1, the SMG is asked to reconstruct history. The group examines past trends and events and directions of emphasis, noting how they have changed in the past and may change in the future. In the mental health center case, the SMG noted external trends and events such as decreases in federal funding, increasing need for health care cost containment, and pressures from its

board to increase productivity. The group identified changes in directions using the four components of any system: market demands, resources, programs and services, and general management practices. Specifically, the SMG of the mental health center envisaged a change in service demands from a historical pattern of free services to a rationing of services. From a resource perspective, the center's SMG viewed the past as typified by the building of facilities, whereas it saw the future as emphasizing full use of those facilities with no new construction. A movement from nonspecialized services for the poor to specialized services for business and industry was envisaged. The SMG saw the center as moving from a reactive to an anticipatory orientation in planning and from management by the staff's clinical preference to management for organizational survival.

A third and final activity in stage 1 has the SMG members create idealized images of the organization five or more years into the future while the analyses of trends and events and of shifting directions are still fresh in their minds. The SMG participants are asked to describe attributes that would make up an ideal vision of their organization. The mental health center's SMG created the following description:

> Balance between decentralization which insures client sensitivity about needs and centralization to maintain high standards of services for all; fiscal balance between income sources (third party, self-pay, levy, state funds, and industry contracts); balance of resources allocated to hospital and residential treatment, day treatment, aftercare, outpatient counseling, crisis and educational programs; and maintain clinical skills development to sustain and increase quality of treatment, use of consultants, in-services, and innovative programs.

The idealized vision of the organization captures the tensions of opposing forces that will take shape as issues. Ideals also provide a target, offering a way to assess movement toward desired ends.

Our first stage gets the SMG members to examine their initial mind-sets by using directions and trends to reconstruct the organization's history. Ideals are used to push the organization's planning horizon forward. Surveys are used to collect this information from each member. The survey results are aggregated and fed back to the SMG to promote discussion and refinement during meetings. Discussion allows the SMG to develop a shared interpretation of the organization's history and its idealized future.

Stage 2: Situational Assessment

The historical context stage brings the strategic management group to an understanding of its past and its idealized future. In the next stage the immediate situation of the organization is considered. To carry out this stage the SMG identifies and ranks the organization's current strengths and weaknesses as well as its future opportunities and threats (Ansoff 1980). The mental health center's SMG perceived its organization's current strengths to include service variety, current financial position, quality of therapists and staff, and leadership and management. Perceived weaknesses included an inadequate billing system, dependency on uncertain public dollars, low levels of revenues from third-party payers, and weak leadership in psychiatry resulting from a long-standing vacancy in its medical director position. In terms of future opportunities, the members of the SMG believed they might increase third-party revenues, get a levy of public support enacted, increase industry contracts for services, and actively market the mental health center's services to new clients. The SMG, as noted earlier, also perceived future threats in the phase-out of federal block grant monies and limits on the amount of levy support it could get county boards to put on a ballot for voter approval. They also were concerned about the capriciously shifting priorities of the 648 board as well as the increasing control of mental health dollars by health maintenance organizations.

Stage 2 is crucial because it makes the SMG candidly confront crosscurrents in the pressures that the organization faces. Reviewing history in stage 1 and conducting a situation assessment in stage 2 make it possible for an

SMG to own up to the organization's weaknesses and threats without attributing blame to others. Clarifying strengths allows the SMG to see capabilities that the organization possesses and reinforces its sense of competence in managing weaknesses and threats. The idealization process stimulates a more active search for opportunities in the direction of the ideals. Finally, the first two stages build great pressure to get at the core issues that must be managed and usher in the next stage.

Stage 3: The Issue Agenda

We define an *issue* as a difficulty or problem that has a significant influence on the way the organization functions or on its ability to achieve a desired future, for which there is no agreed-on response. Issues can be internal or external to an organization, or both.

Public and third-sector strategic management groups typically uncover four to seven high-priority issues for active management, creating what we call the *issue agenda*. It should be noted that the dynamic nature of both the organization and its environment ensures that, over a year or two, the strategic issue agenda will shift as new items enter and old items disappear. For that reason, an SMG should review and update its issue agenda periodically.

Issues are framed (fashioned or formed) in terms of opposing forces pulling or pushing the organization in various directions and away from idealized images of its future. These forces identify the underlying tensions at work on the organization. This format for expressing issues illustrates polar opposites or contradictions within the organization or between it and external actors.

The mental health center uncovered six issues for its agenda, framed as opposites (see Figure 8–1). For example, humanitarian values of service for all, without regard to a client's ability to pay, and the need for a businesslike approach in the collection of fees for service created a fundamental tension. By framing issues as opposites and confronting the historical context and situational assessment, the SMG members felt a strong need to reconcile these contradictory pressures. A second issue, also related to the center's financial stability, was the twin pressures of declining health care subsidies and the need for diversified funding in the face of cutbacks. Again the issue called for a solution that reconciled dual pressures. A third issue concerned the maintenance of a high-quality treatment and the simultaneous demand for more productivity in processing of clients. The center's dependence on the 648 board for its funding, the expected decrease in funds available to that board (resulting from cutbacks in federal subsidies that the board administers), and the potential for independent funding through new ventures by the center caused a tension between independence and dependence, creating still another issue.

The strategic management group uncovers issues, discusses them, and ranks them in one meeting. At the next meeting the top issue is selected for management by the SMG. In our mental health center case, the issue selected was to reconcile humanitarian and business values (see Figure 8–1).

The issue agenda typically is set by the third or fourth meeting and marks a turning point in the process. The remaining sessions focus less on the context and more on identifying substantive actions to manage key issues. It is important to note that our approach does not use specific goals to orient strategic thinking.

Figure 8–1. Issue Precedence Digraph for a Mental Health Agency

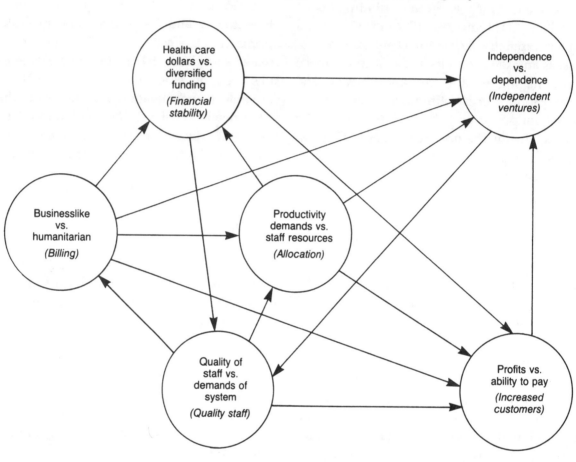

Instead, the participants use reconstructed history and ideals as targets to create an anticipatory mind-set. By shifting to the current operating tensions, an SMG is able to develop an agenda of issues to be managed now rather than goals to be achieved at some distant future. A network of relations (e.g., Figure 8-1) is the underlying focus of action, not a linear movement toward preestablished goals. These tactics help to resolve problems that stem from goal mania. The next stage begins to address our second concern about public and third-sector organizations: the operating environment.

Stage 4: Strategic Options

Strategies are constructed in stage 4. The SMG identifies possible strategies for dealing with each issue on the agenda, beginning with the most important issue to be managed. The list of strengths, weaknesses, opportunities, and threats, identified in stage 2, is reviewed for each issue to see which are most relevant and to uncover new items that had been ignored previously. This is one of the most interesting aspects of our approach. Different issues bring out different configurations of strengths, weaknesses, opportunities, and threats (or SWOTs) and different rankings of the items in each. The shifting SWOT priorities allow a strategic management group to see the complex dynamics at work in its organization. Using the SWOTs as guidelines to generate ideas for action helps the organization to come to grips with its complex dynamics. To identify strategic actions, SMG members are given sheets of paper with the issue and its relevant strengths, weaknesses, opportunities, and threats listed next to it with the following instructions:

> Considering the ideals we have identified for our future, suggest concrete actions we could undertake to manage the issue described below so as to *build* on strengths, *overcome* weaknesses, *exploit* opportunities, and *blunt* threats. Try to find or invent actions that address all four aspects.

Participants list and then swap their sheets of action ideas and add new ideas. Several hundred action ideas often result. The issue focus calls for a synthesis of the forces underlying the issue. For instance, in the mental health case, the billing system philosophy issue called for the reconciliation of humanitarian values with business realities. Strengths, weaknesses, opportunities, and threats suggest actions that can lead to a new billing philosophy.

A strategy is made up of action ideas that have a common theme. The SMG is asked to identify labels for separate bundles of action to suggest themes. Themes may emerge from actions that launch a new program, identify resultant consequences and outcomes, or describe a process.

The strategy selected by the mental health center stemmed from a need to change its past practice in charging for services. Historically, the mental health center had based its fees on the client's ability to pay, negotiated by each therapist for each client. This negotiation allowed therapists to treat low-income clients who could be significantly helped by their services, but it also led to variations in charges for clients with similar resources and problems. Welfare agencies and insurance carriers interpreted this practice as a sliding fee scale, which had two consequences for the center. First, third-party reimbursements were lost. Most welfare agencies and insurance carriers refuse to reimburse unless the provider organization has a fixed fee for services. Second, sliding fees led many clients to view the services of the mental health center as free: fully covered by public funds. With the anticipated cutbacks in federal subsidies, the center's cost recovery from these funds would fall from 80 percent to 50 percent, putting it in an untenable financial position.

The mental health center selected a strategy it called *scholarships*. The scholarship represented that portion of a client's care costs that would be borne by the center, paid for by public funds. Clients would be asked, during admission, to help the center determine how they would pay for the remainder of their care using a variety of sources, such as self-pay, insurance, Medicaid, and so on, and to authorize the center to pursue reimbursement from those payers. This strategy resulted in fixed fees, which allowed the mental health center to pursue aggressive fee collection from welfare and insurance sources and did not call for payments from low-income clients. It allowed the center simultaneously to increase its revenues and to maintain the humanitarian nature of the organization.

When several strategies are developed and

the organization has limited resources to invest, criteria such as cost, feasibility, acceptance, and effectiveness are used to evaluate them. After applying the criteria, the SMG may drop lower rated strategies to sharpen its focus and provide leverage for its limited resources. Having selected one or more strategies for implementation, the SMG does a pre-implementation feasibility assessment and enters a new stage.

Stage 5: Feasibility Assessment

The operating environments of public and third-sector organizations are quite complex. The attempt to introduce new strategies in such organizations ushers in considerations that go far beyond forecasting what services consumers will purchase. Besides the standard concerns for client or customer and employee views of changes, the political, financial, and legal implications of new strategic actions must be considered. To deal with this broader set of considerations a different kind of feasibility assessment is needed. As a result, our approach differs from traditional feasibility assessments in several ways. First, it involves extended discussions of who will be affected by the new strategy and how other parties could affect successful implementation. We call the activity *stakeholder analysis* because it identifies specific parties who can affect or are affected by the strategy to be introduced. We focus on the people or organizations with political, financial, managerial, professional, or other interests or stakes in the strategy, and we try to anticipate how they might respond as the strategy is communicated and implemented. Second, our approach assesses what resources are required to implement the strategy. Here we also extend the analysis to

go beyond finances to consider political, legal, managerial, professional, and other resources and who can supply them. Stakeholder and resource analyses clarify the range of joint commitments that must exist or be built between the organization and its stakeholders and resource suppliers if implementation of the strategy is to be successful. Top management is largely responsible for building these commitments. The operational and technical design and installation activities usually are delegated to others.

The limitations of time and resources call for the targeting of high-priority stakeholders. First, the SMG identifies stakeholders for the strategy under consideration. To aid in this listing, the SMG considers users of services, key providers of support, cooperating units, providers of services, and the like. After the list is completed, each stakeholder is ranked in terms of importance. When assigning ranks the SMG notes the nature of the stakeholder's interest or stake and whether the stakeholder comes from inside or outside the organization. Ranking clarifies how much and what kind of power the stakeholder has, suggesting the extent to which each stakeholder can influence the actions required by the strategy. For example, the mental health center's scholarship strategy called for a movement from a policy of free care to a more aggressive posture toward fee collection. The scholarship would underwrite a portion of the costs of care but would commit clients to help find ways to pay the rest. The SMG lists stakeholders and their stakes or interests in the strategy. Then each stakeholder's importance and posture (support, neutrality, or opposition) is identified to rank stakeholders as shown in Figure 8–2. The ranking puts stakeholders in categories called

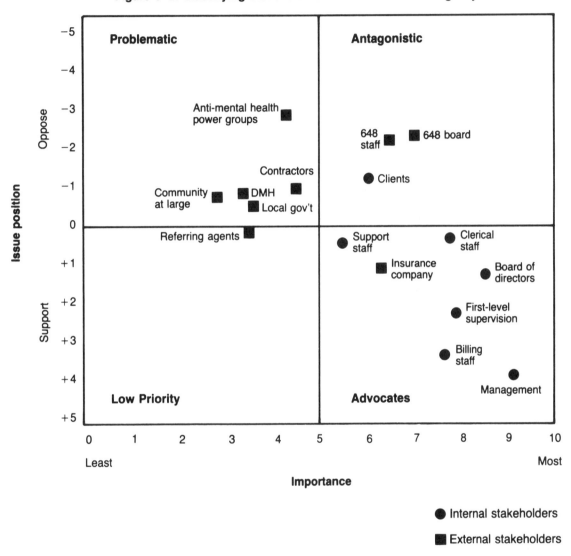

Figure 8–2. Classifying Stakeholders for a Mental Health Agency

low priority, antagonistic, problematic, and advocates for the next stage of the process.

The strategic management group begins resource analysis by listing the types of resources required to carry out the top-priority strategy and who might supply them. Both internal and external suppliers are often relevant. The forms of assistance can be fiscal and nonfiscal

resources, such as manpower, power and legitimacy, status, acceptance, knowledge or expertise, time, and existing programs. After listing resources the SMG assesses actions aimed at securing needed resources, using a ranking procedure similar to that used for stakeholders. Resources required by the strategy are assessed in terms of their criticality (importance) and potential availability (ease of finding or mobilizing). Ranking creates four categories, termed *essential scarcity* (critical with low availability), *core support* (critical with high availability), *auxiliary support* (noncritical with high availability), and *irrelevant* (noncritical with low availability).

Stage 6: Implementation

Our approach to implementation deals with the broad-scale concerns raised by a change in strategy, not with steps to install, for example, the mental health center's new billing procedures. Programs are devised to monitor and evaluate stakeholders' predicted actions and to manage resource suppliers. (Space does not permit a discussion of resource supplier management. Tactics follow the same line of reasoning as that described for stakeholders.)

The SMG applies analyses to each of the stakeholder categories in Figure 8–2. First, the numbers and proportions of stakeholders in each category are determined. Additional analyses are carried out to suggest the extent of each stakeholder's support or opposition; determine the homogeneity of the stakeholders in each category; determine the prospects for a coalition; and identify neutral stakeholders who could be targeted for lobbying. Finally, the SMG identifies tactics for dealing with each of the stakeholder categories (Freeman 1983).

Tactics to consider for potentially *antagonistic* stakeholders include the following:

1. Identifying potential coalitions by determining which neutral actors in the problematic and low-priority categories are closely aligned or related to the antagonistic stakeholders.
2. Taking steps to block coalitions of antagonistic stakeholders with those in the problematic category.

3. Preventing antagonistic stakeholders from undermining supporters.
4. Determining which antagonistic stakeholders must be surprised (kept in the dark) to prevent their opposition from mobilizing.
5. Anticipating the nature of objections and developing counterarguments for selected antagonistic stakeholders.
6. Engaging selected antagonistic stakeholders in bargaining; determining strategic changes that will ensure their neutrality, if not their support.

Potential *advocate* stakeholders are managed differently. The following tactics are suggested:

1. Providing information to reinforce advocates' beliefs.
2. Cooptation by involving key supporters in some of the SMG's deliberations or as members of the group.
3. Asking supportive stakeholders to sell the strategy to those who are indifferent.
4. When a balanced perspective is needed, asking stakeholders who are thought to be nearly neutral to react to the strategy after supporters and critics have taken their positions.

Problematic stakeholders pose fewer management problems. Some precautions are desirable, however, as noted below:

1. Preparing defensive tactics to be used if a coalition of problematic stakeholders emerges and takes a public position opposing the strategy.
2. Targeting moderates for education attempts.
3. Redefining the strategy so strongly that negative stakeholders opt out.

Finally, *low-priority* stakeholders need to be managed only under special conditions, such as when they are homogeneous and numerous. Tactics include the following:

1. Low-cost education for those near the importance boundary.
2. Promoting involvement with supporters to demonstrate depth of support for a strategy.

Figure 8–2 identifies stakeholders for the mental health center and its scholarship strategy. The importance of the stakeholders in the antagonistic category suggested a need for considerable caution. Stakeholders who were closest to a neutral position (clients) were approached initially. The SMG attempted to win these individuals over. The center held public meetings to involve clients in careful discussions of the issues, asking for their suggestions of ways to replace lost sources of revenue. Many of the external stakeholders were problematic, because they were not very important. For the problematic stakeholder, initial implementation avoided prematurely drawing attention to the scholarship strategy. The SMG also assessed those stakeholders to determine whether coalitions among them were possible and the probable implications of such coalitions for the scholarship strategy. For example, a coalition was possible between the department of mental health and local governments, so the SMG took steps to allay local government officials' fears, assuring them that the mental health center did not anticipate asking for funding from local governments. Finally, the community at large was targeted for education attempts using the mass media. From that point the implementation moved to industry contractors. The center made presentations attempting to convert those stakeholders to at least a neutral, if not a supportive, position. At this point, the center was ready to deal with the members of the 648 board and its staff. The 648 board was empowered to contract for men-

tal health services using state funds. These potentially antagonistic stakeholders presented a crucial barrier to implementation. The SMG anticipated objections to dropping the sliding fee scale and developed counterarguments. The center also developed a downside scenario: it described various actions, such as cutbacks in services and the like, that the center would have to take if a larger proportion of its service costs could not be reimbursed. The analysis included the proportion of its costs that it currently captured and showed different targets, associating various downside possibilities with each target. For example, after federal cutbacks revenues would be at 50 percent of costs; therefore, the center articulated scenarios at that level, at 65 percent, and at 95 percent, representing the current untenable situation, a problematic situation, and a good situation, respectively. The mental health center's scholarship strategy was presented as a way to preserve the humanitarian nature of its mental health services while assuring the center's survival.

PLANNING TECHNIQUES

Planning techniques (tools) are used to carry out activities, such as the SWOT analysis, required by each stage in the process (see Table 8–1). As noted above, *search, synthesis,* and *selection* steps are conducted for each of the activities required by each stage. Information and ideas are sought during search; patterns are uncovered in synthesis; and priority actions are identified in selection. For instance, the SMG searches for issues, identifies relationships (order or importance) among the issues, and selects an issue for immediate management. In this section we discuss techniques that can be used to aid the SMG in conducting a search, carrying out synthesis, and setting priorities. It should be noted that some of these techniques deal with all of the steps together. For example, in the nominal group technique (discussed below), participants search for ideas but also create some synthesis when they combine ideas after listing and create a basis for selection when they rank their priorities. Other techniques, specifically developed to aid syntheses or selection, can be combined with the nominal group technique to improve the patterning of information and to make the setting of priorities more reliable. Most search techniques can be improved in this manner (Nutt 1984). Combining techniques creates hybrids that improve results and add variety to the process. In the discussion that follows, we have grouped techniques under search, synthesis, or selection headings in order to highlight their primary use or value.

The Search Step

In the search step, the strategic management group seeks out the information required by each stage of the process, identifying historical context, making a system assessment, and specifying SWOTs, issues, action sets, resources, stakeholders, and other activities as described above. A number of techniques are particularly useful in the search for such information: interacting groups, silent reflective techniques, survey approaches, dialectics, synectics, and focus groups. These techniques can aid the SMG in uncovering ideas, making judgments, and exchanging views. We briefly summarize the techniques to show how each works and how each can be used to support the strategic management process.

Interacting groups. An interacting group has a conventional face-to-face format. Discussion is free flowing and open ended; the only set elements of procedure are an agenda and a leader to keep the discussion focused. *Brainstorming* is a kind of interacting group technique that is specifically useful for planning. In brainstorming, the leader challenges the group into a rapid-fire generation and modification of ideas (Osborn 1963). A key requirement is to keep the idea generation separate from idea evaluation.

Silent Reflective Techniques. Silent reflective techniques require each member of the strategic management group to identify SWOTS, issues, or the like before group discussion begins. A flaw of typical interacting groups is that members often make premature commitments, have inhibitions, or deliver hasty evaluations, thus shutting off valuable lines of inquiry (Bouchard and Hare 1970). Giving group members a chance to reflect before discussion helps to overcome these barriers to candor and stimulates their creativity. The *nominal group technique* (Delbecq and Van de Ven 1971) is a widely used silent reflection group process. In this technique, the group first reflects silently, then systematically considers the ideas generated by members. A four-step procedure is used: silent recording of ideas; listing ideas, giving each member a turn until the ideas all have been presented; discussing the ideas to consolidate the list and share information about the merits of each; and voting to select priority ideas.

Brainwriting (Gueschka, Shaude, and Schlicksupp 1975) is another silent reflection technique. *Cued brainwriting* is one variation of this technique (Nutt 1984). The leader initiates it by placing several written cues (e.g., SWOTs, issues) on sheets of paper in the center of the table. All of these sheets can be identical, or each can have a unique set of items. Each group member is asked to take a sheet, read it, and silently add his or her ideas. When a member runs out of ideas or wants to have the stimulation of another's ideas, he or she puts the list back in the center of the table and takes one returned by another member. After reviewing the new list the member adds more ideas, continuing until ideas are exhausted.

Another variation, called *structured brainwriting,* induces more synthesis among the ideas generated (Nutt 1984). The group leader labels several sheets with particular themes—such as directions (markets, programs, resources, and administrative system) or elements of the SWOTs situational assessment—that represent areas where ideas need to be generated. Each member is asked to list on each sheet ideas that occur related to the theme. After listing several ideas in one category, the SMG members exchange sheets. This process continues without discussion until the group runs out of ideas or time. Structured brainwriting creates synthesis around the themes that the leader initially selects and allows members to sort ideas into theme options, creating a second form of synthesis. These steps improve the quality of ideas without discouraging innovation.

Both the cued and structured versions of brainwriting use the round-robin procedure for presenting and listing ideas, as in the nominal group technique (Nutt 1984). (In the structured form several listing steps are required.) The members take turns, each describing one item on his or her current list, and the leader records the ideas. The listing continues until all members pass. Then the group discusses the ideas, commenting or elaborating on their ideas or the ideas of others. Assigning priorities by vote is the final step.

The *nominal interacting* technique (Souder 1980) introduces "anteroom lobbying" in the idea generation and ranking procedures. Group meetings are held that use the nominal group technique, brainwriting, or some other process, but the procedure is broken off at several points to allow lobbying. After a substantial number of ideas have been generated, the leader calls a break of 30 to 45 minutes; members go to another room, ostensibly to take refreshments. This step permits the emergence of their natural urges to share views and lobby each other. SMG members are encouraged to share opinions, exchange facts, challenge others' views, and bargain during the break. Although votes that assign priorities are confidential, members can ask for one another's ranking and its justification. These informal exchanges create greater mutual understanding and help the group avoid premature closure. Three lobbying sessions typically are needed before a final vote on priorities can represent the level of consensus possible in a particular group. Typically, the first session identifies the diversity of opinions. In the second, members begin to adopt or reject ideas. After the third, judgments can emerge based on new understandings.

Survey Approaches. A survey tests the sentiments in important reference groups, pooling judgments without discussion. The researcher creates a synthetic group by pooling responses from selected individuals. A *traditional* survey can provide a barometer of opinion, if respondents are selected by a random sample, or a reference point for discussion, if respondents are chosen because of their expertise.

In a *Delphi* survey (Dalky 1967) the researcher systematically selects the group and collates their judgments using a series of questionnaires. The first questionnaire solicits ideas, information, opinions, or viewpoints and asks the reasons behind them. Subsequent questionnaires collate the ideas and associated rationales and feed them back to the group. Each group member can review the logic behind the arguments of others, an exercise that can promote consensus. The process continues until the group reaches consensus, obtains sufficient information, or votes. The members' vote assigns priorities to the ideas.

Focus Groups. In the focus group technique, outside experts describe opportunities to the SMG. The experts can be brought in one at a time or as a panel, with the intent of provoking a dispute over their differing positions. Focus groups can be useful in informing the SMG and helping it focus on the most pertinent questions before it.

Dialectic Groups. The systematic examination of an issue from several points of view results in a dialectic (Mason and Mitroff 1981; Emshoff 1980). For instance, subgroups of the SMG can be asked to develop ideas based on radically different assumptions about the environment, constituencies, SWOTs, or the like. One subgroup presents its ideas, and the SMG debates the merits of those ideas. The purpose of the debate is to spell out the implication of each strategy, idea, or SWOT and to challenge it by exposing weaknesses in its underlying assumptions. Discussion of two competing alternatives is *not* a dialectic. A dialectic involves discussion of ideas that are based on different assumptions.

Dialectics have several benefits. First, the debate forces the group to consider a wide range of information. Pet options are subjected to careful and systematic scrutiny in which group members note how internal and external stakeholders would view the situation. This leads SMG members to develop fuller appreciation of each other's rationale, which may lead to synthesis and innovation. Dialectics may not work, however, when an issue is well structured or when there is preexisting conflict between certain group members.

Synectics. The synectics process was devised to promote creativity in groups (Gordon 1971). To enhance group members' comprehension of a problem, the leader uses a metaphor or an analogy to get the group to visualize a new perspective. The process helps purge preconceived notions. Direct, personal, and symbolic analogies are used to help members visualize new options. The group studies one analogy or metaphor after another to come up with an innovative idea. The process is then repeated. In the final step, ideas are modified to make them feasible. For example, Velcro fasteners were identified using this procedure. Their widespread use in apparel stemmed from a proposed, but impractical, application for space suits.

The Synthesis Step

In the synthesis step, the strategic management group seeks generalizations, patterns, or themes in the information (SWOTs, issues, strategic themes, stakeholders, etc.) produced by the search step. Techniques useful for synthesis include the snowball technique, scenarios, morphology, relevance trees, interpretive structural modeling, and policy capturing. These techniques are particularly useful as a group attempts to identify patterns, themes, and generalizations in an unorganized mass of information produced by the search step.

Snowball Technique. A group process for

generating ideas often creates long lists of partially integrated and overlapping ideas. The snowball technique (Greenblat and Duke 1981) is a way of finding labels that identify themes or generalizations that sum up bundles of ideas, such as public awareness, redefining clientele, modifying services, expanding services, and the like. To delineate such categories, the group sorts index cards that list the individual ideas that came out of the group's search step. (Each card might describe an issue, strategic action, stakeholder, or the like.) SMG members are asked to tape the index cards to a wall, grouping similar ideas, and then to label the resulting categories. No ownership of ideas or categories is allowed; anyone can change any label or exchange cards among categories. The SMG's members study the labels or categories and reorganize them without discussion. Stable patterns often emerge after three or four attempts at labeling and content modification. We find that these categories capture a synthesis or higher ordering of the initial idea pool.

Scenarios. Scenarios are constructed as a contingency framework that specifies how various possibilities combine to produce a variety of political, technological, or external event situations in which the strategy may have to function (e.g., Vanston et al. 1977). Different strategies emerge when each of these scenarios is used as a context for strategic management. A two-by-two table that contrasts high and low levels of crucial factors is a useful tool for constructing scenarios. The simplest form of the table is presented in Figure 8–3. (Three-by-three and more complex representations of options that depict intermediate levels of crucial factors are often desirable). For example, the mental health center SMG considered contingen-

Figure 8–3. Defining Scenarios for a Mental Health Agency

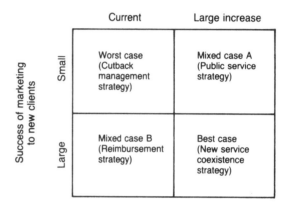

cies based on four situations (see Figure 8–3). The best-case scenario—successful marketing to new clients and enactment of a levy—calls for a strategy of providing new products and programs. Fee-for-service and poverty patients must coexist under this contingency. Plans are drawn with a coexistence strategy as a frame. If neither marketing nor efforts to increase the levy is successful, the worst-case scenario results, calling for a cut-back management strategy that sets priorities on clients' needs and drops low-need, non-paying patients and their providers. The mixed case A scenario results in a public service strategy that calls for an expansion of free care. Mixed case B calls for a reimbursement strategy. When new groups of clients begin to seek services, the mental health center must ensure that its industry-based programs and services can be expanded to produce additional revenues and that reimbursement from third-party payers (e.g., Medicaid) will be sufficient to cover the costs of the other services offered. The group develops a synthesis by finding the common threads in these strategies and treats the remaining strategies as options that could be used if contingencies (as shown in Figure 8–3) emerged.

Morphology. Zwicky (1968) devised the morphology technique to create many diverse options for the strategist to ponder. In morphology, a strategic option is defined by all possible combinations of elements for key components. For example, key components in a mental health plan could be the type of care and its urgency. All combinations of the acute, chronic, rehabilitative, and custodial care elements for the "care" component and the convenient, urgent, or emergent elements for the "urgency" component create nine strategic themes or options, such as acute-convenient care.

Tree Structures. A relevance tree has a hierarchy and subdivisions within hierarchical levels (Warfield 1976). The tree relates an overall objective to intermediate factors. Connections between levels show the relevance of these relationships. The highest level identifies the problem to be solved or objective to be met. Intermediate levels consider issues, such as environment, and would enumerate key elements of the issue, such as regulatory changes in reimbursement policy, as environmental elements. The tree terminates with a list of specific actions. The group can explore the relational properties in a relevance tree by using network techniques, such as interpretive structural modeling.

Interpretive Structural Modeling. Interpretive structural modeling (Warfield 1976) is used to describe relational properties, such as causality, severity, importance or priority, and precedence (order), to make an implicit structure explicit. The technique can be applied to issues,

strategies, problems, objectives, and other items that have relationships to develop a consensus about how they are related. Interpretive structural modeling is particularly useful in sorting out relationships among the mass of items typically produced by a group process. These items, in their raw form, partially overlap and lack any semblance of order. Interpretive structural modeling helps to establish order and eliminate redundancies.

The SMG can use interpretive structural modeling to determine, for example, the order in which issues should be addressed. To capture this ordering the group uses a *paired comparison* ranking technique. To make paired comparisons, each SMG member compares each item (e.g., SWOT, issue) with all other items, determining which should be addressed first. The leader counts how many members judged an item to be more severe, of higher priority, or a first consideration. The count provides an index of severity, priority, or precedence for each item. Alternatively, a consensus about the relative priority of items can be determined using a digraph. In this case, an arrow is used to depict which item of any pair precedes or determines the other. After an initial ranking, the leader allows discussion, encouraging the more informed SMG members to comment on linkages they know best. The discussion allows the SMG to learn about the structure of SWOTs, issues, strategies, and so on. The paired comparison procedure is repeated after discussion so that the final ranking reflects these matured views. The digraph in Figure 8–1 illustrates how issues uncovered by the mental health center were ordered.

Interpreting the digraph offers several kinds of insights. For example, the mental health center decided to consider first the billing issue (at the left of the digraph in Figure 8–1), because it preceded all but one of the other issues. The two issues on the right side of the digraph ("independent ventures" and "increased customers") were preceded by all but one issue, so the center's SMG thought them to be the products of other considerations. These issues were deferred for later consideration. The three circles in the center of the digraph show issues with feedback or interactive effects, shown by arrows that flow both to (depicting influence *by* other issues) and from (depicting influence *on* other issues) these issues. Each of the issues in the center of the digraph must be managed along with the priority issue (e.g., the billing issue). The SMG had to keep financial stability, allocation, and staff quality in mind as it created strategies to deal with the billing issue.

To capture causality among the items being considered, the SMG determines which of two items is causal, using paired comparisons. The arrows in the digraph show the relative strength of each item (e.g., a strategy, SWOT, issue) as both a cause and an effect. These relationships show how actions in one arena enhance or retard actions in another. The SMG then considers those relationships as issues, strategies, or the like emerge.

Policy Capturing. This technique elicits values from important individuals or groups by posing various strategic options defined by all combinations of key factors (Fisher 1979) or by examining the organization's past decisions and inferring the values that lie behind those decisions (Nutt and Hurley 1981). For instance, Fryback, Gustafson, and Detmer (1978) explored components of a medical scarcity policy by creating hypothetical geographic areas described in terms of infant mortality, physicians per 1,000 population, and other determinants of scarcity. Each geographic area represented a policy option that policymakers considered for funding. The researchers asked government policy groups to rank each hypothetical area by desirability. Nutt (1984) describes the "hypothetical decision seminar," in which the group creates strategic options through the morphology or snowball technique, then uses regression techniques to determine the relative importance of hypothetical or actual options. Policy capturing can be used to find which components of a strategy make it acceptable or unacceptable to key individuals and to identify factions within the SMG.

The Selection Step

In the selection step, the strategic management group uses criteria to winnow ideas. The purpose of this step is to set priorities among the generalizations, patterns, or themes that emerge from the synthesis step to provide a focus for action in the next stage of the process. Selection involves organizing the decision-making process in order to set priorities.

Estimate-Discuss-Estimate. This technique is a useful way to organize the setting of priorities. This approach recognizes that the strategic management group often wants time to reflect and regards all choices as preliminary pending more information (Nutt 1977). Reconsideration helps to reduce uncertainty about each member's position (Huber and Delbecq 1972). The estimate-discuss-estimate technique brackets discussion with ranking or rating to create informal lobbying opportunities that encourage disclosure and mutual adjustment among the SMG members. The initial order of priority often shifts after group members share information.

Q-Sort. A Q-sort (Kerlinger 1967) helps the SMG member sort priorities among large numbers of items (more than 60), such as strengths, weaknesses, threats, opportunities, issues, strategic actions, and stakeholders. When the task involves so many pieces of information, demands for information processing can make the ranking process unreliable. The Q-sort procedure has the SMG member first look for the most important items and then the least important ones, switching back and forth until all have been categorized. The number of items considered on each side of each sort is equal. The number of items considered in all of the sorts have the approximate shape of a normal distribution.

Merit Indexes. An index of merit for items on a list can be established using one or more criteria. Useful techniques for setting priorities include *anchored rating scales* (Nutt 1980), *paired comparisons, rank weight* (Huber and Delbecq 1972), *direct weight* (Gustafson et al. 1973), and *pooled rank* (Delbecq, Van de Ven, and Gustafson 1975).

TYPES OF STRATEGY

It is particularly important to carefully consider the nature of strategy being devised in public and third-sector organizations because of their complex environments, laced with politics, and the loose set of internal and external stakeholders that must be managed. Selection of hybrid techniques that recognize the specific needs of these organizations is essential. We use four requirements or expectations to differentiate types of strategy: *quality, acceptance, innovation,* and *preservation* (Quinn and McGrath 1983; Nutt 1977). All combinations of high or low importance accorded these criteria result in identification of 16 strategic types, as shown in Table 8–2.

Quality strategy is defined in terms of the comprehensiveness of considerations and degree of clarity in a strategy. Quality strategies call for services that have desirable performance features such as cost benefit. Acceptance strategy deals with the subjective views of people who can block or covertly subvert either the strategic management process or its product. A strategy with high acceptance has the support of boards of directors and other key groups. An innovative strategy is derived from ideas not previously recognized or attempted, in the hope that some of the ideas will offer a decisive advantage. For example, an innovative strategy may deal with clientele, services, and/or markets never before considered by the organization. Preservation strategy recognizes that requirements to maintain current arrangements and to work within them are often imposed on strategy making. Examples include sacrosanct procedures, policies, programs, or status as depicted by an organization chart that the organization does not want to challenge. The organization seeks to retain this order in the face of the chaos that strategic change may bring. These commitments become real values of the organization, not merely constraints, and thus become performance expectations in their own right. They set out an arena in which people can assume there will be order and continuity and act to preserve certain values.

Specific Strategies

The strategic management process is shaped by performance requirements. The stages of the process were devised to meet the needs of public and third-sector organizations. The hybrid techniques, in contrast, are selected by

Table 8–2. Techniques Best Suited for Each Strategic Type

Strategic Type	Requirements	Search Step	Synthesis Step	Selection Step
1. Comprehensive	Quality, acceptance, innovation	Structured brainwriting with dialectics and synectics	Snowball, interpretive structural modeling and scenarios	Q-sort, estimate-discuss-estimate and paired comparisons
2. Qualified Comprehensive	Quality, acceptance, innovation with important constraints	Cued brainwriting	Morphology	Estimate-discuss-estimate and rank weight
3. Traditional	Quality and acceptance	Nominal group technique	Snowball and scenarios	Q-sort and paired comparison
4. Constrained traditional	Quality, and acceptance with important constraints	Cued brainwriting	Interpretive structural modeling	Estimate-discuss-estimate and rank weight
5. Ideal prototype	Quality and innovation	Delphi with synectics	Snowball and scenarios	Q-Sort
6. Constrained prototype	Quality and innovation with important constraints	Focus group and structured brainwriting	Morphology	Q-Sort
7. Utility	Quality	Brainstorming	Tree structure	Anchored rating scale
8. Qualified Utility	Quality with important constraints	Cued brainwriting	Tree structure	
9. Awareness	Acceptance and innovation	Nominal group technique	Snowball, interpretive structural modeling and scenarios	Estimate-discuss-estimate and paired comparisons
10. Constrained awareness	Acceptance and innovation with important constraints	Cued brainwriting	Interpretive structural modeling	Estimate-discuss-estimate and rank weight
11. Seductive	Acceptance	Nominal interacting	Morphology with policy capturing	Any
12. Constrained seductive	Acceptance with important constraints	Cued brainwriting and nominal interacting	Morphology and policy capturing	Any
13. Idea	Innovation	Nominal group technique and synectics	Snowball and interpretive structural modeling	Estimate-discuss-estimate and paired comparisons
14. Constrained idea	Innovation with important constraints	Cued brainwriting and synectics	Interpretive structural modeling	Estimate-discuss-estimate and paired comparisons
15. Gesture	None	Interactive group	None	Pooled rank
16. Ratification	Recognizing important constraints	Synthetic group	None	Any

their ability to produce specific types of results. Specific performance expectations for the strategy can be matched to the expected merits of planning techniques. The strategic manager identifies the situation he or she believes the organization is confronting by laying out performance expectations and selecting hybrid techniques to meet needs, as shown in Table 8–2.

Comprehensive strategies require quality, acceptance, and innovation but pose minimal constraints; they offer the strategist a wide latitude of action but pose extensive expectations. This type of process would be used when an organization makes a commitment to consider significant changes in its services and clientele. The group processes used for the search step should engage the SMG in far-reaching considerations. As a result, structured brainwriting with a dialectical group process is recommended. Snowball, interpretive structural modeling, and scenarios are recommended to aid in the synthesis of ideas. Q-sort and estimate-discuss-estimate are recommended to prune the idea list and paired comparison to set priorities among items on the winnowed list.

The imposition of constraints calls for a *qualified comprehensive strategy*. A broad search is undertaken but the organization announces core values it seeks to preserve. When constraints are present, the cued brainwriting technique can be used to subtly introduce these requirements into the process without lowering acceptance and innovation. Morphology and estimate-discuss-estimate with rank weight are recommended for synthesis and selection, again to ensure that constraints are recognized.

Traditional strategies do not stress innovation but require quality and acceptance. Such a process could be mounted in response to external agents such as regulators that can impose certain sanctions unless the organization changes its policies or services. For example, Medicare reimbursement policy has forced hospitals to consider expanding outpatient services. Utility regulators call for the use of locally available gas and oil regardless of its storage and transportation costs. The strategy used by respected competitors that are faced with the same external pressures is often mimicked. Nominal group technique is preferred because it promotes both quality and acceptance. Morphology and estimate-discuss-estimate with rank weight are recommended for synthesis and selection tasks. When constraints are added, the process is called *constrained traditional*. For example, a utility may attempt to purchase locally available gas but continue to meet contractual obligations. It continues to transport gas from other states to avoid lawsuits and to ensure adequate gas supplies for worst-case scenarios stemming from extremes in weather. Cued brainwriting, interpretive structural modeling, and estimate-discuss-estimate with rank weight are recommended, for the reasons previously cited.

The *ideal prototype* calls for quality and innovation. The prototype creates a benchmark to gauge future efforts. Such a process can be undertaken by consulting firms to specify the range of strategic alignments that make sense for their current and/or projected clients. Because acceptance is not an issue, Delphi surveys are recommended. The surveys are designed to tap people with state-of-the-art information, by involving individuals inside and outside the firm. The Delphi survey is used to dredge up ideas for SMG consideration before using synectics. Snowball and scenarios are used for syntheses. A Q-sort winnows ideas. A focus group is used to ensure that ideas the organization wants considered get introduced to the SMG and that the group is oriented away from core values the organization wants to preserve in a *constrained prototype*. Structured brainwriting is applied to introduce quality. Morphology imposes a structure and a Q-sort creates a winnowed list of possible options for future consideration. In both ideal prototypes and constrained prototype processes, formal selection awaits selling a strategy to a client.

Strategies devised to seek only quality are called *utility*. This type of strategy is preferred when organizational leaders are both powerful and relatively independent of their board and regulatory agents. Not-for-profit organizations with fee-for-service revenue generation could adopt such a posture. Examples include consulting firms and some state organizations, such as departments of natural resources, that can charge for licenses or inspections mandated by law. Such an environment permits a proactively inclined leader to operate in a highly autonomous manner. When the leader is less interested in what's new than what works, a utility strategy seeking process can be used. The brainstorming technique is suggested. A tree structure can be used to capture the hierarchy being imposed by the CEO. Anchored rating scale offers a quick way to set priorities. A *qualified utility process* (quality and constraints) could be managed by cued brainwriting, synthesis by a tree structure, and selection by anchored rating scale.

Awareness strategy is carried out to inform an SMG about possibilities and to seek acceptance to act on possibilities that seem particularly relevant. Organizations that seek to coopt key stakeholders into exploring possibilities would use this type of strategy. A nominal group technique is proposed for search; snowball, interpretive structural modeling, and scenarios for syntheses; and estimate-discuss-estimate with paired comparison for selection for awareness strategy development. *Constrained awareness* strategies also seek the acceptance of possibilities but impose constraints on the search. For instance, a utility could use such a process to get top management to see new vistas for the organization, while recognizing pet ideas that pose constraints. For these strategies cued brainwriting is suggested for search, interpretive structural modeling for synthesis, and estimate-discuss-estimate with rank weight for selection.

For the *seductive strategy* only acceptance is important. Such strategy can arise when leaders are confronted by board members who insist that the organization devise a strategic plan. For example, business representatives on a school board may contend that schools without a formal strategy are run by the seat of the pants. The school superintendent may have a strategy, but prefers to keep it under wraps, for example, because of impending desegregation litigation, or may not see the merit in a strategic management process. In either case, only acceptance would be sought. Search techniques are preferred that make the member believe that something was accomplished but do not limit the leader's ability to maneuver (Mintzberg and Waters 1982). The nominal interactive process is recommended. Morphology with policy capturing can be used to explore emergent factors, seeking a synthesis of ideas acceptable to all. Any quick voting technique (e.g., anchored rating scale) can be used. *Constrained seductive* strategies (acceptance with constraints) calls for cued brainwriting to introduce constraints and nominal interacting with "plants" (people who lobby for ideas thought to be crucial) to promote acceptance. Syntheses and selection use the same techniques recommended for seductive strategy.

Idea strategies develop possibilities for contemplation, not action. Hospitals that explore ways to replace revenue losses due to reimbursement caps may develop such a strategy to inform themselves about possibilities without the friction of acceptance or the need to make assessments of quality. A creative process is needed for search; calling for synectics with each step of the synectics process managed by nominal group technique. Synthesis calls for snowball and interpretive structural modeling to capture the relationship. Selection is by estimate-discuss-estimate and paired comparison. *Constrained idea* strategies identify areas to be preserved before the organization sorts through possibilities. Cued brainwriting can be used for search, interpretive structural modeling for synthesis, and estimate-discuss-estimate with paired comparisons for selection to identify approximate ordering among a constraint list of ideas.

A *gesture strategy* is created when the process to derive strategy is mounted merely to impress third parties. Such a process may be rational when regulatory or legislative bodies give special consideration to organizations that carry out strategic management or appear to have produced a new strategy. For example, health regulators require evidence of a strategic plan before capacity expansion plans of a hospital will be considered. An interaction group, made up of people that the leader can control, is asked to elicit ideas and act as the SMG for a gesture strategy. The ideas can be recorded and voted on using a pooled rank voting technique. For a *ratification* strategy, synthetic groups are used, because constraints are important. Analysis of the survey can ensure that those constraints are identified. For instance, newspapers use this type of strategy when they conduct surveys of readers' preferences and then ignore preferences that conflict with editorial positions of the paper. Any format that makes voting easy can be used. The synthesis step can be ignored for gesture and ratification strategies.

CONCLUSIONS

Our strategic management approach has three key features: (1) its process, (2) techniques that support the process, and (3) guidelines for technique selection. We call for a movement of six process stages tailored to meet the needs of nonprofit, third-sector, and public organizations. This process recognizes some of the paradoxes and unique problems involved in doing strategic management in those settings, and shows a way to avoid such difficulties. The process moves through six stages, repeating three steps for each of the six stages. The activities and requirements are different for each stage, but each requires moving through the same three steps. Search, synthesis, and selection steps are taken to describe the historical context, conduct situational assessment, form an issue agenda, generate strategy, assess feasibility, and implement. We also describe techniques useful in carrying out the search, synthesis, and selection activities required in each stage. Many of the techniques we suggest are particularly useful in a single step, but most can be applied in many, if not all, of the six stages. Finally, we offer guidelines for the selection of techniques based on performance requirements imposed on the strategy, derived from the strategic manager's expectations.

We have identified several techniques that planners can use to aid a strategic management group as it carries out search, synthesis, and selection. As noted by Kaplan (1964) and others, planners with a repertoire of techniques are more effective than planners who use just a few techniques over and over again. We presented several techniques for each of the search, synthesis, and selection steps so that planners would have a variety of options on which to draw. Planners without such a repertoire tend to rely on past practices, which lead them to overusing favored techniques and failing to use process requirements as a guide to selecting techniques.

The notion of selecting techniques according to strategic requirements has an added benefit: Planners can combine various parts of techniques identified in this chapter. For example, using Q-sort along with the nominal group technique can make selection more effective. The snowball or interpretive structural modeling technique can be used with nominal groups to make synthesis easier. Planners can use brainwriting in place of the nominal group technique to increase variety and incorporate constraints into the search process. Some other hybrids include synectics merged with brainwriting and paired comparisons; nominal group technique with morphology and estimate-discuss-estimate; and brainwriting with snowball and paired comparisons. All possible combinations of the ten ways to search, six ways to synthesize, and seven ways to select make several hundred hybrid techniques planners can use when working with a strategic management group.

We call for planners to combine *thinking about* *action* with *acting thoughtfully* as they support a process to formulate and implement strategy. It is also important for planners to see themselves in roles that are required to support acting as well as thinking if they are to become involved in strategic management (Howe and Kaufman 1979). Our process calls for a planner to be a facilitator, teacher, and politician as well as a technician. Planners are facilitators when they help to carry out the strategy selection process, teachers when they demonstrate the need for each stage, and politicians when they aid in stakeholder management. To assume the role of a facilitator, the planner not only guides the SMG through the process stages and steps but also recommends and helps to apply appropriate techniques. For new strategic management teams, the planner also takes on the role of teacher. Planners must communicate the rationale behind stages and steps, handle informal questions, and provide guidance. Finally, planners help to link the process to political considerations within the SMG and to stakeholders who affect or are affected by the deliberations and actions. Planners provide a means to solicit points of view as a strategy emerges from the process. We believe planners must be prepared to adopt the roles of analyst, facilitator, teacher, and politician in each process stage if they are to deal with the ambiguous and politically sensitive business of fashioning a strategy and promoting its use.

AUTHORS' NOTE

The authors wish to acknowledge the assistance of John Bryson and the editors of the *Journal of the American Planning Association*, whose suggestions made many significant contributions to this chapter.

NOTE

1. The 648 board distributes state mental health funds to multicounty areas by contracting with mental health centers to offer services in those areas.

REFERENCES

Ansoff, H. E. 1980. Strategic issue management. *Strategic Management Journal* 1: 131–148.

Bouchard, T. J., Jr. and M. Hare. 1970. Size, performance, and potential in brainstorming groups. *Journal of Applied Psychology* 54, 1: 51–55.

Bryson, J. M., R. E. Freeman, and W. D. Roering. 1985. Strategic planning in the public sector: Approaches and future directions. Discussion paper 37. Minneapolis, Minn.: Strategic Management Research Center, University of Minnesota.

Dalky, N. 1967. *Delphi*. Santa Monica, Calif.: The Rand Corporation.

Delbecq, A. L. and A. Van de Ven. 1971. A group process model for problem identification and program planning. *Journal of Applied Behavioral Science* 7, 4: 466–492.

Delbecq, A. L., A. Van de Ven, and D. H. Gustafson. 1975. *Group techniques for program planning*. Glenview, Ill.: Scott-Foresman.

Emshoff, J. 1980. *Managerial breakthroughs*. New York, N.Y.: American Management Association.

Fisher, G. W. 1979. Utility models for multiple objective decisions: Do they accurately represent human preferences? *Decision Sciences* 10, 3 (July): 451–479.

Freeman, R. E. 1983. *Strategic management: A stakeholder approach*. New York, N.Y.: Pitman.

Fryback, D., D. H. Gustafson, and D. Detmer. 1978. Local priorities for allocation of resources: Comparisons with IMU. *Inquiry* 15, 3 (September): 265–274.

Gordon, W. J. J. 1971. *Synectics*. New York, N.Y.: Harper and Row.

Greenblat, K. S. and R. D. Duke. 1981. *Principles and practices of gaming simulation*. Beverly Hills, Calif.: Sage.

Gueschka, H., F. Shaude, and H. Schlicksupp. 1975. Modern techniques for solving problems. In *Portraits of Complexity*. Columbus, Ohio: Battelle Monograph Series.

Gustafson, D. H., R. Shukla, A. Delbecq, and G. Wallester. 1973. A comparative study in subjective likelihood estimates made by individuals, interacting groups, Delphi groups, and nominal groups. *Organizational Behavior and Human Performance* 9, 2 (April): 280–291.

Hatten, M. L. 1982. Strategic management in the non-profit organization. *Strategic Management Journal* 3: 89–104.

Howe, E. and J. Kaufman. 1979. The ethics of contemporary American planning. *Journal of the American Planning Association* 45, 3: 242–255.

Huber, G. P. and A. Delbecq. 1972. Gudelines for combining the judgments of individual members in decision conferences. *Academy of Management Journal* 15: 159–174.

Kaplan, Abraham. 1964. *The conduct of inquiry: Methodology for behavioral science*. San Francisco, Calif.: Chandler.

Kerlinger, F. N. 1967. *Foundations of behavioral research*. 2d ed. New York, N.Y.: Holt, Rinehart & Winston.

Mason, R. O. and I. I. Mitroff. 1981. *Challenging strategic planning assumptions*. New York, N.Y.: Wiley-Interscience.

Mintzberg, H. and J. A. Waters. 1982. Tracking strategy in an entrepreneurial firm. *Academy of Management Journal* Vol. 25, No. 3, pp. 465–499.

Nutt, P. C. 1977. An experimental comparison of the effectiveness of three planning methods. *Management Science* 23, 4: 499–511.

———. 1980. Comparing methods to weigh: Decision criteria. *Omega. The International Journal of Management Science* 8, 2: 163–172.

———. 1984. *Planning methods*. New York, N.Y.: Wiley.

——— and R. Hurley. 1981. Factors affecting capital expenditure review decisions. *Inquiry* 18, 2: 151–164.

Osborn, A. F. 1963. *Applied imagination*. New York, N.Y.: Scribners.

Porter, M. E. 1985. *Competitive advantage*. New York, N.Y.: The Free Press.

Quinn, R. E. and M. R. McGrath. 1983. Beyond the single solution perspective: The competing values approach as a diagnostic tool. *Journal of Applied Behavioral Science* 18, 4: 463–472.

Rainey, H. G., R. W. Backoff, and C. H. Levine. 1976. Comparing public and private organization. *Public Administration Review* 36, 2 (March/April): 233–244.

Souder, W. E. 1980. *Management decision methods*. New York, N.Y.: Van Nostrand Reinhold.

Vanston, J. R., Jr., W. P. Frisbie, S. C. Lodeato, and D. L. Poston, Jr. 1977. Alternative scenario planning. *Technological Forecasting and Social Change* 10: 159–180.

Warfield, J. N. 1976. *Societal systems*. New York, N.Y.: Wiley.

Weick, Karl, 1979. *The social psychology of organizing*. Reading, Mass.: Addison-Wesley.

Zwicky, F. 1968. *Discovery, invention, research through the morphological approach*. New York, N.Y.: Macmillan.

External Scanning—
A Tool for Planners

ANN M. PFLAUM
TIMOTHY J. DELMONT

External scanning allows managers and planners in both public and private sector organizations to identify emerging trends, to minimize the number of surprises they encounter, and to enhance strategic thinking and planning.[1]

Although external scanning is newer in the public sector than in the private sector, we are beginning to see it used in a variety of public sector settings. Accordingly, in the first part of this chapter we examine external scanning in 10 public sector organizations selected for their reputations for leadership in the use of this technique.[2]

Five of the 10 public organizations studied are state or local: the Florida Office of Planning and Budgeting; Hennepin County, Minnesota; the Minnesota Department of Transportation; the Minnesota State Planning Agency; and the Toledo Area Council of Governments. Five of the organizations are more national in focus: the Congressional Clearing House on the Future; the Council of State Policy and Planning Agencies; the United Way of America; the University of Minnesota; and the Pennsylvania State University.

In the second part of this chapter we present a model approach to external scanning.

The approach is based on the generally accepted view of the technique as a three-part activity: *scanning,* the identification of key issues and trends; *analysis,* interpreting their strategic importance; and *reporting/referral,* creating products useful for planning and decision making.[3]

Deriving conclusions from this review of practice and theory, we suggest that external scanning is gaining acceptance as a viable technique for public sector organizations; that an in-house volunteer approach to external scanning can be cost-efficient and cost-effective; that a final verdict on its durability is premature; and that the greatest usefulness of the practice is in its use to enhance qualitative rather than quantitative insights.

SCANNING IN 10 PUBLIC SECTOR ORGANIZATIONS

For this overview of external scanning as practiced in 10 public sector organizations, we examine (1) products, purposes, and staffing; (2) analytical techniques; and (3) issues identified. We created this overview through telephone interviews with 10 public sector scanners. Here we summarize the findings from this informal survey, noting, where applicable, points where public practice converges with practice in private sector planning, especially as documented in research (Engledow and Lenz 1985) on external scanning in seven corporations.

Products, Purposes, and Staffing

Newsletters documenting issues and trends identified by the scanning teams were the principal products of five of the organizations studied: the Florida Office of Planning and Budgeting, the Minnesota Department of Transportation, the Minnesota State Planning Agency, the Congressional Clearing House on the Future, and the Council of State Policy and Planning Agencies.

Although such newsletters are aimed at insiders, editors report increasing requests by outsiders—often other scanners—to be added to circulation lists. The purpose of the newsletters was similar among the organizations studied: To identify key issues and trends, primarily for internal audiences.

Comprehensive scanning reports and brief analytical pieces on trends (scans) are also products of scanning in the 10 public organizations studied. The United Way of America produced for its member agencies a comprehensive scanning report titled *What Lies Ahead—A Mid-Decade View: An Environmental Scan Report.* The report was designed as part of United Way strategic planning and was prepared under the direction of a blue-ribbon panel of national advisers, many of them leaders in the field of external scanning. In addition, more than 50 volunteers from United Way communities across the country contributed to the report.

The Pennsylvania State University likewise used a large group to produce a comprehen-

sive environmental scanning report that was designed to initiate strategic planning under a new university president.

Brief scanning reports are prepared as part of the Council of State Policy and Planning Agencies scanning process and have been used at the University of Minnesota and in the Minnesota and Florida state planning agencies.

Seminars offered by the Congressional Clearing House bring national experts on scanning, futurists, and other experts together with members of Congress. The relative success of such seminars and hearings has led to plans to offer similar sessions in a number of legislative districts.

Information exchanges and scanning networks offer an opportunity to connect scanners in the public and private sectors in order to identify emerging issues and to analyze their importance. The University of Minnesota has hosted such sessions quarterly since 1985. Planners from three universities (Minnesota, Pennsylvania State, and Texas) have met on two occasions to exchange information about scanning—both on substantive issues and on analytical techniques. Members report that the Council of State Policy and Planning Agencies network is helpful in making contacts beyond state boundaries and that it enhances their individual scanning efforts.

Scanning as preparation for strategic planning appears to be an important purpose in both private and public sector scanning. Engledow and Lenz (1985), for example, in a study of environmental analysis found that four of seven public corporations studied used external scanning as a part of strategic planning. Of the 10 public sector organizations we surveyed (Table 9-1), five carried out external scanning as part of their planning activities

(United Way of America, University of Minnesota, Pennsylvania State University, Hennepin County, and the Toledo Area Council of Governments).

Even more pronounced than using external scanning as an aid to strategic planning was its use by nine of the 10 organizations surveyed to collect information on emerging issues and trends to reduce the likelihood of being caught off guard by unforeseen events.

On the other hand, the Toledo Area Council of Governments, a consortium of 50 units of government, was the only one of the organizations surveyed that used external scanning primarily as an exercise to inform and structure citizen participation in local government. A part of the Toledo rationale for the citizen education view of scanning was that a galvanized public opinion, when congruent with the judgment of the professional administrators, could produce a coalition around particular issues. That was the case with the issue of rapidly escalating liability and risk management costs, which was identified as strategic both by the citizen scanners and by the professional administrators. As a result, elected officials have supported the professional administrators in exploring the possible strategy of creating a regional pool of risks to lessen liability costs.

Participants and staffing that relied on a combination of paid in-house coordinators or lead people and volunteer inside scanners were used by nine of the 10 public sector organizations. The exception was the Congressional Clearing House, which accords the dominant role in scanning to its full-time professional staff. One result of the part-time staff and volunteer pattern is that efficiency becomes very important, since participants in external scanning are typically fitting this responsibility alongside other responsibilities.

Analytical Techniques Used in External Scanning

Authorities on external scanning note an array of possible analytical techniques: brainstorming, Delphi, impact/probability, issue networks, and scenarios (Morrison and Renfro 1984; Wilson 1983).[4]

Of the 10 public organizations we studied, each reported using some form of group discussion or brainstorming among scanners as the most important tool for helping them to analyze and rank trends and issues identified through scanning. There seemed wide consensus in the literature of external scanning (Morrison and Renfro 1984; Olsen and Eadie 1982; Wilson 1983) that insights of a qualitative or integrative nature are among the most important products of external scanning. Quantitative analytical techniques associated with external scanning have been used only sparingly and sporadically by scanners in both the private and public sectors (Klein and Linneman 1984; Stubbart 1985).

The 10 organizations we surveyed were experimenting with a variety of analytical techniques. The United Way reported using a computerized polling process to assist them in obtaining and rapidly tabulating the views of their external scanning board.[5] Congressional Clearing House staff members reported using scenario generation occasionally; the Council of State Policy and Planning Agencies reported using nominal group techniques to help its advisory board sort issues; and the Minnesota Department of Transportation has been using impact matrices and impact/probability assessments.[6] The two universities in the sample

Table 9–1. External Scanning in 10 Public Sector Organizations

Organization	Products	Purposes	Participants/staffing	When initiated	Analytical techniques	Issues identified	New directions/comments
State/regional							
Florida Office of Planning & Budgeting	Scans; newsletter	To improve planning in Florida; to learn from issues/trends in other states through CSPA network	1 full-time employee spending 2 weeks per month to produce newsletter; 7–9 staff members in planning and evaluation unit, 8 hours a month	1982	Scans ranked by scanning team on a scale of 1–5 of suitability for inclusion in newsletter	Challenges from growth; sees emerging political power of baby boom generation	New administration may bring different priorities that may alter commitment to scanning, but newsletter recipients indicate satisfaction with product
Hennepin County, Minnesota	Trend profiles; strategic issues newsletter	To inform issue identification; to improve county's strategic planning and management	Produced by staff from planning and finance departments; 40 issues studied by 8- to 10-person issue teams	1982	Policy analysis of demography, finances, land use; group discussion	Civil liabilities; declining county tax base; disaster recovery	Newsletter being developed
Minnesota Department of Transportation	Newsletter	To provide agency staff with a broader perspective and new information	3/4-time editor; 4 hours a week; volunteer scanners; 6-person team meeting 2 hours monthly	1986	Matrix/impact probability	Automated highways; career structure within agency; reduced federal funds for highway construction	Scanning aided by contacts with CSPA and Congressional Clearing House planners
Minnesota State Planning Agency	Newsletter; public presentations on emerging demographic trends	To present policy issues early in their development; to exchange information with organizations within the state	Editor/coordinator 1 day a week; 7–9 scanners 8 hours a month	1985	Group discussion	Teen pregnancy; increase in insurance liability costs; indoor air quality (identified as a socially desirable and popular issue for executive leadership)	Reviewing workers' compensation costs and policies
Toledo Area Council of Governments	Brief oral reports on emerging issues	To provide for citizen input to the council; to use citizens as scanners; to increase awareness of emerging issues; to forge better links between professionals and citizens	3/4-time staff liaison works with 15-member citizen committee from different areas	1986	Group discussion; issues divided into 5 areas: health, social, political, international, economic development	Escalating costs in liability/risk management	Proposed strategy: regionally-based risk pooling to lessen liability insurance costs

Table 9-1. (Continued)

National Congressional Clearing House	Issue papers (1–2 pages); new technology summary; seminars with outside experts	To inform legislators and their staffs on emerging issues/trends; to influence context and character of legislation	8 full-time professional scanners/analysts; participating Congressmen; outside policymakers and futurists	1976	Staff generally does not use matrices; does use scenarios; executive board votes priorities annually	Need for alternative health care system; new directions in trade and investment policy; impact of innovative technologies	1986–87 focus: the environment; impact of emerging technologies and demography; hearings and seminars will be brought to legislative districts
Council of State Policy and Planning Agencies	Newsletter; data base; report to governors	To share issues and information among state planning agencies; to inform governors of key emerging issues	1 full-time national coordinator; 18-member national scanning board; 8 participating state scanning groups	1984	Reading/information pooling; national board uses nominal group technique and voting to select issues for governors	Opportunity for enhancing state revenues (e.g., taxing oil revenues in state land); national spread of citizen "initiative" in the political process (from west to east)	Computerized data base being developed. In the future scanners may be able to communicate across state lines
United Way of America	"What Lies Ahead: A Mid-Decade View—An Environmental Scan Report"	To enhance national and local United Way strategic planning	2½ full-time employees work with 35-member scanning board; 50 volunteer scanners in member United Ways also assist	1984	Consensor used to carry out Delphi inquiries; group discussion	Baby boom generation interest in direct participation in philanthropy led to donor options, new United Way links with cancer/heart funds to respond to donor preference for inclusiveness	Scanning creates new dialogues/partnerships as scanners work with urban planners, public officials, and foundations to address community needs
University of Minnesota	Scans; policy papers; seminars for scanning practitioners; national contacts on scanning	To avoid surprises; to enhance planning; to stimulate strategic thinking; to network with other organizations	10- to 12-volunteer team; two 3/4-time employees; two graduate interns at 1/4 time each; external scanning group of professionals	1982	Group discussion	Animal rights movement; opportunities in university/industry collaboration	Since 1982, scanning approaches varied; internal team, graduate interns, coalition of professionals, outside advisers, and shared scanning with peer institutions
Pennsylvania State University	Environmental scan	To influence strategic planning; to legitimize new directions	4-month intensive effort; 6 full-time employees and 60 faculty members	1984	Group discussions; staff research and analysis	Escalating liability costs; choosing appropriate telecommunications systems	Scanning at unit level will supplement universitywide scan

drew upon resident experts on their faculties— economists, demographers, and social historians—to help guide their scanning.

ISSUES AND TRENDS IDENTIFIED THROUGH EXTERNAL SCANNING

What kind of information has external scanning typically produced? We asked the 10 organizations surveyed to identify examples of information generated through external scanning. Obviously, the issues cited represent a snapshot of issues as they appeared in the summer of 1986. Ongoing monitoring may well produce a different listing of issues. The results can be grouped into six categories.

1. *Revenue-related issues and trends* included redefining the U.S. trade and investment policy (Congressional Clearing House); strategies for maximizing income outside the property tax (Hennepin County); taxing oil operations on state rights-of-way (Council of State Policy and Planning Agencies); and creating university/industry partnerships in equipment purchase and entrepreneurial ventures (University of Minnesota).

2. *Social/political value shift trends* included attending to the values of the baby boom generation—as a potential enrollment pool (University of Minnesota); allowing for direct donor option (United Way of America); and acknowledging and planning for an emerging political constituency (Florida).

3. *Computation, communication, and information systems trends* included attending to developments in artificial intelligence and robotics (Congressional Clearing House); building industry ties to expand supercomputing niche (University of Minnesota); assessing the implications for member agen-

cies of technology in the work place (United Way); and use of sensors and robotic technology in traffic monitoring (Minnesota Department of Transportation).

4. *Liability and risk management cost increases* were identified through scanning in four of the 10 organizations studied. Hennepin County has completed an in-depth report on strategies for reducing civil liabilities. The Toledo Area Council of Governments is exploring a regional consortium to create a pool of risk to diminish cost to individual units of government. The Minnesota State Planning Agency has used scanning to create additional time to formulate responses to the threat of premium and cost increases. The Pennsylvania State University also gained time through an early warning; it used the time to develop strategies to deal with escalation in health center liability premiums and with liability exposure related to alcohol use by students.

5. *Health care* figured in the scanning products of the Congressional Clearing House, leading to a focus on cancer and heart research as well as exploration of alternative health care delivery systems. In Hennepin County identification of health care as an issue led to service contracts with health maintenance organizations as well as reorganization of services within the county bureau of health.

6. *Other issues and resulting actions* included developing a plan for disaster recovery and programs for dealing with teen pregnancy (Hennepin County); reassessment of policies on research on live animals (University of Minnesota); consideration of public sector child care delivery (Florida); and strategies for dealing with reduced federal funds for highways (Minnesota Department of Transportation).

Before we move away from the review of external scanning in practice, it is appropriate to reflect on lessons that might be learned from the public sector practitioners of external scanning.

First, there is no evidence to suggest that differences between public and private sectors (Ring and Perry 1985; Bryson, Van de Ven, and Roering 1985; Pflaum and Delmont 1985) make the practice of external scanning inappropriate for the public sector. In fact, differences such as greater susceptibility to political pressure, less flexibility in personnel policies, and fragmented authority may make a practice such as external scanning more valuable in the public sector than in the private sector.

Second, since the use of external scanning is comparatively recent in both the public and the private sectors, it will be important to watch developments in both practice and theory before we arrive at definitive judgments about this practice.[7] At present, we can characterize the mood of the 10 practitioners surveyed as one of cautious enthusiasm. Practitioners have found the networks and contacts made through external scanning valuable and appear reasonably confident that they are identifying significant emerging issues.

Third, discussions on the usefulness of external scanning generally are based on the premise that its greatest potential value lies in insights and information that supplement quantitative analysis (e.g., Wilson 1983; Morrison and Renfro 1984). Stubbart (1985, p. 73), for example, suggests that data bases and forecasts alone cannot equip a planner to deal with turbulent changes. He suggests that being limited to the framework of quantifiable data may well contribute to "an inflexible pattern of thinking." By contrast, he cites as a chief benefit of external scanning "the flexibility of multiple perspectives that it can offer."

Three of the 10 public sector practitioners of external scanning we surveyed said external scanning helped them arrive at insights about their organizations that they might not have gained through other forms of analysis. For scanners connected with the Florida State Planning Agency, that meant seeing growth as a unifying principle connecting a number of separate trends and issues (population patterns, transportation, the environment, education, and politics). An integrative insight observed by Minnesota planners was the increasing competition that the state would face in medical instrumentation and biotechnology industries. Minnesota had entered these fields relatively early, ruling out a role in heavy industry because of the state's distance from eastern markets. As Minnesota's northeastern competitors began to be squeezed by foreign competition in heavy industry, however, they began to invade the medical instrumentation/biotechnology arena. An integrative insight for the University of Minnesota encouraged it to present more forcefully to its constituents its unique character among public universities as a combined international research university, land-grant institution, and urban institution intimately a part of the Twin Cities metropolitan area.

Finally, although there are perceived benefits from information gained on emerging issues and trends, practitioners also cited negatives associated with external scanning. In this regard, practitioners surveyed cited its costs in time and the difficulty of ensuring that information gathered would be the information needed.

A THREE-PART MODEL OF EXTERNAL SCANNING FOR PUBLIC SECTOR ORGANIZATIONS

Scanning

In the triad *scanning, analysis,* and *reporting/referral,* scanning is frequently described by analogies that emphasize its use of readings and other information-gathering techniques to broaden perspectives. Hence images such as "radar" or "helicopter view" are used to describe this activity (e.g., Wilson 1983). The main elements in this phase of the process are clarifying purposes, selecting participants, defining time commitments, and deciding on appropriate structures through which to obtain the desired breadth of view. Below we elaborate on how each of those activities helps ensure success in the scanning phase of this process (see Table 9–2).

Clarifying Purposes. Gaining information on emerging trends and gaining insights for strategic planning are two of the most common purposes associated with scanning—purposes that pertain in both public and private sector contexts. Information on emerging trends can be exchanged at national, regional, or local meetings. Such meetings can attract people primarily from a single field, or they can include people from different disciplines, as might be typical in local or regional meetings. The American Planning Association's annual meeting might be a forum that planners could use to discuss how to carry out external scanning and to discuss key trends and issues that they commonly face.

Scanning also can be used as part of strategic planning. In this context, external scanning is the external information-gathering activity that forms one of the two paramount perspectives in the SWOT analysis.[8] From the combined external and internal perspectives that emerge from the SWOT analysis, planners can deduce strategic direction for an institution or organization.

Clarifying desired purposes for carrying out external scanning is necessary as a first step in establishing this technique, since that decision will guide subsequent ones. The next step in scanning involves making decisions about who should carry out scanning.

Selecting Participants. The selection of participants for external scanning offers several possibilities. We recommend following the fairly common pattern of a designated lead person with volunteer in-house scanners. Most observers agree that the dedication of the lead person is crucial to the success of external scanning (Stubbart 1985; Morrison, Renfro, and Boucher 1983). Ideally, the volunteers to participate in external scanning should come from a cross section within the organization and should include people who are comfortable with reading and discussion (Wilson as quoted in Albert 1983).

The rationale for a volunteer scanning team (typically 10–12 people) with diverse responsibilities is that it creates structural breadth. If at all possible, the team should combine staff and line participants. For the public sector, moreover, we recommend including a cross section of elected officials, professional administrators, and representatives of the general public.

Beyond the scanning team, some organizations have used advisory panels to receive and comment on the information collected (e.g., United Way, Council of State Policy and Planning Agencies, Congressional Clearing House, and Toledo Council). Others have taken the

Table 9–2. A Three-Part Model of External Scanning for Public Sector Organizations

A. Scanning—surveying the external environment to identify key trends that are threats or opportunities
1. Clarifying purposes
   - Identifying emerging trends
   - Minimizing surprises
   - Enhancing strategic thinking and planning
2. Selecting participants
   - Lead person
   - Insider/volunteers; network of volunteers
   - Outside consultants
3. Defining time commitment
   - Annually or quarterly (half-day or full-day session)
   - Monthly (2–3 hours)
   - Bimonthly (2 hours)
4. Deciding on structure
   - Selecting issue categories (e.g., social, economic, political/regulatory, technological)
   - Identifying appropriate sources (professional journals, popular press, conference proceedings, informed people)
   - Interpreting issue cycles (aggregation of events, emergence of opinion leaders, appearance of new writings, action by leading-edge "bellwether" individuals or regions, involvement by larger organizations)
   - Asking key questions (Is the idea or trend new? Does the item come from a surprising source? Does it contradict prevailing wisdom? Is there a pattern of ideas or events?)
   - Developing a simple recordkeeping system (e.g., an initial foray into environmental scanning does not require a computerized keyword tracking system; filing by category will be adequate)

B. Analysis—intepreting the strategic importance of issues and trends
1. Reviewing commonly used tools
   - Brainstorming
   - Delphi
   - Impact/probability matrix
   - Issue network
   - Nominal group technique
   - Scenario writing
2. Selecting techniques that are efficient to use and appropriate to issues identified
3. Deciding on issue status: issues to monitor, issues to refer for immediate action, issues to drop from further consideration

C. Reporting/referral—creating products useful for planning and decision making
1. Preparing "scans," which give a brief statement on selected issues cited through scanning and identified as significant through analysis
2. Developing a comprehensive environmental scan that organizes and compiles the individual scans
3. Developing in-depth policy papers that document high-priority issues—three to five pages that amplify information presented in scans
4. Presenting issues or trends through a seminar or discussion forum that allows for broad discussion of an emerging issue or set of issues
5. Creating a newsletter that selects pertinent scans and presents them to interested audiences
6. Creating networks and partnerships to deal with common issues

approach of having the external scanning team report directly to decision- and policymaking bodies (e.g., in Hennepin County to the cabinet, in Toledo to the executive council, in the Council of State Policy and Planning Agencies to the governors).

Outside consultants on external scanning are also an option—either to offer workshops or training sessions in how to carry out scanning or to offer access to information and data bases. Although major national consultants on futures research (such as SRI and Weiner Edrich Brown) may be beyond the resources of individual public sector organizations, representatives of such consulting firms have assisted public sector scanning by serving on advisory panels (e.g., United Way of America, CSPPA

National Board, advisory board that created the Foresight Task Force). Moreover, experience has shown that scanners in both public and private domains are generous in helping those who are new to the field.

Defining the Time Commitment Expected for External Scanning. This is critical to its success and momentum. Sensitivity to the time demanded of volunteers is a factor that the private philanthropic sector has developed to great effect, and it can be adopted readily and easily, we believe, in the public sector.

Essentially, we see three options (Weisbord 1984; Nanus 1982) for timing of meetings: (1) carrying out external scanning as an annual occurrence—perhaps structured in connection with a retreat or annual meeting—in which case the desirable meeting time might be four to eight hours; (2) carrying it out quarterly—in which case the time spent might be two or three hours each quarter; or (3) carrying it out twice monthly—meeting two to three hours at a time.

Beyond periodic meetings to discuss issues and trends is the time devoted to reading—a foundation activity in scanning. Estimates of the time spent on this vary. The key to success, participants note, is that most professionals devote at least some portion of their time to reading anyway. What external scanning does is provide a shared framework within which to exchange information. Structuring the scanning framework involves establishing agreed-on categories for organizing information and may involve targeted reading of particular periodicals or assigning scanners to particular areas of focus. Once the structure is agreed on and the scanners begin reading, they may not be spending significantly more time reading than they had previously.

Deciding on Structure. At the heart of scanning are five decisions related to structure: selecting issue categories, identifying sources, interpreting issue cycles, asking key questions, and developing record-keeping systems.

1. *Selecting issue categories,* essentially around the core topic areas: social, economic, political, and technological. The reason for issue categories is to have concepts around which to organize information. Often an organization carrying out external scanning may add a category closely tied to its mission and purposes (e.g., the University of Minnesota added education, and the Toledo Area Council of Governments added economic development and health).

2. *Identifying appropriate sources,* including books, periodicals, conference proceedings, newspapers, and informed people likely to have insights into emerging issues. Using volunteers to read widely and to meet with experts and opinion leaders is at the core of the scanning process.

3. *Interpreting issue cycles.* Scholars and futurists believe events have a predictable pattern that allows a trained observer to identify issues early in a cycle. The issue cycle begins with isolated events, proceeds to a convergence of opinion, events, leaders, action by leading-edge groups, increasing media attention, and legislative/regulatory interest. Then the issue begins to subside on the public agenda (Molitor 1979; Foresight Task Force 1983). Accordingly, the scanner can learn to spot where within the cycle a particular issue falls. The goal for the scanner is to identify issues earlier rather than later in such a cycle.

4. *Asking key questions* to identify relevant facts, issues, and trends. Possible questions (*ShellScan Newsletter* 1982) include the following: Is the idea new? Does it contradict prevailing wisdom? Does it come from a surprising source? Is there a pattern of prevailing events? Using such questions can serve to direct the scanner's attention to significant emerging trends.

5. *Developing a record-keeping system* to maintain records of issues identified and discussed. Initially a paper filing system can be built around broad issue categories. The scanner also can consider a computerized keyword data base, although to date there is no single convention on keywords (see Figure 9–1 for the keyword list used by the University of Minnesota). The Council of State Policy and Planning Agencies main-

Figure 9–1. Keyword Checklist Used in Scanning by the University of Minnesota

KEY WORD CHECKLIST

Check all key words which apply. At least three key words must be checked in order for this report to be filled in the data base.

Social/Political
- abortion (abort)
- agriculture (ag)
- animal rights (anl rit)
- apartheid (apart)
- bilingualism (biling)
- business/industry (bus/ind)
- civil rights (civ rit)
- consumer rights (consum rit)
- environment (environ)
- foreign relations (for rel)
- foreign trade (for trade)
- health care (hlth care)
- housing (hous)
- legal issues (legal is)
- military/defense (mil/def)
- social protest (soc prot)

Economic
- economic indicators (econ indic)
- income distribution (incm dist)
- industrial development (ind dev)
- labor force characteristics (lbr frc)
- taxes (tax)
- regulation (reg)
- trade (trade)

Lifestyles, Values Groups
- academic (acad)
- American Indian (am ind)
- Asian (asian)
- baby boomers (baby boom)
- Black (black)
- childhood (child)
- education (ed)
- elderly (elder)
- feminist (fem)
- fitness/health (fit/hlth)
- Hispanic (hisp)
- leisure (leis)
- marriage/family (marri/fam)
- non-western (nonwest)
- poor (poor)
- religion (relig)
- work (work)
- youth/teens (youth)
- Yuppies (yup)

Demography

Population trends (pop trend):
- global/internat'l population (glob pop)
- USA population (usa pop)
- regional population (reg pop)
- Minnesota population (mn pop)

Societal structures (soc struc):
- agriculture structure (ag struc)
- migration patterns (migra struc)
- minorities (minor)
- mobility (mobil)
- socio-economic status (socecon stat)

Science/Technology
- artificial intelligence (art intel)
- biotechnology (biotech)
- computation (comput)
- telecommunications (telecom)

Elementary/Secondary Education
- curriculum (curric)
- enrollments (enroll)
- financing (financ)
- policy (policy)
- reports on (rep on)
- students (student)
- teachers/staff (teach/staff)

Postsecondary Education
- admissions (admis)
- athletics (athlet)
- benefits (ben)
- budgets (budget)
- cocurriculum (cocurric)
- computation (comput)
- computation, communication, Information (cci)
- equipment (equip)
- evaluation (eval)
- facilities (facil)
- faculty salaries/compensation (fac-sal)
- faculty/staff (fac/staff)
- faculty vitality (fac-vit)

Postsecondary Education (continued)
- fellowships (flshp)
- financial aid (fin aid)
- governance (gov)
- graduate education (grad-ed)
- graduate/professional (grad/prof)
- graduate student (grad-stu)
- high ability program (hi-abil)
- higher education (hi-ed)
- honors program (honor)
- industry relations (ind rel)
- interdisciplinary program (interdis)
- international education (int-ed)
- international program (int-prog)
- investments (invest)
- language program (lang)
- legislative appropriations (leg appro)
- lower division (low div)
- marketing/public relations (mark/pr)
- merit pay (mer-pay)
- nontraditional (nontrad)
- other institutions (other inst)
- patent policy (patent)
- planning/management (plang/mgt)
- private contributions (priv contrib)
- remedial (development) programs (dev-prog)
- reports on (rep-on)
- research (res)
- sabbatical (sab)
- SEE (see)
- seminars/symposia (sem)
- service (serv)
- school relations (school rel)
- single quarter leave (sql)
- student experience (stu-exp)
- students (student)
- student services (stud-serv)
- support services (sup serv)
- teaching (teach)
- technology collection/transfer (tech-tran)
- tenure and promotion (tenure)
- upper division (up-div)
- world affairs committee (world-afrs)

Subject Areas/Units:
- agriculture (ag)
- computer center (comput ctr)
- education (ed)
- health sciences (hs)
- liberal arts/humanities (lib art)
- libraries (librar)
- museum (museum)
- press (press)
- professional/graduate schools (prof/grad)
- technology (tech)
- telecommunications (telecom)

tains a network of scanning information that can be shared by participating state planning agencies.

Analysis

The second major element in external scanning is analysis. This phase of the process involves *interpreting the strategic importance* of issues and trends.

Ongoing research in both public and private contexts (Klein and Linneman 1984; Engledow and Lenz 1985) has shown that brainstorming and group discussion are the preferred tools for analyzing issues. As noted above, practitioners of scanning have reported that group discussions of issues raised through scanning have been helpful in developing integrative and innovative ideas. In our experience (see also Morrison, Renfro, and Boucher 1983), however, four techniques have been especially helpful as background to group discussions: brainstorming, impact/probability, issue networks, and scenarios.[9]

Deciding on appropriate issue status. This is the final aspect of the analysis phase of the external scanning process. Among the options, with regard to any particular issue, are (1) identifying issues to monitor in future scanning, (2) identifying issues to refer for action, and (3) identifying issues to drop from further consideration. These decisions typically are reached on the basis of discussion among scanning participants.

Reporting/Referral

The products of the reporting/referral stage of the external scanning process are partly determined by the purposes identified in the first step of the process. Five products are recommended for use in the public sector:

1. *Scans:* brief reports documenting the key elements of a particular issue or trend. Typically the scan provides information on the source of the item and a brief note by the scanner as to why it is worth noting.

2. *Policy papers:* reports in greater depth than the scan. Often such papers may suggest action possibilities with regard to the particular issue.

3. *Comprehensive environmental scans:* reports that synthesize information from individual scans, summarizing issues and trends in the basic information categories—social, economic, political, and technological.

4. *A seminar or forum:* a setting in which either a range of issues or a single issue can be addressed. Outside experts can be invited to participate, as can representatives of other institutions who share an interest in the issue.

5. *Newsletters:* a compilation of selected scans, often edited by the lead scanner. Typically, such newsletters are prepared on a low-cost basis, often mimeographed and intended for internal use rather than for external circulation.

CONCLUSION

We conclude with five points about external scanning in the public sector. First, although somewhat later than its introduction in the private sector, external scanning is beginning to appear with some frequency in the public sector. Furthermore, we have seen no indication that external scanning requires significant modification in order to be carried out in the public sector as opposed to the private sector. In our survey of 10 public organizations carrying out external scanning, we found initial satisfaction with its usefulness as well as a willingness to continue to experiment with ways in which to enhance the benefits to be gained from this practice.

Second, on the basis of the organizations studied as well as our own experience as participants in external scanning, we believe planners should consider a volunteer, in-house scanning effort.

Third, with careful definition of the tasks to be addressed and with equal attention to limiting the time that will be allotted to the process, scanning can complement other professional tools of the planner and can be carried out both effectively and cost-efficiently.

Fourth, enthusiasm for external scanning should be tempered by the recognition that the practice is still relatively new in both the public and the private sector. It will be important, accordingly, for scholars and practitioners to monitor its development.

Finally, we agree with those who view external scanning primarily as a tool to help provide qualitative rather than quantitative insights. Such insights are being used more and more to help the planner synthesize discrete pieces of information into a larger framework, frequently as a part of strategic planning.

NOTES

1. For purposes of the chapter, "external scanning" is used interchangeably with "environmental scanning."

2. Information on scanning by 10 public sector organizations was collected by means of telephone interviews carried out in July 1986. The interviews covered what kind of scanning was carried out, what staffing support was used, what analytical techniques were used, and which issues were identified. There was remarkable consensus that, despite difficulties in justifying external scanning to skeptics, the efforts seemed worthwhile.

3. The proposed three-part approach to external scanning conforms to generally accepted practice, although there are a variety of frameworks within which

to view external scanning. Influential in shaping the approach put forward in this article are works by Ashley (1985); Bryson, Freeman, and Roering (1985); Bryson, Van de Ven, and Roering (1985); Chase (1984); Molitor (1979); Morrison and Renfro (1984); Nanus (1982, 1984); and Wilson (1983).

4. Although this chapter does not offer detailed definitions of the numerous techniques associated with external scanning, readers are referred to Nutt and Backoff (1987) for discussion of a number of them. For purposes of this chapter, however, the authors' understandings of six techniques are described below:

a. *Brainstorming or group discussion.* Most scanning practitioners rely heavily on group discussion to consider the significance of issues and trends. Variations of group discussion also are used (e.g., Delphi and nominal group techniques).

b. *Delphi technique.* This can be done in a written or computerized form using a device called a "consensor." Delphi allows a group to discuss an issue, then refine its discussion through a second or even a third round of information gathering. The advantage of the Delphi over the group discussion is that it prevents overweighting of the opinions of verbal individuals or of individuals to whom a group might defer because of their senior status within the organization. While this iterative process can be time-consuming, with a computerized polling capability such as the United Way's "consensor," results can be tabulated instantly and time delays can be overcome.

c. *Impact/probability assessments.* These typically occur on a matrix allowing issues to be compared, on one axis in terms of impact and on the other axis in terms of the probability that the event or trend will occur (see Morrison, Renfro, and Boucher 1983, pp. 31–33). The technique allows scanners to identify issues or trends that are high in both impact and probability of occurrence.

d. *Impact/networks.* These start from the premises of a single event or trend will occur (see Morrison, Renfro, and Boucher 1983). Starting from the primary event, users of the technique develop a list of three or four of the most important secondary impacts that are likely to take place if the primary event occurs. The impact network can be carried to a third level by asking participants to identify trends that are most likely to flow from those identified in the second level of the matrix (see Morrison, Renfro, and Boucher 1983, pp. 37–39).

e. *Nominal group technique.* This technique calls for

members of a group to identify key ideas in written form; next, each member of the group has the opportunity to speak to his or her ideas before a vote is taken. Finally, the group works toward a ranked list of ideas (Delbecq and Van de Ven 1971 is an authoritative source on this technique).

f. *Scenarios.* These techniques develop a range of internally consistent probable future outcomes ranging from a worst case to a middle option to preferred outcomes (see Morrison, Renfro, and Boucher 1983, pp. 72–76, for a public sector example, and Wack 1985, pp. 73–89, for a private sector example). The scenarios can be refined through group discussion.

5. See Note 4 above.

6. See Note 4 above.

7. We suggest that readers interested in following up on the practice of external scanning consult the reference list. Such sources stem from five traditions: Planning in the public sector (e.g., Christensen 1985; Foresight Task Force 1983; Kaufman and Jacobs 1986; Olsen and Eadie 1982); strategic planning (e.g., Ansoff 1980; Bracker 1980; Bryson, Freeman, and Roering 1985; Nutt 1984; Ring and Perry 1985; So 1984); scanning (e.g., Aguilar 1967; Ashley 1985; Chase 1984; Fleming 1980; Molitor 1979; Morrison and Renfro 1984; Nanus 1982, 1984); futurism (e.g., Naisbitt 1982; Toffler 1970, 1980); and organizational change (e.g., Kanter 1983; Lindblom and Cohen 1979; O'Toole 1981; Peters and Waterman 1982; Ouchi 1984; Quinn 1985).

8. SWOT analysis in strategic planning derives its acronym from assessing *strengths* and *weaknesses* internally and *opportunities* and *threats* externally.

9. See Note 4 above.

REFERENCES

Aguilar, F. J. 1967. *Scanning the business environment.* New York, N.Y.: Macmillan.

Albert, K. J., ed. 1983. *The strategic management handbook.* New York, N.Y.: McGraw-Hill.

Ansoff, H. I. 1980. Strategic issue management. *Strategic Management Journal* 1: 131–148.

Ashley, W. 1985. Issues management. Presentation for the Minneapolis Chamber of Commerce Public Affairs Committee conference, Minneapolis, Minnesota. October 22.

Bracker, J. 1980. The historical development of the strategic management concept. *Academy of Management Review* 5, 2: 219–224.

Bryson, J. M., R. E. Freeman, and W. D. Roering. 1985. Strategic planning in the public sector: Approaches and future directions. Discussion paper 37. Minneapolis, Minn.: Strategic Management Research Center, University of Minnesota. January.

Bryson, J. M., A. H. Van de Ven, and W. D. Roering. 1985. Strategic planning and the revitalization of the public service. Discussion paper 39. Minneapolis, Minn.: Strategic Management Research Center, University of Minnesota. September.

Chase, W. H. 1984. *Issue management: Origins of the future.* Stamford, Conn.: Issue Action Publications.

Christensen, K. S. 1985. Coping with uncertainty in planning. *Journal of the American Planning Association* 51, 1: 63–73.

Delbecq, A. and A. H. Van de Ven. 1971. A group process model for problem identification and program planning. *Journal of Applied Behavioral Science* 7, 4: 466–492.

Delmont, T. and A. Pflaum. 1983. External scanning and issues management: New planning techniques for colleges and universities. St. Paul, Minn.: Association for Institutional Research Upper Midwest. October 3.

Engledow, J. L. and R. T. Lenz. 1985. Whatever happened to environmental analysis? *Long Range Planning* 18, 2: 93–106.

Fleming, J. E. 1980. Linking public affairs with corporate planning. *California Management Review* 23: 35–43.

Foresight Task Force. 1983. *Foresight in the private sector: How can government use it?* Prepared for use by the Committee on Energy and Commerce, U.S. House of Representatives. Washington, D.C.: U.S. Government Printing Office. January.

Hearn, J. C. and R. B. Heydinger. 1984. Formal assessment of the external environment of a university. Chicago, Ill.: Association for the Study of Higher Education. March.

Kanter, R. M. 1983. *The change masters.* New York, N.Y.: Simon and Schuster.

Kaufman, J. L. and H. Jacobs. 1986. A public planning perspective on strategic planning. Paper presented at the National Planning Conference of the American Planning Association, Los Angeles, April.

Klein, H. E. and R. E. Linneman. 1984. Environmental assessment: An international study of corporate practice. *Journal of Business Strategy* (Summer): 66–75.

Lindblom, C. E. and D. K. Cohen. 1979. *Usable knowledge: Social science and social problem solving.* New Haven, Conn.: Yale University Press.

Molitor, G. T. 1979. The hatching of public opinion. In

Corporate planning: Techniques and applications, edited by R. Allio and M. W. Pennington. New York, N.Y.: North American Society for Corporate Planning.

Morrison, J. and W. Renfro. 1984. The application of futures research techniques in strategic planning. Presented at the annual forum of the Association for Institutional Research, Fort Worth, Texas. May 5–6.

Morrison, J., W. Renfro, and W. I. Boucher. 1983. *Applying methods and techniques of futures research*. New Directions for Research no. 39. San Francisco, Calif.: Jossey-Bass.

Naisbitt, J. 1982. *Megatrends: Ten new directions for transforming our lives*. New York, N.Y.: Warner Books.

Nanus, B. 1982. QUEST—Quick environmental scanning techniques. *Long Range Planning* 15: 39–45.

———. 1984. Foresight, strategy, and political communication. Presented at the National Governors Association, Nashville, Tennessee. July 30.

Nutt, P. 1984. A strategic planning network for non-profit corporations. *Strategic Management Journal* 5: 57–75.

——— and R. W. Backoff. 1987. A strategic management process for public and third-sector organizations. *Journal of the American Planning Association* 53, 1: 42–55.

Olsen, J. B. and D. C. Eadie. 1982. *The game plan: Governance with foresight*. Washington, D.C.: Council of State Planning Agencies.

O'Toole, J. 1981. *Making America work: Productivity and responsibility*. New York, N.Y.: Continuum Publishing.

Ouchi, W. 1984. *The M-form society: How American teamwork can recapture the competitive edge*. Reading, Mass.: Addison-Wesley.

Peters, T. and R. Waterman. 1982. *In search of excellence: Lessons from America's best-run companies*. New York, N.Y.: Warner Books.

Pflaum, A. M. and T. J. Delmont. 1985. External scanning in public and private organizations: Implications for strategic management. Presented at the annual forum of the Association for Institutional Research, Portland, Oregon. April 28–May 1.

Quinn, J. B. 1985. Managing Innovation: Controlled chaos. *Harvard Business Review* 63, 2: 73–84.

Ring, P. S. and J. L. Perry. 1985. Strategic management in public and private organizations: Implications of distinctive contexts and constraints. *Academy of Management Review* 10, 2: 276–286.

ShellScan Newsletter. 1982. Abstract analysis session IV. (December): 1–12.

So, F. 1984. Strategic planning: Reinventing the wheel? *Planning* 50, 2: 16–21.

Stubbart, C. 1985. Why we need a revolution in strategic planning. *Long Range Planning* 18, 6: 68–76.

Toffler, A. 1970. *Future shock*. New York, N.Y.: Random House.

———. 1980. *Third wave*. New York, N.Y.: Bantam Books.

Wack, P. 1985. Scenarios: Uncharted waters ahead. *Harvard Business Review* 63, 5: 73–89.

Weisbord, M. R. 1984. Future search innovative business conference. *Planning Review* (July): 16–20.

Wilson, I. 1983. The benefits of environmental analysis. In *The Strategic Management Handbook*, edited by K. J. Albert. New York, N.Y.: McGraw-Hill.

CHAPTER

10

Oak Ridge, Tennessee: Strategic Planning for a Strategic City

JOSEPH C. KING

DAVID A. JOHNSON

Oak Ridge, Tennessee, is not a typical American city. It was secretly created by the United States Army during World War II on a remote site 25 miles west of Knoxville. Using TVA power, Oak Ridge provided the refined uranium for the atomic bombs of the Manhattan Project. Forty years later, Oak Ridge was no longer an Army camp of 75,000, but an incorporated city of 28,000.

From the outset Oak Ridge was a planned community. But because it was planned for a purpose other than housing people and commerce, its initial character and subsequent development yielded conditions that by the mid-eighties called for a stronger commitment to immediate problem solving, as well as long-range urban planning. The community and its municipal government met this challenge with an approach that successfully combined traditional elements of master planning with components of strategic planning. This chapter documents the process and suggests that such a synthesis is both desirable and practical.

SETTING THE STAGE

Oak Ridge today faces a variety of problems comparable to other boom towns, communities with highly educated populations, university communities, and company towns. Some problems simply relate to the fact that Oak Ridge began as an "instant" city; built and populated in a short period of time, its population, economy, and housing stock all show signs of aging at the same rate. Other problems are those usually associated with company towns, only in Oak Ridge the "company" is the federal government. The government employs nearly 20,000 people, dominates the local economy, owns much of the land and, in the view of many residents, does not pay its fair share of taxes. Indeed, it generates no taxes at all, instead making a much lower in-lieu payment. Still other problems derive from the special nature of Oak Ridge and its original mission—the promotion and exploitation of nuclear energy by a cadre of highly educated scientists and technicians. Justified or not, the suspicion of things nuclear eventually cast a pall over Oak Ridge, the "Atomic City." The discovery in the early eighties of mercury contamination in local streams and significant environmental problems on the U.S. Department of Energy's 37,000-acre reservation tarnished the city's favorable image.

The creation and operation of Oak Ridge as a federal reservation shaped the city from the beginning. At the point of its incorporation in 1959, the city found itself without a taxable industrial base and lacking a vigorous commercial sector. The hilly, isolated site selected for the Manhattan Engineering District served well in providing for safety and security required for development of the atomic bomb during the Second World War, but was not at all conducive to residential, commercial, and private sector industrial growth. Moreover, the manner in which land and improvements were transferred from the federal to the private sector yielded very little developable property to support future growth. Unlike the surrounding area, the work force in Oak Ridge traditionally had been unionized. This, coupled with the relatively high wage rates paid at the federal facilities, created an environment not well suited to the types of industries that were likely to locate in East Tennessee communities. Consequently, new industries and new populations, so attracted to East Tennessee's share of the growing Sun Belt, were not especially drawn to the Atomic City.

During the fifties and sixties, Oak Ridge's isolation diminished as Knoxville's suburbs developed. The construction of a four-lane divided parkway in the early seventies linked Oak Ridge to the interstate highway, greatly facilitating movement in and out of the community. While residential development in Oak Ridge occurred at a respectable rate, the surrounding communities began to house an increasing share of the city's work force. The maturing of families that had moved into Oak Ridge during the forties and fifties yielded declining household sizes and a steady drop in school enrollment during the seventies and early eighties.

Oak Ridge had received considerable planning attention over its short life from the Army Corps of Engineers and, in 1948, from Skidmore, Owings and Merrill (SOM), which had laid out some of the elements of a new town combining Garden City principles with Bauhaus buildings. The plan called for self-contained neighborhoods as well as a town center to provide civic identity and urbanity. Much of the SOM plan had been carried out, but the town eventually sprawled down its long valley, exhibiting some of the less desirable aspects of American highway commercial development. The generally well-educated population demanded and enjoyed a high level of municipal services—schools, in particular—but the city lacked physical amenities and a high quality of public landscape and urban design. Oak Ridge ended up looking more than a little like a retired Army base with a gateway commercial agglomeration incorporated into the jurisdiction. Conventional city planning and zoning in later years had brought some order to the development process, but not enough to prevent the accumulation of serious economic and environmental concerns.

During the late seventies and early eighties, the city suffered several economic development setbacks. Plans for a $2 billion synthetic fuels plant were scuttled, as were hopes for a large uranium fuel reprocessing plant. The much contested Clinch River Breeder Reactor

Project was cancelled by Congress after years of engineering and site preparation work. The in-lieu-of-tax contract between the city and the Department of Energy expired and subsequent payments made on a year-by-year basis were subject to termination without notice. The Department of Energy's pending decision to mothball the inefficient K-25 Gaseous Diffusion Plant and terminate uranium gas centrifuge research development and manufacturing activities, plus the potential loss of 2,000 jobs, caused concern to grow to deep apprehension regarding a future tied to the uncertainties of the federal budget. A strong consensus was building among Oak Ridgers that it was time to take actions that would guide the community toward a more stable economic future.

Another important event occurred in 1982 when, after nearly forty years of managing Oak Ridge energy operations for the federal government, the Union Carbide Corporation terminated its contract and a new management contract was won by the Martin Marietta Corporation. The arrival of Martin Marietta and small branch offices of several other national firms such as Boeing, Bechtel, Westinghouse, Gilbert/Commonwealth, Lockwood Greene, and Science Applications International brought to Oak Ridge companies committed to quality community growth. Martin Marietta's executives, and those of other national corporations with branches in Oak Ridge, were enthusiastic about the concept of strategic planning. Why not, they suggested, apply the principles of strategic planning to the problems of Oak Ridge?

Oak Ridge had long enjoyed a reputation of being a well-managed provider of municipal services. A strong emphasis on efficiency and increased productivity resulted in significant staffing reductions during the early eighties and by 1984 cost savings resulting from such efforts exceeded $1 million. Telephone surveys conducted by the city revealed a high level of public satisfaction relating to delivery of services. However, the surveys indicated that the public also saw its municipal government as being responsible for solving long-range problems relating to the issues of growth and development. While the city was seen as performing well in terms of program implementation, it was not perceived by community business leaders as being effective in planning for and managing change. Several expressed a need for a comprehensive plan to better articulate policies, goals, and strategies. Interested citizens formed the "Coalition for a Master Plan," composed of representatives from the regional planning commission, the municipal environmental advisory board, the chamber of commerce, the local chapter of the League of Women Voters, and two growth-oriented groups, to encourage the Oak Ridge City Council to fund and undertake such a planning process.

A PLAN FOR A PLAN

The assistant city manager was assigned responsibility to design and implement a master planning effort for the community. In March 1984, a proposal to develop a comprehensive plan was presented to the city council as part of the city manager's proposed budget. In addressing the development of a comprehensive plan, the proposal cautioned against falling prey to the failings of past efforts. Two land use plans and several special topic plans had been prepared by the city since the 1948 Skidmore, Owings and Merrill master plan. While each served a purpose and to a certain extent had guided development, none was officially adopted, none served as a foundation for day-to-day decisions, and all soon became outdated and of relatively little use. Deficiencies of past planning efforts were obvious—inadequate community involvement; weak commitment and participation on the part of the city council and staff; poor linkage between the plan, policymaking, and operational decisions; and a tendency to be too long-range in scope. Four important criteria were therefore suggested by the assistant city manager as objectives of the planning process:

• The entire community was to be involved.

• The city council was to directly participate in development of the plan and would formally approve the finished product.

• The resulting plan would be easily understood and readily available to the public.

• The plan would be *useful*.

As depicted in Figure 10-1, it was anticipated that the comprehensive planning process would integrate long-term considerations with more incremental short-term management systems already in place. The finished product was to be practical in that it would focus on policies and strategies rather than on unrealistic or restrictive prescriptions. To remain current and responsive to community needs, it would be maintained and regularly updated.

The city staff initially envisioned that the desired integration of long-range planning and existing administrative and budgetary processes could be accomplished with minimal outside assistance from planning consultants. A review of the literature suggested to the staff that small cities making heavy use of outside consultants too often found themselves with documents that were of relatively little use be-

cause elected leaders and the general citizenry did not participate sufficiently in the planning process.[1] The city staff therefore recommended that the bulk of work associated with development of the plan be done in-house. A majority of the budgeted funds were to be spent on engineering studies of transportation and utility systems and any outside assistance that was needed would be sought from the faculty of nearby University of Tennessee. The business community, particularly those national firms with branches located in Oak Ridge, urged more extensive use of outside experts. The final proposal to the city council recommended a compromise that featured extensive staff involvement with support provided by an outside planning firm.

The issue of how the proposed comprehensive plan would look also was deliberated. The city staff saw the need for a detailed working document that might serve as a constant reference to those involved in setting and implementing policy. Some in the business community expressed preferences for a glossy, summary document formatted like a corporate report that could be used to market the community and recruit industry. Again, a compromise allowed both documents to be produced.

The city council approved a $125,000 budget for the comprehensive planning project in its FY 1986 budget. The appropriation subsequently was increased to $144,500 to complete a supplemental traffic study. Under the direction of the assistant city manager, the project team included the planning director and other city staff members, a graduate student serving a special internship, and outside consultants. Rather than use a single planning firm, the city chose to retain three. After evaluating

Figure 10–1. Integrating Strategic and Long-Range Planning: The Oak Ridge Process

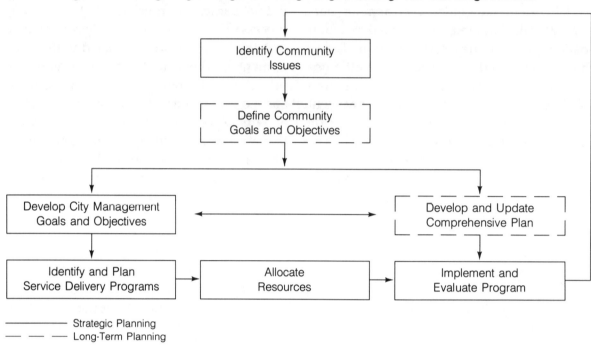

——————— Strategic Planning
— — — — Long-Term Planning

Source: SRI International, *Picket Fence Planning in California* (Menlo Park, Calif., 1978). Modified from Figure 12, page 31.

proposals submitted by comprehensive planning firms, the city selected Bennett, Ringrose, Wolsfeld, Jarvis, Gardner, Inc. (BRW) of Minneapolis, Minnesota, as its primary consultants. Robert C. Einsweiler, Inc.[2] was selected as a special consultant to assist the city in arriving at an operational definition of its comprehensive plan, establishing development goals and objectives, and resolving conflicts between participants in the planning process. George E. Bowen and David H. Folz, both faculty members at the nearby University of Tennessee and doing business as Cherokee Planning and Development Associates, were hired as economic development consultants. The assistant city manager and planning intern assumed responsibility for coordinating citizen participation.

Initial work with the comprehensive plan project team revealed a fundamental conflict between advocates of long-range master planning and those of strategic planning. Traditional comprehensive planning proponents tended to be goals oriented, while those preferring strategic planning were more concerned with community issues. The traditional comprehensive planning proponents suggested a systematic inventory of conditions, setting of formal goals and stating of policies, and development of general plans and programs. Specific, detailed action plans were seen as less important at this stage than was the need to establish policy direction. Adherents of the strategic planning approach expressed a stronger bias for action, arguing that formal goal and policy setting were less important than determining what action the city would take to address major community issues. Ultimately the project team blended the two approaches. The mix of traditional and strategic planning processes balanced the perceived need for a formal policy structure with the desire to focus on specific actions necessary to resolve identified community problems and take advantage of available opportunities.[3]

THE PLANNING PROCESS

As indicated in Figure 10–2, the project was divided into four basic components. The first provided for the framing of community issues and a general inventory of the community—its demographics, physical design, land use and topographic characteristics, and its economic base. This helped the project team focus its assessment of social, economic, and land use trends within the context of problems and opportunities perceived to be the most important to the community. The second component aimed at achieving community consensus regarding major issues, objectives, and policies identified during the initial analysis. The third focused on specific plans and strategies to accomplish identified objectives. The final phase brought all the inventory, issue, policy, and strategy elements together into a formal comprehensive plan that provided a framework from which short-range actions could be taken, the results assessed, and future actions directed. Following adoption of the plan, it was anticipated that the initial product would be embellished with an additional detailed traffic network study that would yield specific roadway improvement plans for the next five to ten years.

Several informal advisory groups were established at the project to represent the interests of major employers, various components of the commercial sector, growth-oriented organizations, social agencies, and organizations concerned with quality-of-life issues. Interactions with these groups were augmented by sessions with the city council, planning commission, board of zoning appeals, environmental quality advisory board, and the general public. Depending on the project phase, general public input opportunities ranged from neighborhood meetings to community workshops and symposia. Opportunities were provided to interact with the informal advisory groups, city council, planning commission, and the general public during each of the four project phases.

As reflected in Figure 10–3, it was anticipated that from an identification of community issues the project team would construct policies that could serve as a framework for specific strategy components. Emphasis was placed on consensus building from the start. The project team sought to reach an agreement among the public and community decision makers regarding not only the issues that should be addressed in the plan, but also on the specific actions that would be taken to solve community problems or take advantage of opportunities. As expected, the process turned out to be a reiterative one. As the focus became more and more specific, earlier assumptions regarding consensus on issues and policies were tested and, where appropriate, issue descriptions, policy statements, and strategy descriptions were modified.

The process for developing initial consensus on strategies in group sessions, as introduced by Einsweiler, follows:

1. Survey the concerns of the group.
2. Capture those concerns insofar as pos-

Figure 10–2. City of Oak Ridge, Tennessee: Comprehensive Plan Project Schedule

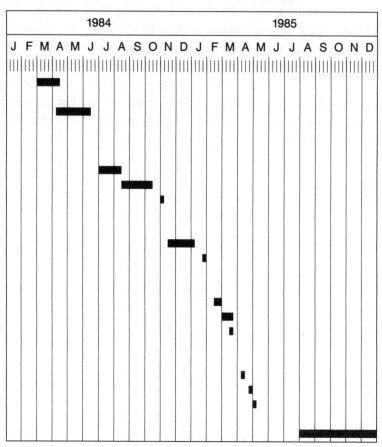

Project Approval

Consultant Selection

Project Components
1. Inventory/Issue Framing
   advisory group meetings
   community workshops
   symposium

2. Issue and Policy Testing
   community meetings
   symposium

3. Strategy and Plan Developing
   advisory group meetings
   community meetings
   symposium

4. Adoption of Plan
   presentation
   public hearing
   adoption

Implementation

sible in the exact language of those who stated them.

3. Organize stated concerns under headings that appear to reflect larger issues.

4. Test the "quality" of capturing concerns by presenting them back to those who stated them and also sharing them with other groups.

5. Test the range of acceptable solutions by asking the same people to propose ways of dealing with those issues and concerns.

6. Coalesce behind proposals that possess desirable attributes and are shorn of undesirable or unacceptable negative effects.

The issue-framing and inventory phase of the comprehensive planning process was initiated in July and completed in early November. Meetings with the consultants and the city council, planning commission, various municipal boards, the city staff, and several of the informal advisory groups were conducted, as were tours of the community, municipal facilities, and Department of Energy installations. The consultants were provided with copies of previous land use and special topics plans, budgets, and other studies. From such interaction and research, a preliminary identification of major community issues was accomplished.

Figure 10–3. Development of a Comprehensive Plan: The Oak Ridge Process

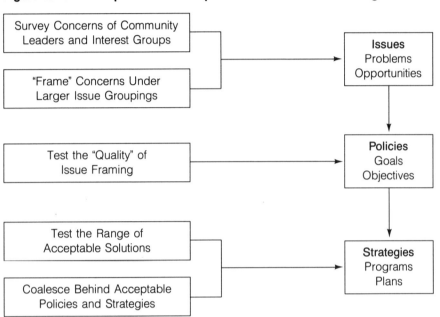

Seventeen workshops were conducted, the first three with the help of the planning consultants and the balance by the city's staff. Sessions were held for the city council and planning commission, advisory groups representing major employers, quality-of-life organizations, lending institutions, builders and developers, real estate agents, retailers, community college and high school students, the clergy, social welfare agencies, and the general public. An analysis of general conditions followed by a review of issues identified in the initial round of meetings and concluded by a solicitation of strategy suggestions by those present was the agenda used for all the workshops. Participants were asked to identify the major community problems and opportunities that should be addressed in the comprehensive plan and to describe the specific means for dealing with them. While participants pro-

duced few strategy and program ideas not already under consideration by the project team, suggestions did reveal the extent of municipal involvement considered appropriate in attempting to resolve problems and take advantage of identified opportunities. From this information, the project team compiled policy statements and where appropriate identified alternative positions for city council and planning commission consideration. The issue-framing, inventory, and analysis phase ended with a public symposium conducted by the planning consultants. A review of the project team's analysis of conditions was conducted along with a presentation of suggested planning policies.

During the late seventies and early eighties, the city council and planning commission frequently found themselves caught between community interests favoring expanded development and those favoring preservation of the community's quality of life. The city staff consequently anticipated two basic concern groups would emerge: one pro economic development and the other pro environmental quality. As the process unfolded, it became apparent that differences centered not on the issue of whether development should take place, but instead on how growth should occur. Consequently, the planning process focused on how development could occur so that both concerns could be adequately addressed. With minor exceptions this pattern repeated itself with regard to other issues. The degree of conflict anticipated by the city staff regarding key community concerns did not materialize. While there were differences of opinion on how problems might be solved or opportunities seized, there was general agreement regarding the issues that should be addressed. The framing of issues yielded four focal points for the comprehensive planning effort:

1. *Employment and economic development issues* including economic uncertainty; conflicting attitudes about methods of economic development; the need for jobs, a balanced economy, and economic self-sufficiency; the adequacy of infrastructure; and the appropriate role of government in fostering economic growth.

2. *Population and housing issues* including declining population; unbalanced age distribution and household status; the type, value, and availability of housing; and deficiencies in the marketing of available housing.

3. *General development issues* including the original town plan's neighborhood concept versus a more market-based approach; urban sprawl, service extension problems, and

the availability of land for development; and the location of special uses.

4. *Quality-of-life issues* including the image of Oak Ridge, the attitudes of its citizens, and the impact of both on housing and economic development policies; concepts of ambience and aesthetics; the need for activity spaces for varying age groups; the need for increased diversity; social issues; and the quality of services.

The second project phase was initiated with work sessions for the city council and planning commission to confirm proper framing of issues and to review and respond to the inventory analysis. Policy choices were then presented to the public in a series of eight neighborhood meetings. A second public symposium was held in late January 1985 to finalize policy formulation and focus on selection of specific strategies and plans. At this session, a preliminary draft of the comprehensive plan was introduced for review.

The plan adoption phase included a round of seven workshops for the city council, planning commission, and informal advisory groups followed in March by three special subject symposia—one on population and housing, one on economic development, and the third on land use and general development. A final draft of the comprehensive plan was presented to the Oak Ridge city council in early April. One month later, following a public hearing and several modifications, the plan was formally adopted.

IMPLEMENTATION OF THE PLAN

The adopted plan includes chapters on population and housing, economic development, general land use and development, public facilities and utilities, parks and public open space, quality of community life, and administration. Each identifies major issues and provides an extensive inventory of conditions, policies expressing community goals and objectives, and specific programs and action plans. For example, with regard to the condition of the community's housing stock, statistics on the age, tenure, condition, and vacancy rates have been collected. Concerns relating to deterioration of housing and maintenance of neighborhood quality have been noted and policy statements regarding stabilization, rehabilitation, redevelopment, and land use control have been adopted. Programs featuring housing rehabilitation loans and grants, scattered-site rehabilitation, maintenance standards, public facility maintenance, and housing inspections have been identified and/or implemented.

The plan has been extensively integrated into the city's management process. Nearly all of the city management's adopted performance objectives are linked directly to the plan. For example, one of the city manager's goals and measures of performance include implementation of a reoccupancy inspection program. The plan provides the framework from which this strategy is launched.

The city's annual and six-year capital improvement budgets are now based on policies and programs prescribed in the comprehensive plan. Based on the outcome of the process, the adopted plan includes a priority framework from which to make capital and operations expenditure decisions. As indicated in Figure 10–4, the first of four priority groups focuses on provision of basic services. The second, third, and fourth groupings represent strategic investments in opportunity areas and address issues of economic development,

housing development and preservation, and quality of life.

In short, the comprehensive planning project has produced a *strategic* plan based on a firm foundation of broad, long-range goals and objectives.

STRATEGIC PLANNING IN OAK RIDGE

What can be learned from the Oak Ridge comprehensive planning process? Perhaps the primary lesson is that strategic planning and traditional comprehensive planning are not mutually exclusive; they can be blended successfully. The Oak Ridge process embodies most of the key elements that are said to characterize a strategic planning process:

• It is a focused process that concentrates on selected issues.

• It explicitly considers resource availability.

• It assesses strengths and weaknesses.

• It considers major events and changes occurring outside the organization or jurisdiction.

• It is action oriented—with a strong emphasis on practical results.[4]

For students of practical strategic planning, the Oak Ridge experience provides an interesting case study. The stimulus to undertake the planning process was provided by community leaders frustrated by slow economic and population growth and the downturn of federal funding cycles critical to the city's economic well being, but the process evolved from the traditional approaches to comprehensive planning. The final product does not reflect a growth-at-all-costs philosophy. The city council was directly involved in the process, as were the planning commission and other citizen boards, but elected and appointed groups generally responded to concerns, issues, and strategies generated by the community-based

Figure 10–4. Relationship of Comprehensive Plan Priority Framework to Budget Resources

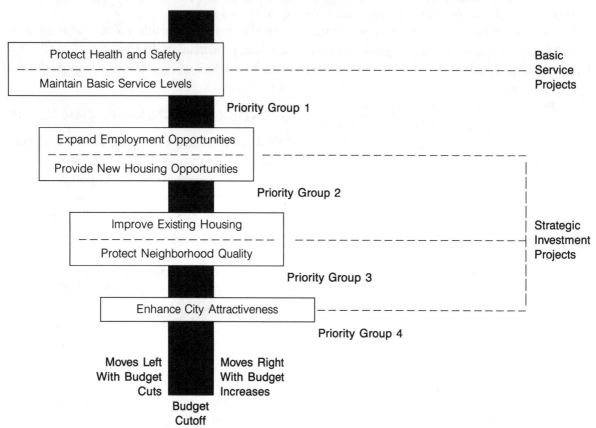

planning process rather than setting their own planning agendas.

The Oak Ridge process generated issue statements by aggregating and clustering specific citizen concerns. Prioritized policies were derived from these statements and specific actions to achieve those stated objectives have been implemented by the city. The Oak Ridge operating and capital budgets, as well as the city staff's management objectives, now are directly linked to the comprehensive plan.

The planning approach undertaken by Oak Ridge has not differed greatly from conventional comprehensive planning approaches

that use a high level of citizen and interest group input. It is unique in its direct linkage with short-term strategies and programs. This should be reassuring to planners who have been told by some writers that comprehensive planning and strategic planning are polar opposites, with the former being all-encompassing, goal and plan oriented, idealistic, and ambitious, and the latter being focused, practical, and results oriented.

The Oak Ridge approach is not without risks. Early in the process, a local newspaper editorial questioned the focus on community concerns rather than positive attributes and potentials. Indeed, had the process ended with the cataloging of problems, little of anything constructive would have been accomplished. But the process in Oak Ridge went beyond consensus on what the problems were to coalescing behind action plans aimed at resolving problems.

The ultimate success of the process will rest in part on its ability to survive changes in key personnel. Since adoption of the comprehensive plan, both the city manager and assistant city manager have moved on to work for different cities. Changes have also taken place in certain private sector positions. Time will tell whether the process was overly dependent on the actions of specific individuals or is successfully institutionalized.

Another problem for Oak Ridge, as for all cities attempting to apply strategic planning, is that many of the strategic decisions affecting the future of the city will be made not by city government alone, but also by other community actors such as the Department of Energy, Martin Marietta, and absentee commercial landowners. The city has its comprehensive strategic plan, but the city is only one among a number of key players. The question is: Are the city's plan and action agenda adequate to structure and guide the actions of the other players whose interests may or may not coincide with those of the city and its residents, or is it necessary to demand that these players also provide strategic plans for their involvement and responsibilities in Oak Ridge? One citizen participant, who is fond of sculling the Clinch River, proposed that Oak Ridge change its nickname from the Atomic City to Rowing Capital of the World. It won't take very long to see if all the strategic rowers in Oak Ridge are pulling on the oars together.

NOTES

1. In an extensive review of local government planning efforts in California, SRI International found this to be true in a number of locations. See Steven A. Waldhorn, Edward J. Blakely, James R. King, and Phyllis A. Guss, 1978. *Picket fence planning in California: A study of local government planning*, Menlo Park, Calif.: SRI International, September.

2. Robert Einsweiler is a professor of planning and public affairs at the University of Minnesota's Hubert Humphrey Institute of Public Affairs, Minneapolis.

3. The successful blending of these approaches can be credited to Robert Einsweiler who brought to the process an effective method of framing community issues and articulating strategies. With a clear reading of community issues and associated strategies that were acceptable to policymakers, the project team was able to back into the process of formally setting goals and policies.

4. Donna L. Sorkin, Nancy B. Ferris, and James Hudak, 1984. *Strategies for cities and counties: A strategic planning guide*, Washington, D.C.: Planning Technology Incorporated, p. 1.

11

Strategic Planning in Hennepin County, Minnesota: An Issues Management Approach

PHILIP C. ECKHERT
KATHLEEN HAINES
TIMOTHY J. DELMONT
ANN M. PFLAUM

Strategic planning has become an increasingly useful approach to public sector management. Elected and appointed government officials have adopted techniques of strategic planning from the private sector chiefly to better anticipate emerging public needs and "to govern with foresight" (Eadie and Olsen 1982; Foresight Task Force 1983; Nanus 1984).

While styles of strategic planning have differed (Taylor 1984; Bryson et al. 1986), one activity has become an essential component of nearly all approaches: the assessment of emerging trends and concomitant issues likely to influence future planning and management decision making (Wilson 1983; Renfro and Morrison 1983; Delmont and Pflaum 1985). The term *issues management* has been applied to an integrated, often sequential set of actions involving the monitoring, analysis, reporting, and preparation of action responses to critical issues and trends (Zentner 1981; Chase 1984; Ashley 1985). These issue management activities have been integrated into the strategic planning processes of selected organizations (Dutton et al. 1983; Lozier and Chittipeddi 1985).

In adopting an issues management form of strategic planning, Hennepin County, Minnesota, has developed a process to identify and resolve issues having broad, countywide significance over the next three to five years. This chapter offers a description and analysis of the county's planning process, one which we believe is a significant initiative because it (1) involves the pragmatic application of an innovative form of strategic planing, (2) uses a planning approach that encourages professional managers as well as elected officials to collaborate in policy and decision-making processes, (3) presents a systematic approach for developing quality public services in an era of limited resource growth, and (4) provides an example of one of the few strategic planning efforts successfully introduced in a large-scale local government entity; that is, a strategic planning initiative covering all departments, all functions, and all levels of service. The county's present efforts offer possible lessons for the improvement of planning practice to professional managers, planners, and elected officials in many levels of government.

The issues management approach the county developed consisted of three major phases:

1. The identification of strategic issues.

2. The preparation and analysis of alternative strategies to address each issue.

3. The development of plans to carry out strategies.

This chapter deals with all phases of the planning process. Section one identifies the factors leading to the adoption of this strategic planning initiative. Section two describes the issues management approach in detail and the county's process of implementation from 1983 to 1986. Section three offers an analysis of the effectiveness of the issues management process. Section four presents conclusions to the study.

This case study methodology involved two procedures: (1) initial in-depth as well as follow-up interviews with a cross section of 14 county board members, managers, and planners who have been consistently involved in the planning effort, and (2) a comprehensive review of all pertinent planning documents and materials prepared in the process.

FACTORS LEADING TO STRATEGIC PLANNING

Hennepin County, the most populous and ur-banized county in Minnesota, serves nearly one million residents in a geographic area covering 611 square miles. Its FY 1986 budget of $681 million—the largest among local government agencies in the state—provides residents with a broad range of health, social service, court, corrections, educational, transportation, library, financial, and licensing services.

Hennepin County government grew rapidly in the 1960s and 1970s, its budget increasing in real terms an average of 6 percent per year. Growth of federal and state revenues as well as the local property tax base permitted the concurrent development of many new programs and the expansion of traditional services. Much of the county's emphasis during this period was on managing growth and planning and guiding development.

The 1980s have produced a clearly different environment for the county. Service needs and demands have continued to grow, while revenue increases have not matched the local rate of inflation. Federal and state funding have decreased dramatically but statutory mandates to provide services have not been reduced. Management's challenge has been to find creative ways to ensure the provision of quality services in an era characterized by continuing cost increases and stable or declining revenues. That task has been complicated further by the emergence of a growing number of complex issues which require multiyear planning and implementation schedules, often also involving the development of public/private sector partnerships (e.g., health care delivery systems, maintenance of water quality standards, long-term care for the elderly).

Because of this changing environment, in fall 1983 the county administrator and planning staff—the Office of Planning Development—

developed a stategic planning process for application across county departments. While the county board did not formally endorse the proposed process at this time, many of its members encouraged the county administrator to introduce the process as quickly as possible. Among the reasons for doing so were the following:

1. To improve the effectiveness of county services by "doing more with less, doing things better."[1] Because of increasing complaints about local property tax rates, the county board and many top-level administrators felt the need to provide demonstrably cost-effective services to the county's constituents and taxpayers. Improved effectiveness, they reasoned, would follow from an assessment of future directions and service options.

2. To improve budget planning. The short-term focus of the annual budget cycle often precluded a careful examination of the long-range implications and consequences of funding decisions. Moreover, in retrenchment periods across-the-board rather than selective budget cuts associated with countywide priorities usually had been emphasized.

3. To develop a systematic approach for investigating alternative policy and program choices, many of which were growing more difficult and controversial as the county's external environment changed.

4. To anticipate and better understand significant issues that were likely to affect county services and performance (e.g., as one respondent suggested, "To get a hold of issues before they became political issues."[2]).

5. To find a method for integrating planning and policymaking functions across county departments and programs. Many signifi-

cant issues were interdepartmental in nature and needed to be addressed in an integrated and cooperative fashion.

6. To focus the attention of the board and top management on priority program and fiscal stategies that required formal board approval.

IMPLEMENTATION OF THE ISSUES MANAGEMENT APPROACH IN HENNEPIN COUNTY

The county defined strategic issues as fundamental policy questions having long-term service and funding implications for county operations. For the most part, these issues were not current problems or crisis situations, nor were they simply or quickly resolved. (See Table 11-1.) Their effective resolution typically involved decisions "on the nature of the services provided, to whom, by which methods, at what cost, and how financed and managed."[3]

The strategic issues arose from conflicts among three essential factors:

1. County policy objectives (the things the county *wanted* to accomplish in terms of service, financial, or management objectives).

2. Service mandates (the things that *must* be done pursuant to statute and regulations).

3. Environmental trends (*real* and perceived changes in demographics, economic climate, social and political trends, service needs, etc.).

The relationship among these factors is represented in Figure 11-1.

To foresee and address these issues effectively, the county developed its three-phase issues management process. Phase 1, the identification of strategic issues, began in September 1983 and continued to September 1984. Phase 2, the preparation and selection of broad, alter-

Table 11–1. Strategic Issues and Areas of Concern: Strategic Planning Process, Hennepin County, Minnesota

Areas of Strategic Concern	Issues
Finance	Erosion of county tax base Maximization of nonproperty tax resources
Changing health mission	Health care mission Financing county health care services Organizational relationships within the bureau of health Relationships with external health care providers
Employment and economic development	Employment and economic development Child day care
Services to the elderly	Elderly
Environmental quality	Hazardous waste Waste resources Solid waste
Transportation	County roadway system Light rail transit
Justice system overload	Justice system workload Driving while intoxicated (DWIs) Correctional services
Technology and information management	Opportunities through automation
Risk/liability management	County litigation and liabilities Workplace health hazards
Development and management of the work force	Employee development Affirmative action Comparable worth Management succession Merit system Performance evaluation and incentive systems
Capital resource management	Downtown property disposition Capital and operating project delivery systems Capital resource allocations
Service contracting policy	Service contracting policy
External relationships	Protection of parklands Overlapping park authority County as service provider Communications to the public
Program fragmentation and coordination	Energy Social services coordination Family violence Juvenile placements Special needs prisoners Delivery of economic assistance programs

Source: "Hennepin County Strategic Planning, Phase I: Management Report," Minneapolis, Minnesota, 1984, pp. i and ii.

Figure 11–1. Factors Influencing Strategic Issues

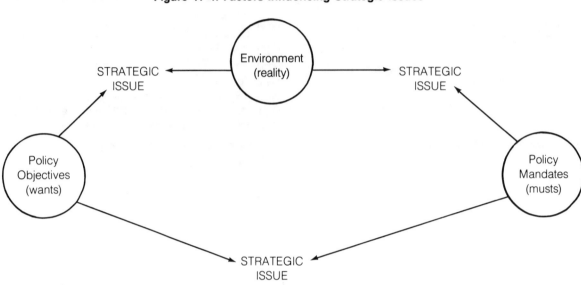

native strategies for issue resolution, occurred from fall 1984 through fall 1986 and, with respect to most issues, is continuing. Phase 3, the identification of actions to carry out selected strategies, was implemented in 1986 for specific issues and will continue through 1987 and beyond for others. A description of the three phases of the planning process follows.

Phase 1

In the first four months of Phase 1, each of the county's 36 departments developed multiple issue statements as requested by the county administrator. These statements included a brief description of the external and internal environmental factors influencing the issue, applicable program or service mandates, county board policy objectives, and a statement of assumed consequences of failure to respond.[4]

Issue statements were prepared by departmental planning teams composed of top managers and staff. These teams were assisted by

the Office of Planning and Development (OPD) which conducted initial workshops on strategic planning concepts, developed planning guidelines, prepared demographic and fiscal trends data, and offered staff support as needed.

To help department planning teams identify strategic issues and distinguish them from operational, short-term concerns, OPD prepared a set of evaluation questions titled "A Litmus Test for Strategic Issues." Among the most pertinent questions identified were: How broad an impact will the issue have on your department? What are the possible consequences of not addressing this issue? How sensitive or "charged" is the issue relative to community social, political, religious, and cultural values?

Much of the planning teams' issue identification work was intuitive in nature, involving brainstorming and unstructured group discussions. Some, but not all, of the teams used the demographic and fiscal data prepared by OPD to stimulate discussion. Assumptions about future trends and their likely impact on county service delivery were, for the most part, professional seat-of-the-pants judgments, varying according to the perspectives of department managers.[5]

County departments submitted 136 issues to the cabinet for review. From January 1984 to May 1984, the county cabinet and OPD staff discussed these issues, consolidating them into a set of 40 strategic issues. Some issues—the anticipated costs of civil liability insurance coverage or the nature of coordination of services for the elderly, for example—were relatively easily defined by the teams or the cabinet. Others, such as the slowdown in growth of the county's property tax base, took much longer to define, required more in-depth analysis, and did not lend themselves readily to easy solution. For these issues, Phase 1 work continued far beyond May.

Phase 2

Phase 2 involved a systematic exploration of strategies for issues resolution. A strategy was defined as a general approach used by an organization in achieving its objectives or in addressing critical issues; it was not defined in detailed terms nor limited to specific fiscal years or other short-term variables. Strategies provided general policy direction to guide detailed planning and management decisions over a multiyear period.[6]

In this phase, the county administrator assigned each strategic issue to a planning team composed of managers representing departments chiefly affected by the issue. A lead department—one most affected—coordinated team planning efforts. Teams identified alternative strategies for resolving the issue and estimated costs, staffing, capital requirements, and probable impact of each strategy developed.

Through 1986 these interdepartmental planning teams had developed strategies for 8 of the original 40 issues that were formally approved by the county administrator or the county board. On the issue of the county's capacity to control and maintain county highways, for example, new strategies included seeking legislative approval for changes in the county's bonding authority and highway funding formulas. With respect to the civil liability insurance issue, a strategy of reviewing insurance policies for departments most likely to face lawsuits was adopted.

The issues for which strategies were initially identified and approved were usually less complicated, better understood, and more amenable to action than other issues.[7] Strategy development for more complicated though no less critical issues required a lengthier period of time, with debate on many of these issues continuing into 1987. This has been the case often because each issue consisted of multiple subissues requiring separate attention by the planning teams. With respect to the issue of the slowdown in tax base growth, for example, the planning team has identified separate strategies for six related subissues. In effect, the total of all of these strategies has become a collective strategy for addressing this major critical issue.

In evaluating alternative strategies and establishing priorities among them, many planning teams used decision criteria developed for the process by OPD. These criteria included public acceptance, availability of financing, nature of capital expenditures, long-term (service impact, staff requirements, compatibility with department mission, relevance to strategic issues, cost effectiveness, flexibility, timing, client and user impact, and coordination/integration with other services or programs (see Table 11-2 for a definition of each of the 12 criteria).

Phase 3

In Phase 3 of the issues management process, many of the interdepartmental planning teams that developed strategies for issue resolution prepared action plans for their implementation. Through 1986, action plans—which chiefly involved changes in program budgets, personnel assignments, or policies—had been developed for strategies dealing with eight issues. For example, the county prepared specific pieces of legislation for submission to the 1987 Minnesota legislature that were designed to increase funding for county highway development and maintenance. To improve communication with constituents—another issue needing attention—the county has added a separate color-coded section for departmental telephone listings in the metropolitan Twin Cities phone directory.

ANALYSIS OF THE EFFECTIVENESS OF THE ISSUES MANAGEMENT PROCESS

Much of the issues management process has been implemented as designed. However, problems also have developed with each major activity of the process. This section highlights the aspects of the activities that worked, the ones that did not, and their impact on the overall effectiveness of the planning initiative.

In the private sector, the issues management process has consisted typically of monitoring the social and political environment, analyzing and evaluating the impact of emerging issues, establishing priorities among these issues, and preparing responses to new developments in the environment.[8] As designed, the county's three-phase model of issues management incorporated these elements. The county specifically moved beyond this private sector approach with its second phase—the identification of alternative strategies to address emerging issues—thereby linking issues management with strategic planning (which many corporations have not yet successfully accomplished).[9]

The conceptual simplicity of the county's three-phase model helped county managers and board members understand the planning process and, we believe, contributed to their acceptance of it as a credible, workable planning approach. In politics as well as administrative operations, attention and response to significant issues is a characteristic role.[10] The county's planning process mirrored this familiar activity rather than requiring participation in an elaborate, wholly new endeavor.

The three-phase process was an effective mechanism for: (1) systematically investigating a broad array of policy issues likely to confront county operations and (2) developing practical policy and program strategies to address these issues. Prior to initiating the planning process, county personnel anticipated that the three phases would follow each other sequentially, with all issues moving through the three-step process simultaneously. The county has found however, that the length of each phase varied for different issues depending on the complexity of the issue being examined. Thus within planning teams work on issues has often overlapped, as have review efforts by top management. As a result, problems have been created in the overall coordination and direction of the countywide planning effort and within individual teams (i.e., unexpected time demands on participating managers and staff,

Table 11–2. Criteria for Evaluating Alternative Strategies: Strategic Planning Process, Hennepin County, Minnesota

Public Acceptance: The resolution of some strategic issues will result in varying levels of public acceptance. The most desirable strategy is the one you perceive will have the greatest public acceptance.

Financing: If additional funding is required, is nonproperty-tax-derived funding available? A desirable strategy will identify alternative financing and/or will not require additional property taxes.

Capital Expenditures: A desirable strategy will better utilize existing county-owned or managed space and available equipment rather than require increased additional capital expenditure. However, in certain cases it may be financially and programmatically prudent to commit to an increased capital expenditure rather than utilize or attempt to upgrade existing assets of questionable value or benefit.

Long-Term Impact: The major thrust of strategic planning is to anticipate future issues that will confront the county and to respond effectively to those issues. The desirable strategy will offer long-term (more than five years) solutions to the issue and have a lasting positive effect.

Staff Requirements: A desirable strategy will allow the resolution of the issues by better utilizing existing county staff capabilities rather than hiring new employees.

Compatibility with Mission Statement: A desirable strategy is one that can be accomplished within or is appropriate to the department's mission statement.

Relevance to Strategic Issue: It is assumed that every strategy will respond to the issue; however, some strategies will better resolve the issue than others. The desirable strategy is the one you anticipate will best resolve the issue as a long-term solution with lasting effect.

Cost Effectiveness: A countywide policy objective is to provide cost-effective service delivery and management. A desirable strategy will improve or increase service and management within the existing budget parameters, or realize cost savings in the long term.

Flexibility: Flexibility in implementing a strategy is a desirable feature. A desirable strategy should lend itself to a trial or test before full implementation.

Timing: When implementing a strategy, timing is often critical. The desirable strategy should enable you to satisfactorily respond to the strategic issue within known time/response constraints.

Client or User Impact: If the delivery of client services is a part of the strategy being considered, a desirable strategy should have a positive effect on the client group.

Coordination/Integration with Other Services or Programs: A desirable strategy would allow for coordination and/or integration with services provided by other agencies.

Source: *Hennepin County Strategic Planning Manual*, Minneapolis, Minnesota, 1983, pp. 2-28 and 2-29.

priority setting in the work agenda, the meeting of deadlines, etc.). This particular finding of the study is consistent with Halstead's observation that a key problem in the issues management process is the lack of coordination both within and between organizations.[11] In sum, however, the county's three-phase approach, while difficult to manage over the nearly four years of the planning process, has

emerged as an useful, implementable format.

The county's decision to adopt a broad scope in its issues identification phase—to require county departments to address a multiple array of issues simultaneously—further complicated the effective implementation of the planning effort.

Among the positive accomplishments of the county's comprehensive approach are: (1) the (often early) detection of issues before they became crises (the erosion of the tax base, for example), (2) it helped managers with policy-making responsibilities and, in some cases, county board members to understand better the administrative and political implications of strategic issues, and (3) in general, it resulted in the county's first comprehensive assessment of the quality and effectiveness of its public services.[12] The scope of the effort ensured that a fundamental review of the purposes, activities, and costs of county programs was accomplished, something not previously achieved in the county's attempts at program budgeting and management by objectives.

The scope of the effort, however—which resulted in the identification of 136 issues initially by planning teams and 40 following central review—helped create irritating although not insurmountable problems. These problems involved the length of time demands on planning teams, slowdown in the movement of issues through the three-phase process, significant reporting requirements, lack of systematic analysis and central review of issues and, most importantly, an inability to identify the selected issues which in an overall sense were most critical to the county. In this regard, the county's experience was consistent with what Halstead also has identified as key problems in issues management: The identification of too many issues as well as too little analysis of the issues.[13]

At the formal conclusion of the first phase in fall 1984, the county faced the formidable task of developing strategies and action plans for 40 issues, a challenge that was not successfully met during the 1984–86 period.

The effort by the county to decentralize the planning process—to create a bottom–up process through the use of multiple planning teams—has been, for the most part, successfully realized. Over the three-and-a-half-year planning period, departmental and inter-departmental planning teams have met consistently to identify significant issues, carefully define and analyze them, prepare detailed alternative strategies for many issues, and, with respect to eight of the issues, persuade the county administrator or county board of the need for action responses. Decentralization has led to more coordination and collaboration among managers and staff within and across departments—many of whom previously had had no knowledge of each other's needs and responsibilities. Thus communication and information sharing on issues of mutual concern was initially established or strengthened.

Collaboration on policymaking between top management and the board on selected issues and between the county administrator and department managers, many of whom headed planning teams, also has been improved. Most respondents further indicated that the team approach to planning has contributed to an increase in morale among managers and a lessening of the feeling of having been isolated from decision processes in this large (7,200-person) bureaucracy.[14]

The widespread use of planning teams also has had its drawbacks. Respondents indicated that the lack of outsiders on teams may have prevented the surfacing of divergent, critical points of view on issues; that foot-dragging on controversial issues—those with especially difficult political overtones—was evidenced; that planning progressed slowly on some teams where leadership was weak; and that information overload sometimes occurred for members and especially chairs of planning teams.

Staff assistance by the OPD has been essential to maintaining the momentum of planning and to the success enjoyed thus far. Staff helped design, skillfully facilitate, and publicize within and outside the county the strategic planning accomplishments of the planning teams and top management. In doing so, OPD has neither made strategic planning decisions nor developed a strategic plan for the county; that has remained the fundamental responsibility of the county's line managers. The scope and direction of the planning process has resulted, however, in the continuingly heavy, and as yet unmet, demand for staff time—the thinning of staff resources.[15]

CONCLUSION OF THE STUDY

The county's issues management approach to strategic planning may be successfully applied, we believe, to other units of local government. Our conclusions to the study address the potential benefits and pitfalls of adopting the Hennepin County model.

The first conclusion is that the county's use of an issues management approach helped integrate strategic planning and operational decision making. In an environment where, as one respondent suggested, "County departments have nothing in common except the property tax base,"[16] the issues management process has prompted the top management, many departmental planning teams, and, with respect to certain issues, the county board to assess complex issues systematically, to weigh long-range policy and program options, to select practical strategies and, in some cases, to implement action steps including budget request or allocation decisions. What is emerging is an attitude among county managers that issues management is "not a project but part

of my job," that planning, in other words, is being perceived as an ongoing or recurring operational responsibility of line managers.[17]

A second conclusion is that the identification of a limited number of critical issues is essential to the effective implementation of the issues management approach. We concur with a recent decision of the county administrator that in the planning process county managers should address no more than 10 issues simultaneously; that, in effect, the team planning approach will be used selectively on major issues to be determined by the cabinet and county board.[18] The bottom–up process will become more of a top–down and bottom–up collaborative effort.

This emerging policy chiefly is a recognition that many complex and some controversial issues carrying potentially adverse political implications for board members may take a lengthy period to move through the planning process—until the timing for action steps is appropriate. A narrowing of the overall issues agenda will improve the management of the planning process by decreasing the number of functioning planning teams, reducing time spent in planning by the teams, easing the burden of coordination and direction of teams, reducing in-kind costs, and permitting a more effective scheduling of staff assistance.

A third conclusion is that the use of a broadly implemented, collaborative planning approach has increased expectations among county managers for organizational development and change. Managers have reported that they feel more ownership and commitment to the management of county services, more a part of a management team giving direction to county operations. In a climate where the raising of questions about the mission of the county, its policy and funding priorities, and the effectiveness of board leadership has been encouraged, improved morale among many managers has resulted.[19] Many planning teams also have experienced direct, positive response to their planning efforts as their proposed strategies and actions have met with board approval and have been implemented. As these initial changes have been made in the delivery of services, expectations among managers that additional changes will be forthcoming have increased.

NOTES

1. Interview with Mark Andrew, Hennepin County Commissioner, September 13, 1985.

2. Interview with Bruce Kurtz, Hennepin County Deputy Administrator, August 8, 1985.

3. "Hennepin County Strategic Planning, Phase 1: Executive Report," 1984.

4. "Hennepin County Strategic Planning, Phase 1: Management Report," 1984.

5. Interview with Sue Zuidema, director, Hennepin County Community Health Department, August 3, 1985.

6. Eckert 1986.

7. Interview with Philip Eckert, director, Hennepin County Office of Planning and Development, November 24, 1986.

8. Zentner 1981.

9. Zentner 1981.

10. Crable and Vibbert 1985.

11. Halstead 1985.

12. Kurtz interview, 1985.

13. Halstead 1985.

14. Interview with Jan Smaby, director, Hennepin County Economic Assistance Department, August 13, 1985, and Zuidema interview, 1985.

15. Zuidema interview, 1985.

16. Interview with Dan McLaughlin, administrator, Hennepin County Medical Center, September 13, 1985.

17. Eckert interview, 1986.

18. Eckert interview, 1986.

19. Zuidema interview, 1985.

REFERENCES

Ansoff, H. Igor. 1980. Strategic issue management. *Strategic Management Journal* 1, 2: 131–180.

Ashley, William. 1985. Issues management. A presentation at the Issues Management Seminar, Minneapolis Chamber of Commerce, Minneapolis, Minnesota. October.

Bryson, John M., R. Edward Freeman, and William D. Roering. 1985. Strategic planning in the public sector: Approaches and future directions. In *Strategic Perspectives on Planning Practice*, edited by Barry Checkoway. Lexington, Mass.: Lexington Books.

Bryson, John M., Andrew H. Van de Ven, and William D. Roering. 1986. Strategic planning and the revitalization of the public service. In *Toward a New Public Service*, edited by Robert Denhardt and Edward Jennings. Columbia, Mo.: University of Missouri Press.

Chase, W. Howard. 1984. *Issue management: Origins of the future.* Stanford, Conn.: Issues Action Publications, Inc.

Crable, Richard E. and Steven L. Vibbert. 1985. Managing issues and influencing public policy. *Public Relations Review* 7, 2: 3–16.

Delmont, Timothy J. and Ann M. Pflaum, 1985. External scanning in public and private organizations: Implications for strategic management in higher education. Paper presented at the 25th Forum of the Association of Institutional Research, Portland, Oregon. April 28–May 1.

Dutton, J. L., L. Fahey, and U. K. Narayanan. 1983. Toward understanding strategic issue diagnosis. *Strategic Management Journal* 4: 307–323.

Eadie, Douglas C. 1983. Putting a powerful tool to practical use: The application of strategic planning in the public sector. *Public Administration Review* September/October, 447–452.

———, and John B. Olsen. 1982. *The game plan: Governance with foresight.* Washington, D.C.: The Council of State Planning Agencies.

Eckert, Philip C. 1986. A public sector model for strategic planning: An overview of the Hennepin County process. Report prepared for Hennepin County government, April 6.

Foresight Task Force. 1983. *Foresight in the private sector: How government can use it.* Washington, D.C.: U.S. Government Printing Office.

Halstead, J. Philip. 1985. Issues management and issues networking: A national and regional plan. Report prepared for the Clorox Company.

Hennepin County strategic planning manual. 1983. Minneapolis, Minn.

Hennepin County strategic planning, phase 1: Executive report. 1984. Minneapolis, Minn.

Hennepin County strategic planning, phase 1: Management report. 1984. Minneapolis, Minn.

Lorange, P. 1980. *Corporate planning: An executive viewpoint.* Englewood Cliffs, N.J.: Prentice-Hall, Inc.

Lozier, G. Gregory and Kumar Chittipeddi. 1986. Issues management in strategic planning. *Research in Higher Education.* 24, 1: 3–14.

Nanus, Burt. 1984. Foresight, strategy and political communications. Paper presented to the National Governors Association, Nashville, Tennessee, July 30.

Renfro, William L. 1982. Managing the issues of the 1980s. *The Futurist* August: 61–65.

Renfro, William L. and James L. Morrison. 1983. The scanning process: Getting started. In *Applying Methods and Techniques of Futures Research,* edited by J. L. Morrison, W. L. Renfro, and W. I. Boucher. San Francisco: Jossey-Bass.

Taylor, Bernard. 1984. Strategic planning—which style do you need? *Long Range Planning* 17, 3: 51–62.

Wilson, Ian. The benefits of environmental analysis. In *The Strategic Management Handbook,* edited by Kenneth J. Albert. New York, N.Y.: McGraw-Hill.

Zentner, Rene D. 1981. Issues and their management. Paper presented at the Critical Issues Management Program, Castine, Maine. June 14–19.

12

Strategic Planning in a Nonprofit Organization: Model Cities Health Center

BRYAN W. BARRY

In 1983, the leaders of Model Cities Health Center decided that their community would be better served if the clinic could spin off from the city of St. Paul and become a free-standing nonprofit organization. Strategic planning was a tool for making that transition.

The clinic began in 1968 as a community program to make health services more accessible to the low-income residents of the Summit–University community of St. Paul. The clinic at that time was staffed by a coordinator plus doctors and dentists who volunteered their time. In 1968, clinic services and staff expanded greatly under Model Cities program funding. An advisory board for the program was established at that time. The clinic became part of the city of St. Paul's Division of Public Health in 1972.

From 1972 to 1984 the clinic experienced several major changes:

• As federal Model Cities funding phased out in 1975, community development block grants became the primary source of the clinic's funding. Other federal funding was obtained in 1979 through HEW.

• Services and staff continued to expand over these years. By 1984, services included internal medicine, family practice, pediatrics, obstetrics/gynecology, podiatry, ophthalmology, minor surgery, lab, X-ray, dental care, pharmacy, health education, and transportation. The clinic's staff of 19 (15 full-time equivalents) served about 5,000 community residents in that year.

• In 1980, the clinic's advisory board began to discuss whether the program might function more effectively as a free-standing nonprofit health center apart from the city. After three years of discussion the clinic's advisory board and health department officials agreed on this direction.

• In June 1984, a capable new executive director was hired. One of the board's expectations was that she would lead the clinic through the transition from city program to nonprofit agency.

In November 1984, the center's advisory board decided that specific plans were needed for becoming a free-standing agency and charting the center's future for the next few years. A board retreat was scheduled for early 1985 to begin work on that plan. The board's chair recommended that a consultant be hired to help with the retreat. The board chair contacted a suggested consultant and asked that he meet with the clinic's executive director, then prepare a proposal for board review.

After meeting with the executive director and the board chair, the consultant prepared a project proposal with the following objectives:

1. Develop a six- to twelve-month plan for Model Cities Health Center to manage the transition from city program to nonprofit organization. The plan will include key tasks, responsibilities, and time lines.

2. Develop a three- to five-year strategic plan for Model Cities Health Center that describes the center's:

- Mission
- Target population
- Services
- Financing
- Staffing
- Structure
- Governance
- Marketing
- Facilities
- Implementation steps

The advisory board, which would become the new organization's board of directors, reviewed and accepted the proposal. The February retreat would be used to introduce the board, key staff, and a few outsiders to strategic planning and begin developing a strategic plan for the Center.

After the retreat a smaller planning team would be charged with developing a first draft of the plan. Part of the retreat would also focus on outlining immediate tasks that needed attention over the next six months in order for the center to become a free-standing nonprofit entity.

THE RETREAT: INTRODUCTION TO STRATEGIC PLANNING

The full board, three key staff members, an administrator from a prominent hospital, a city health department official, and a staff member from the Department of Health and Human Services in Chicago were then invited to attend a one-day planning retreat at a local conference center. The consultant began the retreat with a 30-minute orientation to strategic planning, which was defined as the process of determining *what* an organization intends to be in the future and *how* it will get there. Strategic planning was further defined as finding the best fit among the three sets of forces described in Figure 12–1.[1]

A general model for developing a strategic plan was also reviewed (Figure 12–2).[2] The consultant then reviewed with participants the process that would be used to develop the center's strategic plan. In earlier discussions, the center's executive and board had expressed a desire for a relatively compact planning process—one that would take no more than five or six planning sessions over a three-month period. The planning process in Figure 12–3 was developed to meet these time constraints. Retreat participants reviewed this planning process and approved it without modification.

SITUATION ANALYSIS

After the strategic planning orientation, the retreat participants reviewed the center's history, current situation, mission, opportunities/threats, strengths/weaknesses, and critical issues using the worksheets in Figure 12–4. After participants completed each worksheet, their responses were listed, prioritized, and then discussed. This analysis led to a summary

Figure 12–1. Finding the Fit

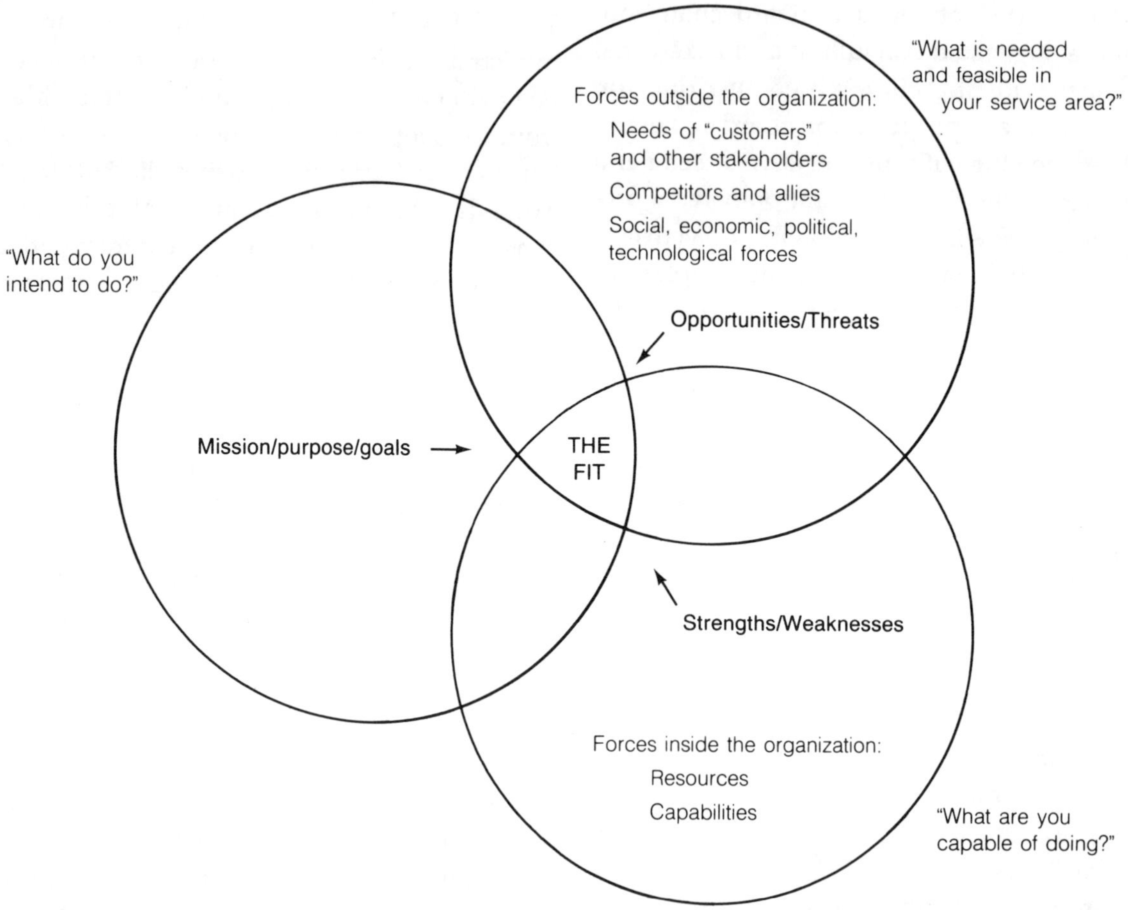

"What do you
intend to do?"

Forces outside the organization:

Needs of "customers"
and other stakeholders

Competitors and allies

Social, economic, political,
technological forces

"What is needed
and feasible in
your service area?"

Opportunities/Threats

Mission/purpose/goals →

THE
FIT

Strengths/Weaknesses

Forces inside the organization:

Resources

Capabilities

"What are you
capable of doing?"

From *Strategic Planning Workbook for Nonprofit Organizations*, Bryan W. Barry. Amherst H. Wilder Foundation, 1985

of the center's most critical issues and choices for the future.

During this phase of the planning, the planning team did not attempt to resolve these issues, but to get the issues on the table. For example, a review of the center's *history* showed that the organization had adjusted its mission and services over time to meet the priorities of funders. Several board members suggested that community needs, not funder priorities,

should be stressed in charting the center's course for the next three to four years. The discussion of the center's *mission* focused on whether the organization should expand its services both geographically and to middle-income people. Would such a shift bring the center new vitality or take it away from its historic identity and strength? A review of *opportunities and threats* highlighted a possible loss in patients from competing head-to-head with

Figure 12–2. Steps to Develop a Strategic Plan

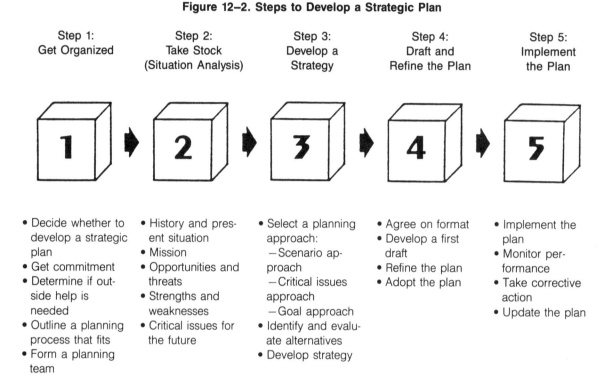

Step 1: Get Organized	Step 2: Take Stock (Situation Analysis)	Step 3: Develop a Strategy	Step 4: Draft and Refine the Plan	Step 5: Implement the Plan
1	2	3	4	5
• Decide whether to develop a strategic plan • Get commitment • Determine if outside help is needed • Outline a planning process that fits • Form a planning team	• History and present situation • Mission • Opportunities and threats • Strengths and weaknesses • Critical issues for the future	• Select a planning approach: —Scenario approach —Critical issues approach —Goal approach • Identify and evaluate alternatives • Develop strategy	• Agree on format • Develop a first draft • Refine the plan • Adopt the plan	• Implement the plan • Monitor performance • Take corrective action • Update the plan

From *Strategic Planning Workbook for Nonprofit Organizations*, Bryan W. Barry. Amherst H. Wilder Foundation, 1985.

HMOs, a growing need and market for medical services in their changing community, and federal budget cuts that would likely affect the center's funding. *Strengths* of the center included its director and strong community support built over the years. *Weaknesses* included the center's free clinic image and unstable funding. At the end of this discussion the planning team summarized the analysis by listing seven critical issues or choices that the center faced related to community support, target population, staffing, the board, funding, image, and facilities. Appendix 12A is a summary of this analysis.

NEXT STEPS

After identifying the critical issues, the board and key staff outlined how the strategic plan would be completed. A smaller planning team consisting of board (4), staff (2), and the health administrator were charged with developing a first draft of a three- to five-year plan for the center. The plan would then be brought to the full board for review. The situation analysis developed at the retreat was summarized by the consultant and executive director, then mailed to participants for comment.

Figure 12–3. Strategic Planning Process: Community Health Center

Steps	Responsible
1. Get agreement on planning steps.	Executive director Board chair Consultant
Meeting 1 *(5-hour meeting with board and key staff)*:	
2. Orient board and staff to strategic planning.	Consultant

3. Do situation analysis:
    History and present situation
    Mission
    Opportunities and threats
    Strengths and weaknesses
    Critical issues for the future
	Participants
	Consultant

4. Form board/staff team to complete the plan.	Board chair Executive director
5. Summarize situation analysis (between meetings).	Executive director Consultant
Meeting 2 *(2 hours)*:	

6. Develop scenarios for the future (scenario approach)
    Develop scenarios.
    Note areas of agreement and choices.
	Planning team
	Consultant

7. Summarize scenarios and choices (between meetings).	Executive director Consultant
8. Gather information to test feasibility of scenarios (between meetings).	Executive director
Meeting 3 *(2 hours)*:	
9. Evaluate scenarios (e.g., fit with mission, fit with needs, financial feasibility). Select the best scenario.	Planning team Consultant
10. Develop first draft of strategic plan. Include sections on mission, services, staffing, finances, facilities, and implementation (between meetings).	Executive director Consultant
Meeting 4 *(2 hours)*:	
11. Review first draft. Note suggested improvements.	Planning team Consultant
12. Revise first draft (between meetings).	Executive director Consultant
Review, adopt, and implement plan:	

13. Review second draft with
    Board
    Staff
    2-3 outsiders
    Note reactions and suggestions for improvement
	
	Board chair
	Executive director
	Executive director

14. Review reactions and make needed revisions; prepare final draft.	Planning team Consultant
15. Adopt plan.	Board
16. Implement plan. Review progress every 6 months. Update plan yearly.	Executive director Board

Total meeting time, including review sessions: 18-20 hours.
Time to develop plan: 3 months.

Figure 12–4. Situation Analysis Worksheets

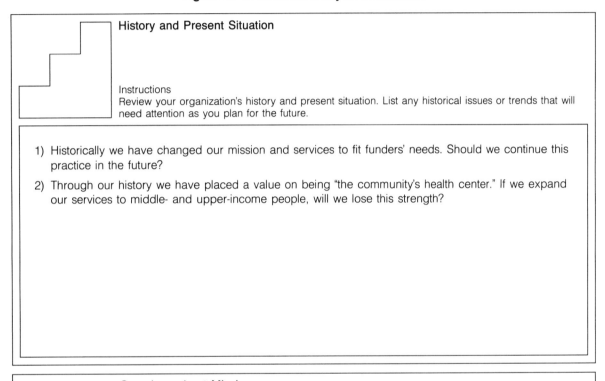

History and Present Situation

Instructions
Review your organization's history and present situation. List any historical issues or trends that will need attention as you plan for the future.

1) Historically we have changed our mission and services to fit funders' needs. Should we continue this practice in the future?

2) Through our history we have placed a value on being "the community's health center." If we expand our services to middle- and upper-income people, will we lose this strength?

Questions about Mission

Instructions
1) Describe below what you understand your organization's mission or purpose to be.
2) List any questions, ideas, or concerns you have about your present mission.
3) Consider what might be the best mission for your organization in the future. Describe what your organization might accomplish in coming years and who will be served.
4) Discuss your responses with the planning team and note areas of agreement and disagreement.

Present mission or purpose
Serve as the principal medical, health care, and health education resource in the _____ area. With emphasis on health promotion and disease prevention, the project's mission must permit a wide range of health delivery programs designed to advance quality health care. In pursuit of this mission the center will develop and provide a wide range of medical and health-related services that respond to community and city needs.

Questions about current mission
1) Present mission statement needs to be revised: too long, too activity-focused.
2) Mission has shifted over the years.
3) Should the center broaden its target population to reflect the present makeup of the community?
4) Should geographical boundaries also be broadened?

Possible changes in mission for the future
What we want to accomplish: 1) Raise the health status of community. 2) Meet the medical needs of people served.
Who will be served—target groups: Low-income people in community. Middle- and upper-income people will be attracted too.

Figure 12–4. (Continued)

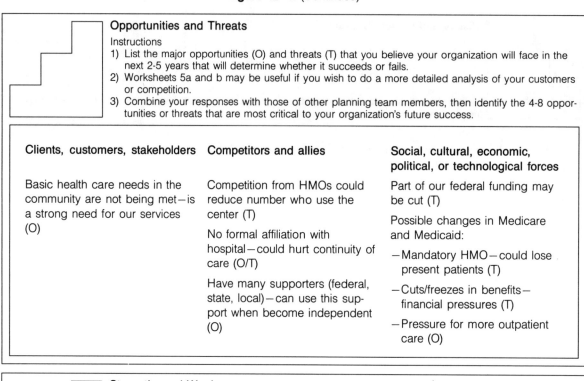

Opportunities and Threats

Instructions

1) List the major opportunities (O) and threats (T) that you believe your organization will face in the next 2-5 years that will determine whether it succeeds or fails.
2) Worksheets 5a and b may be useful if you wish to do a more detailed analysis of your customers or competition.
3) Combine your responses with those of other planning team members, then identify the 4-8 opportunities or threats that are most critical to your organization's future success.

Clients, customers, stakeholders	Competitors and allies	Social, cultural, economic, political, or technological forces
Basic health care needs in the community are not being met—is a strong need for our services (O)	Competition from HMOs could reduce number who use the center (T)	Part of our federal funding may be cut (T)
	No formal affiliation with hospital—could hurt continuity of care (O/T)	Possible changes in Medicare and Medicaid:
	Have many supporters (federal, state, local)—can use this support when become independent (O)	—Mandatory HMO—could lose present patients (T)
		—Cuts/freezes in benefits—financial pressures (T)
		—Pressure for more outpatient care (O)

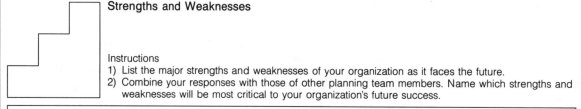

Strengths and Weaknesses

Instructions

1) List the major strengths and weaknesses of your organization as it faces the future.
2) Combine your responses with those of other planning team members. Name which strengths and weaknesses will be most critical to your organization's future success.

Strengths and assets

1) Strong director
2) Support of the people served
3) Services are responsive to community needs—effective
4) Good political support from mayor, council, others

Weaknesses and liabilities

1) Our image as a "free clinic"
2) Unstable funding base—federal dollars are vulnerable
3) Lack of clear plan for the future
4) Inadequate facilities
5) Presently understaffed—hard to keep good medical people

Figure 12–4. (Continued)

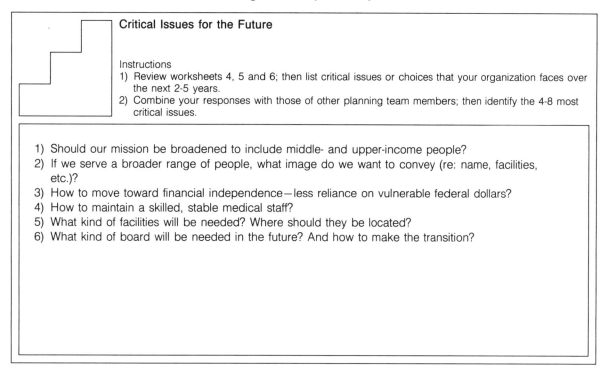

Critical Issues for the Future

Instructions
1) Review worksheets 4, 5 and 6; then list critical issues or choices that your organization faces over the next 2-5 years.
2) Combine your responses with those of other planning team members; then identify the 4-8 most critical issues.

1) Should our mission be broadened to include middle- and upper-income people?
2) If we serve a broader range of people, what image do we want to convey (re: name, facilities, etc.)?
3) How to move toward financial independence—less reliance on vulnerable federal dollars?
4) How to maintain a skilled, stable medical staff?
5) What kind of facilities will be needed? Where should they be located?
6) What kind of board will be needed in the future? And how to make the transition?

The Plan

After the retreat, the smaller planning team developed the first draft of the center's strategic plan in three two-hour meetings. At its first meeting, the team identified several alternative scenarios or futures for the center using the following exercise:

Imagine that it is three years from now and the center has been put together in a very exciting way. Imagine that you are a newspaper reporter doing a story on the organization at that time. You have thoroughly reviewed the center's mission, services, personnel, finances, relationships, etc. Describe in a few phrases or a picture what you see.

Each team member's scenario was then reported. Scenarios included:

1. Continue as a division of the city's health department.
2. Break off from the city. Become a free-standing community health clinic with ties to hospitals and other clinics.
3. Become a community health and human service center that houses the center and several other agencies serving the same target population.
4. Become a component of a consolidated medical program, similar to an HMO, that offers basic health services as well as several specialized services. Participating health centers would provide other specialties.

The executive director subsequently was asked to talk with several other organizations to determine if there might be interest in strategies 3 or 4.

At a second two-hour meeting, the executive director reported her findings. Team members rated each scenario on several factors (fit with mission, fit with community needs, financial feasibility), then listed the relative advantages and disadvantages of each scenario. By the end of the meeting a general strategy for the agency was agreed upon:

> Break off from the city. Become a free-standing community health center, housed in our own building. Establish a new and clearer identity. Expand our target group to include middle-income people—also slightly expand our service area. Improve staffing ratios. Ask two to three other organizations with complementary services (mental health, financial counseling, and perhaps day care) to have offices in the building. Develop and maintain ties with several hospitals and health clinics. Negotiate reimbursement from several HMOs.

The planning team discussed this scenario with board and staff between team meetings and received authorization from the board to test whether this scenario was feasible.

At a third planning meeting, the team identified areas needing more investigation, then resolved as many questions as possible in the time remaining. After the third meeting the executive director and consultant translated the preferred scenario into the first draft of a strategic plan (see Appendix 12B). The plan painted a picture of the center over the next three years. Major sections described the center's mission and overall strategy; specific service, staffing, and financial plans for each year; facility plans; key relationships and next steps for implementing major strategies. Our experience has shown that a relatively brief plan in outline form is a more effective communication and management tool than a long narrative plan.

The draft of the three-year plan was reviewed with the full board, staff, and two knowledgeable people outside the organization. Needed changes were made, then the plan was reviewed and adopted by the board.

Implementation

After adopting the plan, the center completed negotiations with the city to become a free-standing nonprofit health center. Each task in the implementation plan was begun roughly according to schedule. By the end of year 1, plans for the building site changed and the backup site was used. The center was unsuccessful in obtaining one new source of funding, but was more successful than anticipated with other sources so that overall projections for the year were met.

In reviewing the strategic planning one year after the plan was approved Beverley Hawkins, the center's executive director, noted:

> Strategic planning was the best thing we could have done for our organization. I used the planning to expand our service delivery system, diversify our services, and coordinate and link those services with other health and human service agencies. The plan has become an extremely valuable tool in our financial planning as well.
>
> Since the plan was approved we have made significant progress. The services that we identified in our plan are now being carried out with the staff indicated. We have control of a parcel of land on which we will develop and own a new health facility. We have developed a marketing and community relations strategy that links us with community agencies, hospitals, units of government, and churches. Every piece

of our plan is in some stage of implementation.

It took real commitment on the part of the agency, including both board and staff, to make the planning and implementation successful. It was hard work, but well worth the effort.

Lessons

Model Cities Health Center's experience highlights several strategic planning principles:

Tailor the planning to fit the organization. One key to successful strategic planning is designing a planning process that fits. This can be done by staying focused on an organization's critical choices and using planning methods that will resolve the issues. The majority of planning time was spent on the center's most critical issues:

• Which services should be provided to which target groups.

• Future sources of revenue.

• The staff needed for the future.

• A new facility.

• How to mobilize and maintain community support.

The center used a relatively simple planning process to identify and resolve these issues by adjusting the planning process for practical factors such as:

• An organization's experience with planning—a simple, manageable process often works better for beginners.

• Commitment of organizational leaders—get it.

• Leadership available for the planning effort—appoint, hire, or borrow someone who understands planning and can guide a group through the planning process.

• Technical or political problems—consider early how technical and political issues will be handled.

The center had virtually no experience with strategic planning. For this reason it used an experienced consultant to orient the board and staff to strategic planning and ride herd on the planning process. Both staff and board preferred a brief, focused planning process to a more involved approach. Knowing that technical issues regarding the health care industry would arise, the planning team included two people who were familiar with the latest developments in that field—a seasoned hospital administrator and an attorney who specialized in health care law. City and federal officials who would eventually need to support the plan were also involved in its design. Model Cities Health Center designed, then executed, a planning process that was likely to work for it.

Leadership is a key. Success or failure of a strategic planning effort often hinges on how well that effort is led. Model Cities Health Center was fortunate to have a capable, energetic executive director who was determined to develop a workable plan for the future. A retreat early in the planning process had the effect of building board interest in and commitment to the planning process. An experienced consultant was found to help keep the planning efficient, moving, and on track. Effective strategic planning involves an organization's leaders deeply in the process.

Quicker can be better. In consulting on a great number of strategic planning projects we have found that sound strategic plans can be developed in relatively brief periods of time. Since 1982 the average time needed to develop a strategic plan has dropped by 50 to 80 percent. Model Cities Health Center developed the first draft of its strategic plan after three team meetings. The draft was then refined in structured reviews with staff, board, and outsiders.

Recent research on successful innovations indicates that strategic planning systems often inhibit strategic thinking.[3] People get entangled in and distracted by the very methods that are intended to evoke good strategies for the future. A brief, focused planning process that concentrates on an organization's most critical choices is often preferable to an extended planning process that tends to wander.

Strategic planning is a way of thinking. The plan is never perfect or complete. Through their strategic planning, the health center's staff and board understood more clearly the relationships between services, staffing, finances, and relations with other organizations. In addition to charting a course for the future, the plan has provided a framework for making midcourse corrections as circumstances change.

A tool for transition. Model Cities Health Center used strategic planning as a tool to make a major transition—from a program of the city to free-standing nonprofit organization. Since 1982 there has been growing interest from nonprofit organizations and governmental units in strategic planning. Such planning can be a very useful tool for managing organizational changes in turbulent times.

REFERENCES

Allio, Robert J. and Malcolm W. Pennington, eds. 1979. *Corporate planning: Techniques and applications.* New York, N.Y.: AMACOM.

Andrews, Kenneth R. 1980. *The concept of corporate strategy.* Homewood, Ill.: Dow Jones-Irwin.

Barry, Bryan W. 1986. *Strategic planning workbook for nonprofit organizations.* St. Paul, Minn.: Amherst H. Wilder Foundation.

Bryson, J. M., A. H. Van de Ven, and W. D. Roering. 1987. Strategic planning and the revitalization of the public service. In *Toward a New Public Service,* edited by R. Denhardt and E. Jennings. Columbia, Mo.: Extension Publications, University of Missouri.

Hardy, James M. 1984. *Managing for impact in nonprofit organizations: Corporate planning techniques and applications.* Erwin, Tenn.: Essex Press.

Kotler, Philip. 1982. *Marketing for nonprofit organizations.* Englewood Cliffs, N.J.: Prentice-Hall.

Marrus, Stephanie K. 1984. *Building the strategic plan: Find, analyze and present the right information.* New York, N.Y.: John Wiley & Sons.

Naylor, Thomas H. 1979. *Corporate planning models.* Reading, Mass.: Addison-Wesley.

Porter, Michael E. 1985. *Competitive advantage: Creating and sustaining superior performance.* New York, N.Y.: The Free Press.

———. 1980. *Competitive strategy: Techniques for analyzing business, industry and competitors.* New York, N.Y.: The Free Press.

Rowe, Alan J., Richard O. Mason, and Karl Dickel. 1982. *Strategic management and business policy: A methodological approach.* Reading, Mass.: Addison-Wesley.

Steiner, George A. 1979. *Strategic planning: What every manager must know.* New York, N.Y.: The Free Press.

Tichy, Noel M. 1983. *Managing strategic change, technical, political, and cultural dynamics.* New York, N.Y.: John Wiley & Sons.

Tregoe, Benjamin B. and John W. Zimmerman. 1980. *Top management strategy: What it is and how to make it work.* New York, N.Y.: Simon & Schuster.

United Way of America. 1984. *Scenarios: A tool for planning in uncertain times;* 1986, *Strategic management and United Way;* 1985, *What lies ahead: A mid-decade view.* Alexandria, Va.: United Way.

APPENDIX 12A
MODEL CITIES HEALTH CENTER:
SUMMARY OF SITUATION ANALYSIS

The following text is a summary of the Model Cities Health Center's situation analysis performed by the center's planning team. Tables 12A–1, 12A–2, and 12A–3 also provide summary information.

HISTORY

1. Center was started as a Model Cities program—lots of money. Mission was to provide health services to the community.
2. Primary funding shifted to other services (Medical Assistance, other federal and state grants, fees). Mission changed to raising the health status of the community—more emphasis on preventive health care. Became tied more closely to the city's health department.
3. Now engaged in negotiations with the city to become a free-standing nonprofit organization.

Themes

1. Serve the community.
2. Shape mission and services to fit funding.
Comment: These two themes could conflict.

Values

1. We are "the community's health center": responsive to needs, board and staff are representative of community.
2. Quality services.

COMMENTS AND QUESTIONS ABOUT THE CENTER'S MISSION

1. The center's general statement of mission has changed over the years:
• From providing health services to the community to
• Raising the health status of the community to
• Present "Statement of Missions and Goals"
2. The present "Statement of Missions and Goals" may not be a good statement for the future—too long and too focused on activities (vs. results).
3. To what extent should funding concerns influence the center's mission?
4. Who should the center's target population be?
• Present clientele (mainly low-income people)
• Whoever lives in the community (include middle- and upper-income people)
• Other: Focus on women and their children
5. Should the center broaden its geographical service area? If so, what should that area be?
6. Should the center's mission be stated in terms that are achievable?

Table 12A–1. Model Cities Health Center: Strengths and Weaknesses

Votes (14 possible)	Strengths	Votes (14 possible)	Weaknesses
11	1. Strong director	12	1. Image: "free clinic"
10	2. Support of the people served	10	2. Unstable funding—reliance on federal dollars that may not be there in the future
10	3. Good political support (mayor, council, etc.)	8	3. Lack of a plan for the future
10	4. Length of service in the community—range of services, responsive, how service is delivered	7	4. Inadequate facility: not enough space, appearance, distractions, lights, etc.
9	5. Key staff	7	5. More promotion and marketing needs to be done
6	6. Board represents a good mixture or cross section of people	7	6. City control: personnel issues, contracts, political risks
5	7. We have "a franchise" to serve our area	6	7. Staff shortage; Only one doctor—discontinuity of medical care, clerical turnover
5	8. Some funding sources are stable	6	8. Collection of patient revenues
4	9. Dedication and creativity of staff and board	5	9. Relative newness of the board as a governing body—complexity of the issues
4	10. Good medical people on staff and board	5	10. Location
4	11. Some staff have a lot of potential to be developed	5	11. Name
3	12. Good board chair	4	12. Lack a good management information system
2	13. Location—been there a long time	3	13. Hours of services—no night hours (have some now)
		2	14. Staff development, training and motivation

Table 12A–2. Model Cities Health Center: Opportunities and Threats

Votes (14 possible)	Statements of Opportunities (O) and Threats (T)
7	1. Competition from HMOs may reduce the number of people who use the center. Some people who might like to use the center may not be able to. (T)
6	2. There is a market for our services. We are in a medically underserved area. (O)
6	3. Federal funds for programs like ours may be cut. (T)
6	4. The center is not meeting several federal indicators (pharmacy and physician/client ratio). This could affect funding. (T)
6	5. Changes in Medicare and Medicaid may: • Force people into HMOs (T) • Cut or freeze benefits (T) • Move health services into more outpatient care (O)
6	6. Lack of full and formal affiliation with a hospital may hurt continuity of service. (T)
6	7. The center has many allies: (O) • Federal (grants management staff) • State (health department) • Metro (metropolitan health planning board) • Local (community services, mayor)
4	8. The center could become part of a new consolidated medical program (CMP). (O/T)
3	9. Changes on the block we want to move to: • Make that street a good place to move to (O) • Necessitate changes in our image (O/T)
3	10. The "feminization of poverty" will mean that there will be more women with children under six in need of child care. Perhaps the center should provide such child care. (O)
3	11. There is an opportunity for the center to get into community-based education and continuing education through the public schools, university, etc. (O)
3	12. There will be more senior citizens in the community in need of health care in coming years. (O)
3	13. The center lacks support from the medical and dental community.
1	14. The center needs to be able to shift its services to meet epidemic shifts (e.g., AIDS, herpes, etc.). (O/T)
1	15. The center could tailor its services to the needs of the minority populations it serves. (O)
1	16. The center could conduct continuing education events for health care professionals. (O)
1	17. With growing depersonalization in the health care field, the center can provide personalized care—e.g., people are able to get the same doctor here. (O)
1	18. The center needs more funders as allies. (O)
1	19. There is potential for increased/new money from the city and county—similar to funds received for other community clinics. (O)

Table 12A–3. Model Cities Health Center: Issue Identification

Votes (14 possible)	Critical Issues for the Future
10	1. **Community Support.** How can the center develop and maintain support from: • Neighborhood? • Political and funding communities? • Medical community?
10	2. **Mission and Target Population.** • Should the center expand its services to middle- and upper-income people? If so, how will they be attracted? • Should our geographic service area be expanded?
7	3. **Staff.** • How can the center maintain a skilled, stable medical staff?
5	4. **Board.** • What kind of board will be needed in the future? • What will be the board's role (vs. staff's role) in leading the agency?
5	5. **Funding.** • How can the center move from position of financial dependence to independence?
—	6. **Image.** • What is the image that the center wants to convey to the community? How will it be conveyed (e.g., name, facility, etc.)?
—	7. **Facility.** • Should the center move out of its present facility to its own building? If so, where should the building be located? How should it be financed?

APPENDIX 12B
MODEL CITIES HEALTH CENTER: THREE-YEAR PLAN

The following text is a first draft of the Model Cities Health Center's strategic plan, based on the planning team's preferred scenario. Information shown in Tables 12B–1 through 12B–6 also were part of the planning team's preferred scenario.

MISSION AND STRATEGY

The mission of Model Cities Health Center is to improve the health status of residents in the Summit-University community. Over the next three years the center will provide affordable primary medical, dental, and related services to community residents, with particular emphasis on serving those most in need.

Over the next three years, the center will expand and improve its health services. The center also will expand its services to a broader segment of the community. More middle- and upper-income residents will use the center's improved services. A new child development program will be operated in the center's new building by either the center or another agency. The total number of people served by the cen-

ter will increase from 4,800 this year to more than 6,700 in year 3.

In year 1, the center will move to a new facility developed to fit its needs, and will also provide services in several outreach locations.

The staff of the center will be increased to provide those services, from 14.7 present full-time equivalents now to 32.8 in year 3.

Center services will be financed through a broadened base of support. The center will continue to request federal, state, and city grants, and will also request support from the county. Foundation grants will be used to fund the costs of moving into the new center and start up the child development program. Payments from patient fees, Medical Assistance, insurance, Medicare, and HMO payments will also increase with the center's expanded target population and association with at least two major hospitals.

The center's internal operations and board of directors will also be strengthened. The center will have a strong management information system that has accounts receivable, accounts payable, and statistical analysis capability.

In addition, the center will strengthen its relationships with area hospitals, other community clinics and human service providers.

Table 12B–1. Model Cities Health Center Strategic Plan Elements: Service Plans[1]

A. Service Description

Services	Description	Target Group Most in need	Other
1. Basic health care		70%	30%
a. Primary care	Internal medicine		
	Family practice		
	Pediatrics		
	Obstetrics/gynecology		
b. Other health services	Podiatry		
	Ophthalmology		
	Surgery		
	Lab, X-ray		
c. Dental	Dental care		
d. Pharmacy	Prescriptions		
2. Related Services			
a. Health education	Screenings	50%	50%
	Classes: smoking, weight loss, exercise, etc.		
	Health fairs, presentations		
b. Transportation	Transportation to and from clinic	100%	0%
c. Child development/day care[2]	Day care with child development emphasis	45%	55%

B. Levels of Service

Services	Units of Service	Projected Service Levels Base Year	Year 1	Year 2	Year 3
1. Basic Health Care					
a./b. Primary care and other health services	People served	4,300	4,485	5,085	5,890
	Visits	16,000	18,040	22,430	25,960
c. Dental	People served	500	550	800	800
	Visits	1,000	1,500	2,900	3,000
d. Pharmacy	Prescriptions	12,000	13,200	14,520	15,972
2. Related Services					
a. Health education (medical and dental)	People served	1,596	1,750	4,000	4,400
	Events	20	30	50	50
b. Transportation	Patient trips	3,840	4,800	6,000	6,500
c. Child development/day care	Children served	0	0	40	40
	Capacity	0	0	30	30

1. See Appendix A for program assumptions.
2. A feasibility study will show whether the child development should be operated by the center or another organization.

Table 12B–2. Model Cities Health Center Strategic Plan Elements: Staffing Plans

Positions	Full-Time Equivalents			
	Base Year	Year 1	Year 2	Year 3
Basic health care				
Medical director	0.8	0.8	1.0	1.0
Internists	1.0	1.0	1.0	1.0
Family practice	—	1.0	1.0	1.0
Pediatrician	0.1	0.2	0.5	1.0
Obstetrics/gynecology[1]	—	1.0	1.0	1.0
Podiatrist	0.2	0.3	0.5	0.5
Ophthalmologic team[2] (in-kind)	(0.1)	(0.1)	(0.1)	(0.1)
Nurse practitioners[3]	1.0	1.0	1.5	2.0
Medical assistant	1.0	2.0	2.0	2.0
Nurse midwives (in-kind)[4]	(0.1)	(0.1)	(0.1)	(0.1)
Dentist	0.5	0.5	1.0	1.0
Dental hygienist	0.3	0.5	0.75	1.0
Dental assistant	0.7	0.75	1.0	1.0
Dental team[5] (in-kind)	(0.1)	(0.1)	(0.1)	(0.1)
Pharmacist	1.0	1.0	1.0	1.0
Lab/X-ray technician	—	1.0	1.0	1.0
Total basic health staff	6.9	11.35	13.55	14.80
Related Services				
Medical records technician	—	1.0	1.0	1.0
Health education coordinator (RN)	1.0	1.0	1.0	1.0
Pediatric nurse (day care)	—	—	2.0	2.0
Head teacher	—	—	1.0	1.0
Teacher's assistant	—	—	1.0	1.0
Teacher's aide	—	—	1.5	1.5
Cook	—	—	0.4	0.4
Van driver	1.0	1.0	1.0	1.0
Nutritionist	0.1	0.1	0.1	0.1
Total related services staff	2.1	3.1	9.0	9.0
Administration				
Director	1.0	1.0	1.0	1.0
Financial manager	1.0	1.0	1.0	1.0
Grants manager		1.0	1.0	1.0
Office manager	1.0	1.0	1.0	1.0
Billing clerk	1.0	1.0	1.0	1.0
Receptionist	1.0	1.0	1.0	1.0
Patient information specialist	1.0	1.0	1.0	1.0
Office accountant	—	—	1.0	1.0
Clerical assistant	—	—	1.0	1.0
Total administrative staff	6.0	7.0	9.0	9.0
Total staff	15.00	21.45	31.55	32.80

1. Start date July, Year 1
2. From county medical center
3. Includes clinic coordinator
4. From county medical center
5. From the Army Reserve

Table 12B–3. Model Cities Health Center Strategic Plan Elements: Financial Plans[1]

A. Operating Budget

	Base Year	Year 1	Year 2	Year 3
Revenue				
Federal grants (UHI)	$298,500	$305,000	$ 305,000	$ 305,000
State grants (family planning, sexual assault, etc.)	17,307	93,061	98,061	25,000
City	78,532	78,532	78,532	78,532
County grant	0	62,024	62,024	62,024
Private foundation/corporation grants	10,542	30,000	40,000	30,000
United Way/Federated campaign	0	0	25,000	25,000
Health education program income	0	500	2,000	5,000
Patient fees (medical, dental, pharmacy)				
Sliding fee scale	35,947	97,360	148,232	226,764
Personal insurance	3,503	7,800	10,800	13,440
Medical Assistance	101,246	108,160	140,250	152,640
Medicare	4,849	10,920	15,750	22,400
HMOs	5,000	7,852	12,060	24,320
Job voucher	3,000	5,600	0	0
Pharmacy	19,174	21,120	27,456	27,731
Contributions from churches	0	30,000	10,000	0
Early child development project	0	0	96,980	104,000
Contributions for individuals	0	8,000	10,000	10,000
Miscellaneous income	3,990	8,100	9,000	9,500
Total Revenue	$581,590	$874,029	$1,091,145	$1,121,351
Expenses				
Personnel/fringe	$320,545	$374,986	$ 684,735	$ 790,972
Contractual services	157,125	234,850	52,000	10,000
Supplies/inventory	50,807	55,500	70,000	87,500
Space	38,000	59,000	96,000	96,000
Program support	14,000	30,000	50,000	50,000
Staff development	0	2,500	4,500	4,500
Equipment/maintenance	3,600	5,000	6,000	6,000
Equipment/purchase-lease	0	20,000	15,000	10,000
Total Expenses	$584,077	$781,836	$ 978,235	$1,054,972
Surplus/(Deficit)	$ (2,487)	$ 92,193	$ 112,910	$ 66,379

B. Building Budget

Item	Source	Base Year	Year 1	Year 2	Year 3
Assuming New Site					
1. Moving and equipment costs (including furnishings)	Foundation grants United Methodist Church	$ 0	$ 15,000	$ 0	$ 20,000
2. Leasehold improvements	City	0	48,000	0	0
3. Funds to purchase building (exercise purchase option)	Foundation grants Mortgage*	0	250,000	300,000	225,000
Total funds needed		$ 0	$313,000	$ 300,000	$ 245,000

Table 12B–3. (Continued)

Item	Source	Base Year	Year 1	Year 2	Year 3
Assuming Backup Site (new construction)					
1. Acquisition	Foundation grants	$ 0	$ 12,500	$ 0	$ 0
2. Design/construction	Foundation grants City of St. Paul Excess program income Bank loan	0	200,000	200,000	400,000
3. Relocation		0	0	10,000	0
4. Equipment	United Methodist Church	0	5,000	10,000	20,000
Total funds needed		$ 0	$217,500	$ 220,000	$ 420,000

1. See Appendix 12A for financial assumptions.
2. Mortgage of up to $400,000 can be afforded if fund raising goals are not reached.

Table 12B–4. Model Cities Health Center Strategic Plan Elements: Facility Plans

In year 1 the center will move into a four-story building at the corner of Selby and Dale. The space will be built to the center's specifications by a private developer. The first floor of the facility will be clinic space and the second floor will be offices. The ground floor will house a child development center operated by either the center or another agency. The fourth floor will be leased to other organizations with complementary programs (e.g., mental health, services for women and children, financial counseling, etc.).

Each of the floors leased by the Center is 4,000 square feet; 12,000 square feet will be needed with the child development center, 8,000 square feet will be needed without it.

Most of the center's services will be provided at the Selby-Dale location, but the center will also provide outreach services at such locations as Thomas Dale Community Center, Martin Luther King Center, Mt. Airy, and Lexington-Hameline.

The developer will finance the development and construction of the building. Leasehold improvements of clinic space will also be financed by the developer unless the center wishes to raise money to cover those costs. The center's rent will be no more than $8.00 per square foot (or $96,000 per year for 12,000 square feet) with a three- to five-year lease. If the center chooses to raise money for leasehold improvements (approximately $48,000), the developer will reduce rent costs accordingly. The center will also have an option to buy the facility. Money will be raised in years 1 to 3 to exercise that option in year 4.

Table 12B–5. Model Cities Health Center Strategic Plan Elements: Linkages

Over the next three years the center will strengthen its relationships with the following groups and organizations:

1. **Outreach locations:** The center will provide outreach medical, dental, and health education services in several locations; Thomas-Dale Community Center, Martin Luther King Center, Mt. Airy, and Lexington-Hamline are likely locations.

2. **County medical center:** St. Paul Ramsey Medical Center will continue to provide hospitalization and specialty care to center patients, as well as in-kind ophthalmologic and nurse midwife services.

3. **United Hospital:** United Hospital will continue to provide hospitalization and specialty care to center patients. Prepayment arrangements will be investigated.

4. **Other hospitals/medical facilities:** Several other hospitals will also provide hospitalization to the center's patients. Current providers also include University of Minnesota Hospital and Mt. Sinai Hospital. A dental team from the Army Reserve will continue to provide in-kind services at the center.

5. **Other community health clinics:** The center will undertake several joint programs with other community health clinics, including joint community health education and research projects. In addition, the center will provide pharmacy services to several clinics.

6. **HMOs:** The center will continue to serve as a provider clinic for _____ and _____ HMO. Reimbursement from at least one additional HMO will be arranged by year 2.

7. **On-site services from other organizations:** The Urban League will continue to provide home health services to the center's patients. Family Service will continue to provide counseling services. Several new services (women and children's program, financial counseling) will also be provided by other organizations in the new facility.

8. **Nonprofit and for-profit agencies:** The center will increase its services to nonprofit and for-profit agencies in the provision of services to target populations and employees (e.g., physical examinations, health education, health screenings).

9. **Referrals:** The center will strengthen referral relationships with other service providers that can address the needs of our target population.

10. **Health organizations:** The center will strengthen relationships with local affiliates of national health organizations (e.g., _____).

11. **Provider clinic:** The center will continue to serve as a provider clinic for Minnesota Services for Children with Handicaps and Coordinated Health Care, Inc.

Table 12B–6. Model Cities Health Center Strategic Plan Elements: Implementation Plans

Steps	Responsible	By When
1. Determine the feasibility of operating a child development/day care center in the new facility. • Define questions and issues • Review findings • Outline course of action for the center	Planning committee Executive director	October, this year
2. Arrange new prepayment arrangements for health services. • Clarify unit costs and review pricing • Discuss options with several existing and new providers • Select providers • Negotiate contracts	Associate director	December, this year
3. Clarify facilities plans. • Continue negotiations on preferred site • Proceed with plans for backup site, if needed	Executive director	December, this year
4. Continue to improve board functioning. • Review progress • Clarify responsibilities and composition desired for the future	Executive committee Nominations committee Executive director	January, year 1
5. Outline and implement development plans for the center. • Complete program and overall financial plans • Outline a plan for raising needed monies • Implement plan	Finance committee Executive director Assistant director	January, year 1
6. Develop marketing plan.	Marketing/community relations committee Executive director	January, year 1

Strategic Planning in the Federal Government: Lessons from National Energy Policy

GREGORY A. DANEKE

Strategic planning of the sort that is supposed to go on in major corporations is a fairly rare occurrence in government and is an even rarer commodity at the federal level. The public sector is unique, particularly in terms of the dispersion of political influence and the ambiguity of performance criteria. Moreover, recent decline in the prestige of private sector planning (*Business Week* 1984, pp. 62-68) raises significant questions about applicability of comprehensive approaches. Nevertheless, something like strategic planning (or what is now being called strategic management) will continue to be important to both private firms and public agencies, albeit in modified form.

Planning will proceed because – as a few scholars of institutions have observed (Galbraith 1967; Lodge 1975; Solo 1982) and as the national energy policy case confirms – planning goes on whether sanctioned or not. However, most national planning is either of the special interest variety (Friedman 1973) or so poorly done that few would think of it as planning. This is especially the case in the energy realm (Daneke 1982). Energy policy certainly

provided an opportunity for a model kind of comprehensive strategic planning, but the opportunity was lost due to neglect of consensus-building requirements. Outlining these failures might be valuable in improving future efforts.

Many of the observations that follow are somewhat anecdotal. They were drawn from a series of interviews with Department of Energy and White House Energy Policy staffs between Spring 1978 and Fall 1979. These interviews and extensive analysis of policy memos and other documents were part of a major inquiry by the General Accounting Office (GAO) into the process and products of national energy planning. Additional informal interviews were conducted by phone with Reagan administration energy policy advisors in Fall 1981 and Summer 1986. Unfortunately, the nature of this information does not lend itself to more systematic presentation. It is hoped the reader will accept these bits of folk wisdom in the spirit of so many of the recent best-selling management guidebooks and not judge them by the canons of social science research.

A BRIEF HISTORY OF
NATIONAL ENERGY PLANNING

With the sweeping legislation that in 1977 consolidated diverse energy programs into the Department of Energy (DOE), came one of the clearest mandates for national-level strategic planning (Title VIII, Public Law 95-91). In essence, this act suggested that DOE would produce every two years a detailed plan that would provide supply and demand projections, establish clear goals and objectives, and set forth specific proposals for meeting those objectives. The plan also was to evaluate those programs in terms of their social and environmental impacts.

National energy planning, however, actually predates its official sanction by several years (see Table 13-1). Following the first oil shock of 1973, the Federal Energy Administration published its *Project Independence Report* (1974), which, in its own words, was "the most comprehensive energy analysis ever undertaken." Comprehensive or not, the project merely reconstituted President Richard M. Nixon's energy proposals (Nixon 1973), which in turn drew heavily on a study conducted by the National Petroleum Council (1972). However, involving staff from the Federal Energy Office and the recently expanded Office of Management and Budget (OMB), Project Independence created an image of sophisticated analysis because of the use of an elaborate model called *PIES* (the Project Independence Evaluation System).

The PIES effort actually was quite crude by today's standards, and the entire exercise was plagued by inaccurate assumptions. The model projected—assuming as an iron law that an exponential growth in energy demand is needed

Table 13-1. Chronology of National Energy Planning

December 1972	National Petroleum Council publishes its *U.S. Energy Outlook*.
April 1973	Nixon gives energy message to Congress and outlines his "comprehensive, integrated national policy."
October 1973	OPEC oil embargo begins.
November 1974	*Project Independence Report* is officially released.
December 1974	Influential Ford Foundation project report is published under the title, *A Time to Choose—America's Energy Future.*
December 1976	Carter informally commissions his own energy plan.
January 1977	Carter takes office and promises energy plan within 90 days.
March 10, 1977	Public involvement on energy plan initiated.
October 1978	Department of Energy releases preliminary outline for *National Energy Plan II.*
March 1979	Iranian shortfall begins to be inordinately reflected in U.S. gasoline production system.
April 1979	White House staff meet to devise new energy plans.
May 1979	Department of Energy publishes *National Energy Plan II* without fanfare.
May 1979	Carter administration pursues new institutional arrangements to "fast track" "synthetic fuels" and other development programs.
August 1979	Congress approves Synfuels Corporation.
June 1980	Congress votes down the conference committee version of the Energy Mobilization Board.
November 1980	Ronald Reagan is elected.
July 1981	National Energy Policy Plan is published.
May 1985	Draft of Policy Plan II is circulated among energy modelers.
December 1985	Synfuels Corporation is officially terminated.

to drive GNP growth—a year 2000 energy menu in excess of 200 quads (quadrillion BTUs), or a doubling of demand. Then, using a simple linear program, the model optimized energy production primarily through the substitution of numerous inordinately expensive nuclear power plants for foreign oil. Aside from the small problem of electricity not servicing all of the end-uses of oil, initial runs of the model failed to account for such things as reductions in demand brought about by ever-accelerating costs, or what economists call price elasticity. Moreover, even under extremely optimistic assumptions about capital formation, such an expansion of nuclear capacity would virtually bankrupt the economy. Thus, a blind commitment to the original Project Independence scenario would mean a great amount of expensive electricity, but little else.

Actual policy commitment, however, was quite modest. The Nixon and Ford administrations introduced several pieces of legislation aimed at increased incentives and reduced regulations but only were able to get Congress to expand the energy research and development budgets. President Gerald R. Ford's campaign, however, promised a new concerted effort to implement Project Independence. Fortunately, this first major exercise in energy planning was aborted by the voters, and history has pretty much forgotten it. DOE continues to use, however, a modified version of the PIES model for mid-range energy forecasts.

Most people associate the idea of national energy planning with the ill-fated administration of President Jimmy Carter. Here again the planning process was initiated well before the congressional mandate. During his campaign, Carter had acquired a set of energy advisors and actually commissioned an energy plan prior to his inauguration. Given this head start, he did not think it was unreasonable to promise the American people a formal plan within 90 days of taking office. Apparently, his distinguished energy brain trust, made up of David Freeman (director of the Ford Foundation Energy Study), Robert Nordhaus (aide to John Dingell and the House Commerce and Energy and Power Subcommittee), James Schlesinger (former secretary of defense and member of the Atomic Energy Commission), and Al Alm (from the Environmental Protection Agency), had brought with them all the ideas they needed. These ideas, untainted by any energy industry experience, were essentially drawn from the speculations of the Ford Foundation Report (1974), augmented by Nordhaus's analytical work on utility rates and gas pricing. Conspicuously absent from these speculations were the views of industry experts. The sum and substance of these ideas constituted a radical departure from the supply expansion growth policies of the Nixon and Ford administrations (see Table 13–2). Emphasizing conservation strategies, the Ford Foundation report contradicted the iron law of energy growth, and contested that the historical growth rate of 7 percent could reasonably be reduced to 2 percent without adversely affecting the GNP. While these ideas have proven to be fairly well founded, their translation into specific policies and programs was at the time a revolutionary undertaking. Moreover, the basic plan was made more untenable by the fact that, aside from some vague notions about increased coal and solar substitution, the plan completely neglected supply issues.

A belated, and obviously promotionally oriented, public involvement effort was launched

Table 13–2. Basic Objectives of the Various National Energy Plans

Project Independence
- Increased subsidies to the nuclear power industry.
- Streamline power plant licensing.
- Delay air quality implementation.
- Increased coal leasing.
- Deregulation of natural gas.

National Energy Plan
- Incentives/disincentives for conservation (e.g., the gas guzzler tax).
- Incentives for nonconventional technologies.
- Required coal conversion.
- Regulated by higher natural gas prices.
- Crude oil equalization tax, with higher prices, but subsidization of low-income consumers.
- Utility rate reform.

National Energy Plan II
Very similar to National Energy Plan I with the exception of the following elements:
- Emergency measures for future shortfalls.
- Heavy emphasis on synthetic fuels.
- New oil pricing strategies.
- New breeder reactor program to replace Clinch River, and other inducements for nuclear power.
- Removal of regulatory barriers for new energy-producing facilities.

National Energy Policy Plan
- Strong emphasis on market forces.
- Complete deregulation of oil and natural gas.
- Regulatory rollback, especially environmental regulations.
- Increased leasing of public land and offshore for coal and oil development.
- Reintroduction of breeder reactor programs, and further supports for nuclear power development.
- Cut back of synfuels programs.

National Energy Policy Plan II
Takes credit for world oil glut and oil price reductions, provides few new objectives, and no analysis aside from new projections to 2020.

well after the plan was in its final formulation stages. Written comments were requested (even though copies of the plan were not circulated),

nearly a dozen town hall meetings were held across the country, and a set of miniconferences were held at the White House (actually the Executive Office Building). These ex post facto efforts did little to reduce the isolation of the planning team. And, of course, they did not defuse interest group antagonisms.

Hence, Carter had his PR work cut out for him when he eventually went on national television to make his plea for the "moral equivalent of war." Instead of selling energy conservation as a way of doing more with less, the sweater-clad president asked the American people merely to do less, without fully explaining why. While the United States would make amazing strides in energy efficiency in the coming years, the Carter approach made it appear more painful than it proved to be.

The Carter salesmanship was perhaps at its worst when it came to convincing Congress. It is, of course, important to note that the Georgians were always outsiders in Washington, and their legislative liaison was dismal on many fronts. Moreover, the Republicans had little luck on the energy front as well. However, one might argue that it was his poor handling of the energy issue which really started Carter's continuous problems in congressional relations.

Beyond establishing the Department of Energy and sanctioning more planning, Congress did little on energy during the early months of the Carter administration. It took it 18 months to bludgeon what remained of the proposals derived from the original plan into the National Energy Act of 1978. (See Table 13–3.)

While its battles on the hill were raging, and DOE was trying to reorganize itself, the Carter administration embarked on another plan, or

Table 13–3. Congressional Action on Proposals Derived from Original National Energy Plan[1]

Proposal	House Action	Senate Action	Conference	Final Action
Tax credits for home insulation	Approved	Approved	Maximum of $300 credit approved	Approved Oct. 15, 1978
Increase in gasoline tax	Rejected	Rejected by committee	—	—
Tax on gas-guzzler cars	Approved	Rejected; ban on production	Approved	Approved Oct. 15, 1978
Rebate of gas-guzzler tax to buyers of gas-saving cars	Rejected by committee	Not considered	—	—
Mandatory energy-efficiency standards for home appliances	Approved	Approved	Approved	Approved Oct. 15, 1978
Extension of natural gas price controls, with higher ceilings	Approved	Rejected; ended price controls for new gas	Agreement to end price controls on new gas by 1985	Approved Oct. 15, 1978
Tax on crude oil	Approved	Rejected by committee	Killed by conference	—
Tax on utility and industrial use of oil and natural gas	Approved with changes	Approved in weaker version than House	Killed by conference	—
Coal conversion	Approved	Approved in weaker version than House	Compromise	Approved Oct. 15, 1978
Electric utility rate reform	Approved	Rejected in committee	Compromise	Approved Oct. 15, 1978

1. Adapted from *Congressional Quarterly*, 1979, p. 6.

the National Energy Plan II. Directed out of Al Alm's Office of Policy and Evaluation at the assistant secretary level within DOE, this version attempted to integrate the various programmatic elements of DOE (and their associated congressional constituencies) into the planning process. However, this attention from on high merely intensified the conflict between DOE's competing fiefdoms. This pluralistic approach brought a number of supply issues into the plan, but ultimately was not much more successful than the earlier elite approach (GAO 1980).

In fairness, it can be said that circumstances conspired against the Carter administration. While its planners were struggling to get fac-

tions within DOE and the society at large to look at the year 2000 and beyond, the Ayatollah Khomeini was seizing power in Iran. Despite the fact that Iran's production easily could be taken up by noise in the world oil system, a number of factors, including oil company profiteering and DOE's allocation strategy, created a second energy crisis in the gas-line summer of 1979. It was about at this point that the Carter administration seemed to decide to abandon its pluralistic approach and withdrew to Camp David to draft National Energy Plan II in relative isolation.

In what has become typical of analysis in Washington, proposals by White House staff were given to DOE modelers for them to come up with numbers to justify them. Nevertheless, the plan itself reflected an earnest attempt to placate diverse interests, in that it took a kitchen sink approach—throwing a number of supply elements in with recycled conservation options. In particular, National Energy Plan II rekindled national interest in synthetic fuels (or synfuels) from coal, oil shale, and tar sands; options whose government programs had failed in the 1960s.

Not trusting DOE to overcome its infighting and implement National Energy Plan II (assuming Congress would legislate it), the Carter administration also planned an institutional end-run around the bureaucracy and its legislative subgovernments. The White House wanted an Energy Mobilization Board (EMB) to fast track energy projects and to have the authority to override state as well as federal regulatory barriers; it also wanted an Energy Security Corporation to specifically aid the commercialization of synfuels. For those congressmen who had lived through the Great Depression, these projects created an eerie feeling of deja vu. Yet what is perhaps more eerie is how near the projects came to being approved by Congress. What finally came out, however, was only a version of the Energy Security Corporation, renamed the Synfuels Corporation.

Both the EMB and the synfuels programs were criticized by environmentalists, many of whom felt betrayed. The Carter administration obviously believed, however, that given its earlier conservation initiatives it could maintain the base of support among environmental and public interest groups while moving to embrace the energy supply-siders. With the National Energy Plan II and its new institutional strategies, the Carter administration lost

many of its friends, and only gained the support of a few coal state congressmen.

The coming months brought a calming of the energy crisis and more ill-conceived responses to problems (such as the Iranian hostage crisis), further demonstrating the ever-increasing alienation of the Carter administration. As students of electoral behavior suggested, the election of Ronald Reagan was not so much a mandate for conservatism (although it certainly has become one) as it was an indictment of the Carter presidency. It also has proven to be a repudiation of national planning.

Energy planning, as a visible process, has essentially been put out of business by the Reagan administration. Reagan's first plan, now called a policy plan (1981), was a brief (only 24 pages) but euphonious affirmation of the market system. Its objectives center on deregulation and decontrol. Aside from this thrust, increased yet quite modest support for nuclear developments is its only significant governmental initiative. Prior to its release, and in the months that followed, conservation and alternative energy programs were cut back drastically, and a half-hearted attempt was made to do away with (actually redisperse) DOE altogether.

In the 1985 version of the plan, the rhetoric of deregulation remained and a rationale for doing away with Synfuels Corporation was forwarded. Beyond extending the supply/demand projections out to the year 2020, the latest energy plan was fundamentally the same as National Energy Policy Plan I. These projections, by the way, now correspond to the once-heretical prognostications of the various soft-path advocates (e.g., Lovins 1976). While the Reagan programs (or nonprograms) are very different, there is at least consensus that in the twenty-first century the United States will use about half of the energy it did when the first oil shock occurred, with or without a national energy planning process.

LESSONS LEARNED AND UNLEARNED

In some senses, the debacle of national energy planning is so much of a caricature that the lessons are both painfully apparent and difficult to fully appreciate. Few instances of government-supported strategic planning will acquire the power and exposure to generate such levels of arrogance and ignorance. Moreover, since hubris knows no economy of scale, there may even be lessons for prospective planners operating at more modest levels of enterprise with less modest approaches.

In general these lessons stem from a phenomenon all too common to government: the failure to achieve a modicum of accommodation between conflicting interests and values (Thurow 1980). Such accommodation is crucial to the forward movement of sweeping programmatic change. As the energy policy case makes clear, it is certainly possible to have both planning and energy policy without much consensus, but policy change requires new coalitions or crisis. Effective change demands both, plus a smattering of systematic analysis and a measure of luck.

The first and most fundamental lesson from energy policy is that *there is no such thing as not planning.* As George Cabot-Lodge observed, "The American state no longer seems to have any real choice between planning and not planning. It will either choose to plan well and comprehensively, or badly and haphazardly." (1975, p. 265)

What is interesting about the energy case is how even the Nixon and Ford administrations mixed comprehensive proposals in with their defense of the free market. Neither their new incentives (for such things as breeder reactors) nor the deregulatory measures would have established even a small semblance of genuine market signals. But then neither were the Democrats prepared to cut through the Gordian knot of existing artificial incentives, which by 1976 were averaging over $12 billion per year in direct subsidies alone (see Table 13–4).

Table 13–4. Estimated Costs of Incentives Used to Stimulate Energy Production[1]

Energy Source	Time Period	Cost in Billions (1976 dollars)
Nuclear	1950–1976	15.3–17.1
Hydro	1933–1976	9.2–17.5
Coal	1951–1976	6.8
Oil	1918–1976	77.2
Gas	1918–1976	15.1
Total		123.6–133.7

1. Adapted from Cone et al. 1977.

This raises a rather Machiavellian corollary to the first axiom: *It is easier to plan under a cloak of antiplanning rhetoric.* While this lesson may not be axiomatic, partial proofs develop in the energy experience. It proved a particularly potent weapon for those who had special interest planning in mind. Goodwin, in his detailed history of energy policy, explains that:

By and large private firms in energy markets feared that the consequences of planning would be nationalization, prosecution for antitrust violations, or enforced divestiture of some operations. Consequently, they were quick to give strength and muscle to the critics of planning. In any event, what was seldom made clear was that where free markets were prevented from operating there was really no alternative to planning of some sort, even if it was only by one market participant in its own interest. [1981, p. 671]

Another major lesson is that *it is very difficult to use "rational" methods without clear goals.* While every first-year planning student knows this well, it was amazing how often energy administrators fell prey to the famed Cheshire Cat problem of getting directions before they knew where they wanted to go. Given a continuation of the misconception that goals came prepackaged by the political process or the failure to realize the role they played in that process, it is not surprising that energy analysts began their work assuming consensus on goals would somehow magically occur. Moreover, those highly trained in rational analytical techniques (like the Rand analysts Arthur M. Schlesinger brought with him to the Carter planning team) tended to see most problems as matters of efficiency when the issue was more often one of seeking agreement on direction of effectiveness. Herman Daly described quite eloquently this problem:

> We can make a collective social decision regarding energy use and attempt to plan or shape the future under the guidance of moral will; or we can treat it as a problem in predicting other peoples' aggregate behavior and seek to outguess a mechanistically predetermined future. Future energy requirements are usually estimated in the second way, by prediction. As the art of foretelling the future has shifted from the prophet to the statistician, the visionary goal-oriented element and the accompanying moral exhortation have atrophied, while analytical number crunching has hypertrophied. . . . It is an unsuccessful retreat from the responsibility of choosing goals, and is unworthy of any or-

ganism with a central nervous system, much less a cerebral cortex. [1979, p. 232]

Most of the energy planners had forgotten to ask "energy for what?"—that is, what are the social goals energy is to serve? The PIES modelers had made energy an end in itself and might have allowed energy to completely "cannibalize the economy" (Commoner 1982). This provides a corollary to the second lesson: *Clear goals don't help if you can't get there from here.* While the enormous capital demands of the nuclear construction scenario might have quickly caused a detour along the Project Independence path, it also might have taken years and massive economic dislocations for the ship of state to change course.

Such arguments against the pell-mell pursuit of preoptimized objectives are certainly well taken. Nevertheless, linear-programming-type techniques (including single-attribute models such as benefit–cost assessments) do have their place in strategic planning, despite the fact that they are more appropriate for tactical analysis. To the extent that they often can establish parameters of reasonableness, they obviously are useful in the choice of objectives. However, since the fundamental task of planning is the achievement of consensus on goals, objective analysis (even when possible) can not be substituted for subjective choice.

These arguments, of course, can be combined with observations about the limits of human comprehension, etc., to defend an "incremental approach" (i.e., Lindblom 1965). Such a defense is not intended here, for another lesson from energy planning is that *effective political adjustments are predicated upon a strategic assessment.* This may seem like a catch-22 given that political negotiation is involved in the choice of strategy. However, as Carter learned during the National Energy Plan II process, without a set of unifying themes, purposeful muddling deteriorates quickly into blithering (Daneke 1982).

Incrementalism also implies moving slowly enough so that everyone who wants to can get involved. Yet herein lies the real irony of planning in a democracy, and another energy lesson: *Planners are rarely called upon to devise strategy until it is too late to involve everyone and plan effectively or both.* In other words, most planning is only undertaken in the midst of a crisis. When most people think of national planning they point to the Great Depression or Sputnik era. These crisis situations—when planners had sufficient public acquiescence to allow them to throw programs at a problem—in effect represented failures of previous nonstrategies. Carter had an opportunity to do some careful strategizing, providing meaningful involvement to interest groups and his own energy bureaucracy, but he opted to act as if a crisis had already emerged and gave his planning team an unrealistic deadline. When a real crisis did appear, the planners were still reeling from their initial process failures, and quickly fell in to a fire fighting mode. Furthermore, they were caught in what might be called the vicious cycle of planning failures that intensifies the participatory problem. George Cabot-Lodge suggested that if the U.S. chooses to

> plan haphazardly. . .there is likely to be chaos, resulting inevitably in more crisis, which in turn will cause inexorable demand for more planning plus more coercion. Should the crisis prove great enough, and democratic processes not appear capable of dealing with it, there will be a natural call for dictatorial measures. [1975, p. 265]

The Energy Security Corporation and Energy Mobilization Board might have exhibited such tendencies had the crisis not diminished (Moe 1979; Lovins 1980)

The other side of this irony is another lesson that Carter knew well: *Without a crisis, achieving consensus for comprehensive policies is very difficult.* But Carter wanted to move comprehensively before he had planned comprehensively. Commitment to continuous, comprehensive planning is the only way to break out of the above cycle. This addendum to the final two lessons is perhaps the most profound point for would-be public sector planners. For a lack of a better designation, this might be called the strategic planning imperative: *Successful planning usually requires the preexistence of a number of strategic processes.* Without mechanisms in place for goal clarification, interest accommodation, and so forth, most planning quickly goes awry. As Donald Michael (1973) described in his comprehensive study of strategic planning in business and government, administrators must learn to plan by planning to learn.

CONCLUSIONS

The current frenzy over strategic planning on the part of public officials from the Environmental Protection Agency (EPA 1985) to the parks department in Podunk may well be a fad just like zero-base budgeting or management-by-objectives. However, each of these panaceas was used to grope for essentially the same goal classification and programmatic coherence that are the raison d'être of strategic planning.

Pursued as a quick fix for all managerial ills, strategic planning, too, will fail the test. Pursued modestly but continuously as a precursor to more systematic analysis, strategic planning can provide the missing link in many of the earlier ill-fated management reforms.

It is hoped that during the current era, where antiplanning rhetoric is being heard even in corporate board rooms, public administrators will not forget the lessons of energy planning, particularly that the failure to do careful planning merely means poor planning in which special interests dominate and where dictatorial measures always are waiting in the wings for policy breakdowns. These lessons are especially important as the United States moves into an era in which the international challenges to its economic well-being will be more complex and acute than the disruption of oil imports.

AUTHOR'S NOTE

The author would like to acknowledge the insights and assistance of his colleagues on GAO's National Energy Policy Review Team; however, neither they nor the U.S. General Accounting Office are responsible for the interpretations rendered here.

REFERENCES

Business Week. 1984. The new breed of strategic planner. September 17, 62–68.

Commoner, B. 1982. Prologue: energy, economics, and the environment. In *Energy, Economics, and the Environment,* edited by G. A. Daneke. Lexington, Mass.: D. C. Heath.

Cone, B. W. et al. 1977. *An analysis of federal incentives used to stimulate energy production.* Richland, Wash.: Battelle Northwest.

Congressional Quarterly. 1979. Energy policy. Washington, D.C.: *Congressional Quarterly.*

Daly, H. 1979. On thinking about future energy requirements. In *Sociopolitical Effects of Energy Use and Policy,* edited by C. T. Unsell. Washington, D.C.: National Academy of Sciences, CONAES, Paper 5.

Daneke, G. A. 1982. Towards a craft of energy policy: Constraints upon and opportunities for strategic planning in the U.S. Department of Energy. *Journal of Public Policy* Vol. 2, Part 3, August.

Department of Energy. 1981. *The national policy plan.* Washington, D.C.: DOE, July.

Environmental Protection Agency. 1985. *Integrating planning, policy and management at the EPA.* Washington, D.C.: Environmental Protection Agency.

Executive Office of the President. 1977. *The national energy plan.* Washington, D.C.: Government Printing Office.

Federal Energy Administration. 1974. *The project independence report.* Washington, D.C.: Government Printing Office.

Ford Foundation. 1974. *A time to choose—America's energy future.* Cambridge, Mass.: Ballinger Publishing Company.

Friedman, J. 1973. *Retracking America: A theory of societal planning.* New York, N.Y.: Doubleday.

Galbraith, J. K. 1967. *The New Industrial State.* Boston, Mass.: Houghton-Mifflin.

Goodwin, C. D. 1981. The lessons of history. In *Energy Policy in Perspective,* edited by C. D. Goodwin. Washington, D.C.: The Brookings Institute.

Government Accounting Office. 1980. *Letter to Congress: A review of the energy planning process.* Washington, D.C.: GAO.

Lindblom, C. E. 1975. *The intelligence of democracy.* New York: Free Press.

Lodge, G. C. 1975. *The new American ideology.* New York, N.Y.: Knopf.

Lovins, A. B. 1976. Energy strategy: The road not taken. *Foreign Affairs* (Fall): 65–96.

———. 1980. Democracy and the Energy Mobilization Board. *Not Man Apart* (February): 14–15.

Michael, D. 1973. *On learning to plan and planning to learn.* San Francisco, Calif.: Jossey-Bass.

Moe, E. C. 1979. Government corporations and the erosion of accountability: The case of the energy security corporation. *Public Administration Review* 566–71.

National Petroleum Council. 1972. *U.S. energy outlook: A summary report.* Washington, D.C.: NPC.

Nixon, R. M. 1973. Presidential energy message to Congress. In *Basic Documents on Energy.* Washington, D.C.: Commerce Clearing House.

Solo, R. 1982. *The positive state.* Palo Alto, Calif.: South-Western.

Thurow, L. C. 1980. *The zero-sum society.* New York, N.Y.: Basic Books.

14

The Future of Strategic Planning for Public Purposes

JOHN M. BRYSON
ROBERT C. EINSWEILER

The chapters in this book offer some indicators of the future of strategic planning for public purposes. This final chapter highlights those indicators and explores their implications.

The most important conclusions may come from Bryson and Roering in Chapter 2:

1. That strategic planning for public (and nonprofit) purposes probably will become part of the standard repertoire of public (and nonprofit) planners, and

2. That, nevertheless, planners must be very careful about how they engage in strategic planning, since not all approaches are equally useful and since a number of conditions govern successful use of each approach.

Strategic planning is likely to become a part of every planner's repertoire because strategic planning is a set of concepts, procedures, and tools designed to help decision makers in organizations and communities deal with a number of the challenges they face. Strategic planning can help them deal with environments that are increasingly turbulent (Emery and Trist 1965) and interconnected (Luke 1988). Strategic planning provides insights and methods for the management of complexity and change in situations in which the decision makers are

held accountable for the nature and quality of their organization's or community's interactions with stakeholders and environments.

Effective strategic planning in practice, however, will almost certainly remain an art, not a science. Strategic planning to date comprises a number of approaches (i.e., bundles of concepts, procedures, and tools) that vary in their applicability and usefulness to different situations. While additional practical experience and research will improve our understanding of which approach works best under what circumstances and why, planners and decision makers always will have to be careful about how they engage in strategic planning. The same, of course, can be said of any other type of planning. The reason for a special cautionary note is simply that strategic planning is relatively new to the public and nonprofit sectors (outside of military and foreign policy operations) and, therefore, may be prone to misuse by inexperienced practitioners.

Another related reason for caution is that strategic planning to date has been designed primarily for use by *organizations* to help them figure out what they should do and why, given the situations they face. Our case study chapters demonstrate in part that strategic planning can be and has been applied to communities, functions, programs, projects, and all levels of government in addition to nonprofit organizations. But the fact remains that most of the development of strategic planning concepts, procedures, and tools in this century has been focused on improving organizational performance—particularly for-profit organizational performance. We should not assume that insights and experience from private sector strategic planning practice can be transferred without modification to public and nonprofit organizations or to communities or functions that cross organizational boundaries. Much probably can be transferred, but careful thought should precede application and care should be taken during application to make sure that desirable results are produced.

The rest of this chapter will be organized into sets of conclusions related to different aspects of strategic planning. The topics covered include: (1) citizen participation in strategic planning; (2) a discussion of what appears to be necessary to initiate and succeed with strategic planning; (3) our comments about what elements of a strategic planning system probably can be institutionalized by organizations and communities; (4) criteria that might be used to assess the value of strategic planning; (5) a discussion of the implications of strategic planning for planning generally and for planners' roles; (6) implications for planning education; and (7) topics for future research.

CITIZEN PARTICIPATION IN STRATEGIC PLANNING

Strategic planners typically use the stakeholder concept to sort out the various issues concerning who should be involved when, why, and how in the strategic planning process. (Recall that Bryson and Roering in Chapter 2 defined an organization's stakeholders as "any individual, group, or other organization that can place a claim on the organization's attention, resources, or output or is affected by that output." Their definition can be modified easily to define a community's or other entity's stakeholders.) The stakeholder concept prompts planners to list all the stakeholders who might be involved or affected by a process, identify their interest or "stake" in the process, formulate what the response might be to the various stakeholders, and clarify what the stakeholders might contribute to the process.

Traditionally, democratic theory has offered two basic rationales for citizen participation in decision making; namely, that citizen participation is likely to produce better decisions and better citizens (Pateman 1970). Better decisions are supposed to result because more complete knowledge or expertise results in informed decisions and because citizen interests will be better articulated and (presumably) better accommodated. Legitimation and implementation of strategies are likely to be easier to the extent that citizens are satisfied their various interests are adequately addressed. Citizenship is supposed to be enhanced when citizens shoulder part of the responsibility for the formulation or implementation of decisions. Active participation educates and empowers citizens at the same time it commits them and makes them responsible for the life of the polity.

The stakeholder concept can help tap both rationales for citizen participation in strategic planning, but to date strategic planning has been concerned principally with producing better decisions, not better citizens. The stakeholder concept helps differentiate the variety of citizen *interests* likely to be present in any strategic planning process, as well as the *knowledge* or *expertise* different citizens might contribute. We will consider the question of citizen interests first.

A stakeholder analysis is likely to uncover the variety of different—sometimes conflicting, sometimes complementary—*interests* that a simplistic concern for citizen participation is likely to miss. For example, citizens as taxpayers may have one view of a government or a public corporation akin to the view of a private corporation's stockholders. Citizens as service recipients may have another view, while citizens who are government employees may have yet another. Taxpayers, service users, and employees each represent stakeholder groups. While a citizen who is simultaneously a taxpayer, service user, and employee obviously will have to establish some internal calculus to deal with the potential conflicts among different stakes, for planning purposes only the expectations of the different stakeholder groups must be addressed. Ultimately some sort of reconciliation of conflicting stakeholder interests may be necessary, but not necessarily in all cases. The key point is that the stakeholder concept can help satisfy more citizen interests because it differentiates among them and therefore permits a more targeted response and a more specific basis for citizen support for the process and implemented strategies. (Whether more citizen interests actually are satisfied in any particular case, of course, will depend on the nature of the situation and the choices of key decision makers.)

The stakeholder concept also helps clarify potential citizen contributions of knowledge and expertise to the process. In our experience and the cases presented in this book, the ex-

tent of citizen participation—both to gain knowledge and expertise, along with legitimacy for the process and acceptance of the decisions that result—appears to vary depending on whether the strategic planning exercise is focused on an organization, program, or community. (Our statement is not prescriptive, merely an observation of what appears to occur most often.) We offer the following possible explanations for why this variation might occur.

When an organization is the principal focus of attention, as in the Hennepin County case, there usually is little citizen participation in the strategic planning process other than that of elected or appointed policy board members. One reason may be that the organization may already possess the necessary knowledge and expertise in-house and therefore citizen involvement to gain such information would be redundant and excessively time-consuming. Further, citizen participation may not be necessary to legitimize the process because an elected or appointed policy board already is directly involved , in keeping with the idea that we are a representative, not a direct, democracy. The absence of participation by ordinary outsiders would parallel private sector corporate planning practice.

Program-focused strategic planning appears to be much more likely to involve citizens, particularly in their capacity as users. Citizen involvement in program planning thus is roughly analogous to extensive consumer involvement in private sector marketing research and development projects. For example, transportation planning typically involves a great deal of citizen participation. Citizens may provide information concerning travel needs and desires, reactions to various transportation system design alternatives, and advice on ways to resolve conflicts that arise during the process. Park planning also typically involves substantial citizen participation. Unfortunately, because the use of transportation systems or parks by citizens typically is broadbased, users and citizens-at-large often are equated. Such an equivalence, however, is hardly ever justified, as it probably masks great variety in stakeholder concerns about and contributions to the process. A stakeholder analysis can help keep the various citizen interests and contributions analytically separate.

Finally, we have yet to see an example of strategic planning on behalf of a community that did not involve substantial citizen participation. (Further, there does not appear to be any direct private sector equivalent of community strategic planning, except for the development of totally private new towns. Of course, for-profit corporations and their lobbying and community service agents, such as chambers of commerce, often participate in community-focused strategic planning exercises.) Unfortunately, community-focused strategic planning appears most likely to treat all citizens alike and to assume that each citizen is interested in the community as a whole—two assumptions at odds with most studies of political participation (e.g., Verba and Nie 1972). Application of the stakeholder concept to community strategic planning would help avoid these errors.

Thus, there does appear to be some patterned variation in the extent of citizen participation. Nonetheless, the extent of citizen participation in any particular case still appears to be hard to predict, and is even perhaps idiosyncratic. Further, it is not clear what effect differing levels of participation have on the out-comes of the process. We will only know what kind and amount of citizen participation works best for which purposes, under which circumstances, and why, when more communities experiment with strategic planning and more studies of those experiments are undertaken.

WHAT IT TAKES TO INITIATE AND SUCCEED WITH STRATEGIC PLANNING

The chapters in this book and the growing body of literature on strategic planning for the public and nonprofit sectors (e.g., Olsen and Eadie 1982; Barry 1986; Bryson 1988) help us draw some conclusions about what seems to be necessary to initiate an effective strategic planning process. At a minimum, any organization, interorganizational network, or community that wants to engage in strategic planning should have:

1. At least one sponsor—that is, a stakeholder—in a position of power and authority to legitimize the process.
2. At least one champion to push the process along.
3. A strategic planning team.
4. An expectation of disruptions and delays.
5. A flexible attitude toward what constitutes a strategic plan.
6. An ability to pull information and people together at key points for important discussions and decisions.
7. A willingness to construct and consider arguments geared to very different evaluative criteria.

We will discuss each of these points in turn.

Successful initiation and completion of a strategic planning process appears to depend on the presence of at least one powerful stakeholder to sponsor and legitimize the process, even if that stakeholder is not especially supportive. Further, multiple sponsorship is possible, and probably desirable. In each of the successful cases discussed in this book, there was some sort of multiple sponsorship of the process by people in positions of power and authority to legitimize the process. In the one clear failure—national energy planning—the process was sponsored by persons in positions of power and authority, but their power and authority did not cover much of the domain for which the plan was made—that is, private energy production and consumption. This conclusion is in accordance with the findings of Olsen and Eadie (1982), Barry (1986), and Bryson and Roering (1988).

Successful initiation and completion of strategic planning also appears to require a strong "process champion" (Bryson and Roering 1988). Process champions believe that strategic planning will produce desirable results and help organize and push the process along. Process champions have a good understanding of the need to tailor the strategic planning process to the situation at hand. The process champion plays a role similar to the more familiar private sector "product champion" (Kotler 1976, p. 200) or "idea champion" (Kanter 1983, p. 296) who does whatever it takes to promote and operationalize a product or idea against bureaucratic and political inertia, indifference, or hostility. The cases discussed in this book do not highlight this role, but the reason may be that several of the authors were the champions in their cases and they did not emphasize their own contributions.

The case chapters in the book and our experience indicate that strategic planning typically involves a strategic planning team. A team appears to be necessary for several reasons. The issues in organizationally based strategic planning usually have cross-organizational impacts. A team can assure that necessary information is acquired and that proposed solutions are more legitimate (Galbraith 1977). Also, a team often is necessary simply to get the work done well in the shortest possible time. Similar arguments underlie the need for a strategic planning team in community-based strategic planning. In community-based strategic planning, the team is likely to consist of one or more task forces or committees and to involve broad community participation along with use of consultants.

Strategic planning may be particularly prone to disruptions, delays, or disintegration because of the people who should be included and because of conceptual and political difficulties. First, strategic planning is designed for use by decision makers—whose time is notoriously hard to manage (Mintzberg 1973). Second, strategic planning focuses the attention of key decision makers on what is truly important for their organizations, interorganizational networks, or communities—when muddling through or ignoring the important questions may be the line of least resistance. Third, strategic planning evokes a comprehensive view of an organization's, interorganizational network's, or community's actual and potential roles, while it promotes a very selective action focus. Organizations and other entities often find the move from broad view to specific action difficult, particularly when major policy or strategic shifts are required. Fourth, resolution of strategic issues that emerge from strategic planning often requires the assembly of different "decision sets" (Hickson et al. 1986). The assembly of these different groups of decision makers can produce logistical and political problems. Finally, the temporary or permanent loss of key staff (e.g., sponsors, champions, or consultants) and the various other crises (Bryson 1981) that characterize much organizational life can delay or disrupt the process.

Organizations, networks, and communities should remember that a strategic plan can take many forms. The plans developed by each of the organizations or communities discussed in our case chapters differed in format, style, and substance from one another. There is no one correct form for a strategic plan. Plans should differ according to the circumstances surrounding their preparation and the purposes the plans are to serve (Rider 1983).

For strategic planning—or any planning for that matter—to work, the organizations involved must be able to pull together key people and key information at key times. That is because strategic planning requires (1) a focus on what is truly important for the unit (2) through discussions among key decision makers (3) accompanied by attendant decisions and actions (Bryson and Roering 1988). While this requirement is conceptually simple, it is quite difficult for many organizations to implement. Strategic planning will not work unless key decision makers want it to work and since most strategic issues involve or affect more than one key decision maker those decision makers must get together to discuss the issues, decide what to do about them, and oversee the implementation of solutions. Further, the discussions and decisions must be tied appropriately to important organizational decision points, such as the adoption of budgets.

Finally, organizations and people involved in strategic planning must be willing to construct and consider arguments geared to very different evaluative criteria. Strategic planning typically requires planners to consider what an organization, network, or community should do in relation to various stakeholders. These stakeholders can be expected to use different—sometimes complementary, sometimes competing or contradictory—criteria to judge organizational performance. Organizations, networks, and communities engaged in strategic planning will have to work to ensure that proposed solutions to strategic problems are technically workable, politically acceptable, and morally defensible. Strategic planning in this sense can be viewed as a kind of argumentation (Goldstein 1984) in which planners try to construct strategies that can be defended from a variety of viewpoints.

WHAT CAN BE INSTITUTIONALIZED?

Some strategic planning practices probably can be institutionalized by most governments, public agencies, and nonprofit organizations. The following elements of a strategic planning system (see Chapter 2) probably can become a permanent part of organizational life (Bryson and Roering 1988):

1. A formal or informal "cabinet" of key decision makers.

2. Mission statements.

3. Policy objectives that emerge from the sense of purpose embodied in the mission, or from a review of past decisions (see Chapter 11) and the mandates the organization faces.

4. Periodic situation analyses.

5. Periodic strategic issue or problem identification exercises.

6. Strategic issue management practices, for example, appointment of issue managers and task forces, strategy development exercises, development of decision packages, and issue-monitoring processes (see Chapter 2).

7. More formal multicriteria proposal-evaluation procedures.

It should be noted that it probably would be much harder to institutionalize these practices in interorganizational networks or communities because it would be harder to reach agreement on why and how to do so.

There are a number of reasons why we think these elements can be institutionalized. Many organizations have formal or informal cabinets. The development of mission statements is standard practice for many organizations—and most of the successful strategic planning cases noted in this book included preparation of a statement of organizational purposes. Also common is preparation of policy objectives to detail desired performance in key policy areas related to mission and mandates. (If the objectives reflect past decisions, they are more likely to be effective guides to action.) Further, situation analyses are relatively simple, not too time-consuming, and useful. Such audits are especially valuable for their emphasis on the external as well as the internal environment, because an external focus is often crucial to achievement of satisfactory organizational performance.

Strategic issue identification and the development of strategies to deal with the most important issues are also relatively easy to do and can be seen in many successful cases of strategic planning. (Of course, strategic planning also can be successful when the process is driven by goals, scenarios, or, more generally, problems.) Issues management approaches (Delmont and Pflaum 1983) are quite common, particularly in the public sector, because issues are typically on different time frames and, at different stages of development, require differ-

ent teams to handle them, and require different decision sets to resolve them. Finally, decision makers in the public and nonprofit sectors usually use more than one criterion to make important decisions, so developing multicriteria decision-making procedures should not be too difficult—and such procedures can improve the quality of decisions.

The institutionalization of any one of the items in this set might not be a big change for any organization. The institutionalization of the entire set, however, can help guarantee the success of strategic planning. In other words, any organization that can institutionalize all of these items should be well on its way to addressing what is truly important for the organization. As Kaufman and Jacobs note in Chapter 3, public planners have been advised to act more strategically for some time. What is special about strategic planning is that it offers public and nonprofit planners and decision makers a set of relatively simple practices that can help them do just that.

At this point we must note what is perhaps the most important paradox of strategic planning: Strategic planning is probably most needed where it is least likely to work. Strategic planning would appear to work best in units or places that have effective policymaking boards, strong and supportive process sponsors, superb process champions, good strategic planning teams, enough slack in their systems to cope with disruptions and delays, experience in coping with major disruptions, and a desire to address what is truly important for the organization or place. Any organization or place with those features probably already uses some sort of strategic thinking and acting process. Introducing such a unit or community to a formal strategic planning process probably would constitute minor tinkering with an already excellently governed and managed organization or community and should not result in dramatic improvements in performance. On the other hand, just because strategic planning probably will be hard to do where it is most needed does not mean it should not be tried. On the contrary, strategic planning can be used in such cases to build the infrastructure that will make it more likely to work.

CRITERIA OR STANDARDS TO JUDGE THE EFFECTIVENESS OF STRATEGIC PLANNING

What criteria or standards should be used to judge the effectiveness of strategic planning in the public and nonprofit sectors? To begin with, strategic planning by governments and public agencies should be judged by different standards than used for private sector, corporate strategic planning. The nature of the public sector militates against exact duplication of private sector practice, as Crow and Bozeman argue in Chapter 4. The more numerous stakeholders, the conflicting criteria they often use to judge organizational or community performance, the pressures for public accountability, elected policy boards, and the fact that the public sector generally does (among other things) what the private sector cannot or will not do, all preclude holding governmental strategic planning practice to private sector standards. Few governments or public agencies will be able to follow the linear, sequential strategic planning models of the business policy textbooks or will be able to prepare the public sector equivalent of the slick corporate plan. (On the other hand, strategic planning by certain nonprofit organizations such as major

hospitals, health care organizations, or social service agencies probably can be judged according to certain private sector standards, since these organizations often operate much like their private sector counterparts.)

Perhaps with more practice, a more formal and routine strategic planning process might occur in public sector organizations, along with development of the public sector equivalent of private sector strategic plans. But the possibilities for such developments vary depending on the focus of the strategic planning efforts. A government department probably is most likely to develop such a process and plans. General purpose governments are less likely to develop such a process and plans, although the Hennepin County example demonstrates it can be done in county–board executive or council-manager forms of government. Single function interorganizational networks are perhaps somewhat less likely than general purpose governments to do so. While focus on a single function may facilitate agreement, the fact that "sovereign" organizations are involved is likely to make agreement more difficult. Finally, communities would be least likely to develop a formal, routine strategic planning process and standardized strategic plan.

It is important to keep in mind that a more linear, sequential process and slicker strategic plans may be neither necessary nor desirable in the public sector. After all, strategic planning systems have been known to drive out strategic thinking (*Business Week* 1984; Porter 1987; Bryson et al. 1987). Until public sector units gain more experience with strategic planning, it seems best to judge their strategic planning according to the extent to which it: (1) focuses the attention of key decision makers on what is important for their organizations or communities, (2) helps set priorities for action, and (3) generates those actions.

These criteria obviously constitute a *minimum* set and are focused narrowly on strategic planning as a set of concepts, procedures, and tools to help decision makers focus and act on what is important for their organizations, networks, or communities. What we have left out are criteria that might be used to judge whether or not better decisions result from the use of strategic planning. Decision makers can be expected to attend to the criteria that their organization's stakeholders use to judge organizational performance, but there is no guarantee that decisions will be legally, ethically, and morally justifiable. There appears to be nothing inherent in strategic planning as a set of concepts, procedures, and tools that might make it more difficult to produce legal, ethical, and moral decisions; but there also is nothing that guarantees the production of such decisions, either.

IMPLICATIONS FOR PLANNING AND PLANNERS' ROLES

Strategic planning raises several issues for planning as a field and for planners' roles. We will discuss the role issues first.

A review of the chapters in this book—especially the case chapters—evokes the old debate about the proper role for planners. The advent of strategic planning does not resolve the debate; it simply raises it in a new form. For example, in many cases, the planners are not people with the job title planner, but are in fact policymakers or line managers. The people with the title planner often act primarily as facilitators of decision making by policymakers or line managers, as technical experts in substantive areas, or both. This conception of the planner's role goes back at least as far as

Walker's (1950) treatise, in which he argued that the proper role for planners is to advise a government's chief executive, and Kent's (1964) view that an important role for urban planners is to advise a municipality's chief legislative body. Both Walker and Kent sought planners with good process facilitation skills and substantive area expertise. These planners would then use their skills and knowledge to help chief administrators or elected policymakers make better decisions.

In other cases, planners operate in a variety of different roles. Sometimes the planner is an "expert on experts" (Bolan 1971) who eases different people in and out of the process for different purposes at different times. At other times planners may act as technicians, politicians, or hybrids (Howe and Kaufman 1979; Howe 1980). We believe that what is most important about strategic planning is the development of strategic thought and action, and therefore, it may not matter who does it. However, it does seem that strategic planning done by policymakers, line managers, or both, is most likely to be implemented. (Line managers in government are not usually charged with making important political trade-offs, politicians are. An effective government strategic planning process therefore probably needs participation by both.) Exactly how people designated as planners fit into that formulation is unclear and is an important subject for further investigation. At the city level, for example, strategic planners might serve best (as a starting point) as facilitators of discussions among the heads of major departments, getting them to think more comprehensively about the city government—and city—as a whole, and to examine impacts of actions in one functional area on another. Our own view is that planners (whatever their formal title) are most effective when they are good process facilitators and have expert command of the subject matter at issue, but believe that final choices on how to frame the issues and acceptable solutions rest with their clients (whatever their titles or positions might be).

The implications of strategic planning for the field of planning are also important. The rise of strategic planning can expand planning's domain and usefulness. Public planners, for example, can add strategic planning to their existing interest in comprehensive planning, project planning, and operational planning, and to their various topical planning specializations, such as transportation, housing, and health. Further, because strategic planning usually embraces all of a government's existing and potential agenda, strategic planning can expand planning's agenda beyond the traditional agenda of comprehensive planning (Kaufman 1974).

For urban and regional planners, however, this expansion of the domain of planning offers both opportunities and threats. The opportunity is to be more truly comprehensive than traditional comprehensive planning usually allows, and to be more useful to their governments and the people they serve. The threat is the loss of identity. The ultimate issue, however, is probably one of balance. If urban and regional planners become too narrow and too isolated from key decision makers, they become irrelevant. If they become too broad and too close to key decision makers, they may be hard to distinguish from public managers generally, and may lose their ability to critique and inspire from a relatively autonomous organizational position.

There also is an organizational twist to the discussion. If planning is tied to a set of operational concerns—as, for example, when a city government has a department of planning and economic development—it may be very difficult for the planners in that department to facilitate strategic planning by the government as a whole. The reason is that they will be viewed as partisans in any potential cross-departmental bids for power, influence, or resources. In such circumstances, a strategic planning function attached to the chief executive or legislative body is needed to oversee strategic planning for the organization as a whole.

In effect, the rise of strategic planning stimulates a demand for two sets of strategic planners. Functional areas—such as public works, parks, education, and economic development—need their planners. But then so do policymakers and appointed executives with cross-functional responsibilities. The planners working with policymakers or executives have a different agenda toward which they apply their talents. They retain their role as planners, but may lose the adjectives *urban* and *regional*, if to be an urban and regional planner implies an exclusive focus on land use, land management, or development.

The rise of strategic planning would seem to raise fewer troubling issues for nonprofit organizational planners. Strategic planning can simply help them help their organizations cope better with their changing circumstances.

IMPLICATIONS FOR PLANNING EDUCATION

The rise of strategic planning also has a number of implications for planning education. First, planning schools probably should institute special courses on strategic planning. Strategic planning consists of a number of concepts, procedures, and tools that can and should be taught. We believe that every planning student should gain an understanding of strategic planning, and hope that books such as this one can help them gain such an understanding.

Second, we believe that coursework in strategic planning will draw students from a wide variety of fields and disciplines. That certainly has been our experience at the University of Minnesota. The majority of the students in our strategic planning courses have always come from outside the Humphrey Institute. Strategic planning coursework, therefore, can open up new markets for planning schools at the same time that it helps spread the message of planning's importance. As Kaufman and Jacobs argue in Chapter 3, at a time when traditional planning is often under attack, strategic planning can help the profession gain new adherents who otherwise might not learn of the importance of planning and the planning profession.

FUTURE DIRECTIONS

What directions should strategic planning research and practice take if strategic planning is to fulfill its potential for improving public and nonprofit organizational and community performance? Several answers are suggested by the cases in this book.

First, public and nonprofit organizations, networks, and communities need more experience with and knowledge of strategic planning. The examples presented in this book illustrate a variety of approaches to strategic planning. But more studies of the effectiveness of various strategic planning approaches need to be undertaken. Strategic planning as a focus of practice—and of research—is simply too new to say

anything truly conclusive about the effectiveness or applicability of alternative approaches. Particularly valuable, given the current state of knowledge, would be development of more—and more detailed—case studies, for both teaching and research purposes.

Second, most approaches to strategic planning are noncontingent in that they do not specify clearly the boundary conditions of the model or how each should be applied in specific circumstances. Bryson and Roering in Chapter 2 have outlined some of the more important conditions governing use of a variety of approaches, but clearly more work will be necessary to give practitioners detailed advice about which models to use, when, and why.

Third, the relationships among strategic issues, goals, and scenarios need to be explored in greater detail. Ring, in Chapter 5, has pushed the field ahead by presenting in more than usual detail an approach to the identification of strategic issues. Since strategic issue identification is at the heart of most strategic planning models, his work is a real service. But under what circumstances is strategic issue identification the wrong place to start? When, in other words, should one begin with goals or scenarios? And how are issues, goals, and scenarios connected? If you start with one, should you end up with the others, or not? In Chapter 1 we discussed some of the possible connections among issues, goals, and scenarios, but obviously more work needs to be done to advance our understanding and supply additional practical advice.

Fourth, questions remain about how to formulate specific strategies for dealing with strategic issues, or achieving goals, or realizing scenarios, once they have been identified or formulated. Some of the strategic planning approaches outlined by Bryson and Roering in Chapter 2—for example, the portfolio and competitive analysis models—prescribe specific strategies for firms depending on where the model positions them. But these content models have been applied rarely in the public sector. As Bryson and Roering note, most public and nonprofit sector strategic planning approaches are process models. The models outline a process for formulating a strategy, but they do not say which specific strategies should be pursued in a given circumstance. Rubin in Chapter 6, Wechsler and Backoff in Chapter 7, and Backoff and Nutt in Chapter 8, all advance our understanding of which strategies might be pursued most usefully in different circumstances. But obviously more work is necessary before we understand more fully how to construct strategies, including all of the necessary detail, that are likely to be most effective in given circumstances.

Fifth, most models of strategic planning are not formally or explicitly political, although many of the chapters in this book help address this criticism. The literature on strategic planning for public and nonprofit purposes is not very instructive about dealing with the political aspects of strategic planning, except to recognize that politics plays a part. The strategic planning approach that comes closest to being explicitly political is the stakeholder approach (see Chapter 2), and it would seem wise for public and nonprofit planners to incorporate stakeholder analyses and involvement into their efforts. Additional work, however, is needed on the politics of strategic planning.

Sixth, additional work is needed on how to deal with the plural, ambiguous, and often conflicting goals and objectives in the public sector. Most strategic planning models do not highlight this difficulty beyond prescribing the formulation of explicit goals and objectives. Such an approach, however, may not always be wise, depending on how or if it is done at all. In other words, the formulation of explicit—but numerous, ambiguous, or conflicting—goals may not help anybody. The stakeholder approach may help since it calls attention to different goals, objectives, and interests of various stakeholder groups. Such specification should prove useful to strategic planners, even if the results are not made public. In other circumstances, it may be best simply to identify strategic issues and strategies to address them, or to develop scenarios and strategies to implement them, and never to discuss goals and objectives at all. Obviously we need more guidance about when to plan with and without goals (McCaskey 1974) and when goals should or should not be plural, ambiguous, and conflicting.

A related question is whether or not mission statements ought to be prepared in all cases. Earlier in this chapter we argued that many organizations probably could develop and institutionalize mission statements. But doing so may not always be possible or wise. Some situations are so ridden with conflict that no agreement on mission can be reached. The best that might be expected is agreement on the means or the next actions or steps that might be taken by the organization. Participants do not necessarily have to agree on mission or goals to agree on next steps (Cleveland 1973). However, one possibility is the preparation of a mission statement that incorporates different missions for different constituencies or stakeholders. Such an approach is often used in the private sector, for example, in which different missions might be outlined for customers, employees, stockholders, and communities in which the firm operates. As long as the mission statements remain general enough, it may be possible to live with the potential conflict implied by different missions for different stakeholders.

Seventh, most models of strategic planning are not clear on how to link tools and processes. Many of the tools are actually antithetical to process. The portfolio and competitive analysis approaches, for example, are analytical tools that prescribe an answer. Process is irrelevant and might in fact block the way to determining the correct solution to the organization's strategic problems. Among the few exceptions in the literature are Nutt (1984) and Backoff and Nutt in Chapter 8. In those two pieces a strategic planning process is described, the use of specific tools is prescribed for different phases of the process, and generic strategies are outlined based on the conjunction of processes and tools.

Eighth, the appropriate unit of analysis or application is unclear for many of the models. In the case of portfolio analyses, for example, what should a city government emphasize if it is the organization engaged in strategic planning? Should portfolio analyses focus on the region, the city as a place, the city government as an organization, or specific lines of business that the city might pursue? In the case of Bryson's strategic planning process model (see Chapter 2), should it be followed by the city government as a whole, by each department separately, or both? Although this book represents an attempt to overcome the problem, the fact remains that there is little general literature, and even less of an empirical nature, on how best to apply either tools or processes.

Ninth, more work needs to be done on how to relate strategic planning to other kinds of planning, such as comprehensive, project, and operational planning, capital improvements programming, and planning for specific functions and subareas, such as neighborhoods (Rider 1983). The Oak Ridge experience indicates that comprehensive planning and strategic planning can be linked, but we need much more experience on how to link strategic planning with the variety of other planning approaches and focuses.

Finally, much of the literature on private sector strategic planning assumes a competitive model in which firms compete with one another for volume, market share, and revenue. While private sector strategy formulation may involve major collaborative efforts with competitors—as, for example, through trade association activity, joint ventures, or price fixing—the strategy formulation and implementation activities of governments, public agencies, and nonprofit organizations may involve even more collaborative activity. The literature is not particularly helpful on how to engage in collaborative efforts at strategy formulation among different organizations (Porter 1985).

SUMMARY

Planning as a field has always been one of change (Scott 1969; Teitz 1974). The rise of strategic planning simply represents one of the latest in a series of changes for the profession. We believe that the profession should embrace strategic planning because to do so will enhance the standing of the profession and will further public and nonprofit organizational purposes.

We think that the 14 chapters in this book present a useful overview of the variety of approaches to strategic planning for governments, public agencies, and nonprofit organizations; the relationship of strategic planning to more traditional public planning (that is, traditional comprehensive or master planning) and to public management generally; the nature and sources of strategic issues; the varieties and dynamics of strategy in public and nonprofit organizations; the linkage between a strategic planning process and specific techniques; the process and tools of environmental scanning; and the variety of experiences organizations at various levels have had with strategic planning. We hope that the chapters have made clear that public and nonprofit sector planners can and often do engage in highly effective strategic planning. We hope that they will do more, and hope that this book will help them do it more effectively.

REFERENCES

Barry, Bryan W. 1986. *Strategic planning workbook for nonprofit organizations.* St. Paul, Minn.: Amherst H. Wilder Foundation.

Bolan, R. S. 1971. Generalist with a specialty—Still valid? Educating the planner: An expert on experts. In *Planning 1971: Selected Papers from the ASPO National Conference.* Chicago, Ill.: American Society of Planning Officials.

Bryson, J. M. 1981. A perspective on planning and crises in the public sector. *Strategic Management Journal* 2: 181–196.

Bryson, John M. 1988, forthcoming. *Strategic planning for public and nonprofit organizations: A guide to strengthening and sustaining organizational achievement,* San Francisco, Calif.: Jossey-Bass.

——, A. H. Van de Ven, and W. D. Roering. 1987. Strategic planning and the revitalization of the public service. In *Toward a New Public Service,* edited by R. Denhardt and E. Jennings. Columbia, Mo.: Extension Publications, University of Missouri.

—— and William D. Roering. 1988, forthcoming. Mobilizing innovation efforts: The case of government strategic planning. In *Research on the Management of Innovation,* Vol. 1, edited by A. Van de Ven and H. Angle. Cambridge, Mass.: Ballinger Publishing Company.

Business Week. The new breed of strategic planners. *Business Week* 2680: 62–68.

Cleveland, H. 1973. *The future executive.* New York, N.Y.: Harper & Row.

Delmont, T. and A. Pflaum. 1983. External scanning and issues management: New planning techniques for colleges and universities. St. Paul, Minn.: Association for Institutional Research Upper Midwest, October.

Emery, Fred and Eric Trist. 1965. The causal texture of organizational environments. *Human Relations* 18 (February): 21–31.

Galbraith, Jay R. 1977. *Organization design.* Reading, Mass.: Addison-Wesley.

Goldstein, H. A. 1984. Planning as argumentation. *Environment and Planning by Planning and Design.* 11: 297–312.

Hickson, David J., Richard J. Butler, David Cray, Geoffrey R. Mallory, and David C. Wilson. 1986. *Top decisions—Strategic decision making in organizations.* Oxford: Basil Blackwell.

Howe, E. 1980. Role choices of urban planners. *Journal of the American Planning Association* 46: 398–409.

—— and J. Kaufman. 1979. The ethics of contemporary American planners. *Journal of the American Planning Association* 45: 243–255.

Kanter, Rosabeth Moss. 1983. *The changemasters.* New York, N.Y.: Simon and Schuster.

Kaufman, Jerome L. 1974. Contemporary planning practice: State of the art. In *Planning in America: Learning from Turbulence,* edited by D. Godschalk. Washington, D.C.: American Institute of Planners.

Kent, T. J., Jr. 1964. *The Urban General Plan.* San Francisco, Calif.: Chandler Publishing Co.

Kotler, Philip. 1976. *Marketing Management.* Englewood Cliffs, N.J.: Prentice-Hall.

Luke, J. 1988, forthcoming. Managing interconnectedness: The challenge of shared power. In *Shared Power: What Is It? How Does It Work? How Can We Make It Work Better?* edited by J. M. Bryson and R. C. Einsweiler. Lanham, Md.: Universty Press of America.

McCaskey, M. B. 1974. A contingency approach to planning: Planning with goals and planning without goals. *Academy of Management Journal* 17 (2) (June): 281–291.

Mintzberg, Henry. 1973. *The nature of managerial work.* New York, N.Y.: Harper and Row.

Nutt, Paul C. 1984. A strategic planning network for non-profit organizations. *Strategic Management Journal* 5: 57–75.

—— and Robert W. Backoff. 1987. A strategic management process for public and third-sector organizations. *Journal of the American Planning Association* 53, 44–57.

Olsen, J. B. and D. C. Eadie. 1982. *The game plan: Governance with foresight.* Washington, D.C.: Council of State Planning Agencies.

Pateman, Carole. 1970. *Participation and democratic theory.* London: Cambridge University Press.

Porter, Michael. 1985. *Competitive advantage.* New York, N.Y.: Free Press.

Porter, M. 1987. The state of strategic thinking. *The Economist* May 23, 21–28 passim.

Rider, Robert W. 1983. Making strategic planning work in local government. *Long Range Planning* 16(3): 73–81.

Scott, Mel. 1969. *American city planning.* Berkeley, Calif.: University of California Press.

Teitz, Michael B. 1974. Toward a responsive planning methodology. In *Planning In America: Learning From Turbulence,* edited by D. Godschalk. Washington, D.C.: American Institute of Planners.

Verba, Sidney and Norman H. Nie. 1972. *Participation in America: Political democracy and social equality.* New York, N.Y.: Harper and Row.

Walker, Robert. 1950. *The planning function in urban government.* Chicago, Ill.: University of Chicago Press.

Index